Building Aerodynamics

BUILDING AERODYNAMICS

Tom Lawson *FREng*

University of Bristol

ICP Imperial College Press

Published in India by

Cambridge University Press India Pvt. Ltd.
under the imprint of Foundation Books
Cambridge House
4381/4 Ansari Road
Daryaganj,
New Delhi - 110 002

This reprint edition 2010
Reprinted 2015

ISBN- 13: 978-81-7596-757-1

This edition of *Tom Lawson / Building Aerodynamics,* is published by arrangement with World Scientific Publishing Co. Pte. Ltd.

This edition is for sale in India, Pakistan, Sri Lanka, Bhutan, Nepal, Maldives, Afghanistan and Bangladesh only, not for export elsewhere.

Printed in India at Akash Press, New Delhi 110 020

Acknowledgements

It is impossible to mention, or even be conscious of, all those people whose work and contact have affected one's thinking or have implanted ideas which have later flourished. To try to do so would produce omissions which one would regret and which would never be fully redeemed. I would like, therefor, to thank all who have educated me in Wind Engineering, and hope that they think that I have done the subject justice in this book.

However, I would like to express my delight that Nick Cook and Wayne Pearce have come to Bristol to carry on the work of Wind Engineering here, and to thank them for all the help them have given me in the writing of this book. I would like to thank Colin Wood for his help in filling the gaps in my knowledge.

Several of the photographs, which are Crown Copyright, appear in the text and do so by courtesy of the Director of the Building Research Establishment.

I would like to thank Pauline, whose encouragement and backing made me accept the contract to write this book in the first place, and who has kept me in comfort while I finished it.

Acknowledgement

Preface

This book is written specifically for the practicing Architect and Engineer. The various interactions of the wind with buildings are considered in their separate Chapters, each of which has an Introduction in which the interaction is explained in general terms. Detailed data are presented in the rest of each chapter explaining the extent of quantifiable information which can be made available by the Wind Engineer to the Design Team so that the best compromise between the requirements of wind and all the other competing considerations can be made. Typical Tables and Figures from real situations are presented as illustrations of all measurements and calculations. Theory has been kept to a minimum, and is only presented when, in the author's opinion, the analysis is not well known or is central to the argument.

It is hoped that the introductions to all the chapters will be of interest to everyone, but to try to prevent a reader from being put off by long detailed discussions which might not interest him, a Summary for each chapter is presented under "Summaries" which suggests the parts of the chapter which can be omitted by some readers without loss of envolvement in the team discussions, whilst, at the same time, drawing the same reader's attention is to those parts of the chapter which are appropriate to his detailed understanding of the subject.

Although written for the practicing Architect and Engineer, it is appropriate to the student Architect and Engineer because his needs are the same.

Contents

3. Wind Loading 57

Summaries

The introductions to each Chapter are of interest to all readers who want a minimum acquaintance with the involvement of wind with the subject matter of the Chapter

To allow this book to be used as a reference book, the contents of each chapter are summarised separately for the architect and for the relevant engineer. For example, the relevant engineer for the chapter on Fire matters will be the Fire Engineer. Obviously everyone can read all the book, but the important parts for the particular reader will be highlighted in these Summaries.

S.1. The Wind.

S.1.1 To the Architect.

This is generally an introduction to the generation of the wind and is, or may be, of interest but is not essential .

S.1.2. To the Engineer.

Likewise it is mostly background reading.

However the description of the Van der Hoven spectrum in Section 1.3.3 is of importance in understanding the split in values of wind speed between the data supplied by the Meteorologist and the Wind Tunnel Engineer.

Section 1.5 summarises the needs of the Engineer, in particular Section 1.5.2 on the Reference Wind Speed, and Section 1.5.3 justifying the use of strong wind data in wind tunnel studies.

S.2. Flow around Bluff Bodies in Turbulent Flow.

S.2.1. The Architect.

Section 2.2 will be of interest if the Architect wants to understand the reason behind the General Points and Pitfalls in Section 4.2.

S.2.2. The Engineer.

This is general reading for all engineers and lays the background for much detail work which follows.

S.3. Wind Loading.

S.3.1. The Architect.

Choose a good Structural Engineer and leave it to him. The introduction contains all that is needed. It would be worth asking whether any part of the construction could suffer dynamic effects, if the answer is "No", the probable reason is a matter of size and Section 3.3.7 might be consulted.

S.3.2. The Engineer.

For nearly all structures the Quasi-Static Approach is satisfactory. If in doubt start with the Mildly-Dynamic approach, and read Section 3.3.7 early on.

Section 3.1.8 is interesting if the client is suggesting that the design loads, although quasi-static, are on the high side.

Otherwise a general reading of Sections 3.1 will allow the Structural Engineer to decide whether a wind tunnel investigation is necessary, and to get the most out of a wind tunnel investigation if one has been conducted.

If the structure proves to be dynamic, read Sections 3.2 and discuss the results with a colleague who is conversant with dynamic structures. Sections

3.2 do not give the structural information required for an assessment of the problems, only explains how the Wind Engineer will present his data for the Structural Engineer to bring his analysis to a successful conclusion.

S.4. Wind Environment.

S.4.1. The Architect.

This Chapter is mainly the concern of the Architect. Section 4.2 (with flashes back to Chapter 2) should be read and applied in the early stages of the design where decisions about shapes and massing are being undertaken. It is often useful to involve a Wind Engineer at this early stage so that decisions, which have adverse wind effects, are not taken in ignorance of the wind effects, when different decisions would have met all the other interests, without entailing wind problems.

A full wind tunnel investigation is only economic if carried out on the final design. If such a study is required to obtain Wind Loading data, then the addition of a Wind Environment study involves little additional cost, and is well worth while. If no loading study is to be undertaken, then a simple wind environment investigation is the only way to obtain a quantifiable assessment.

If it is decided to carry out a wind tunnel investigation, an understanding of Sections 4.3 will allow a meaningful discussion between the Architect and the Wind Engineer to the benefit of both. It will also allow the Architect to put to the Wind Engineer the worries of his client or planning authority, and obtain a detailed answer. It is often advantageous to have a meeting at the Wind Tunnel between the Client, the Planning Authority, relevant Engineers, the Architect and the Wind Tunnel Engineer. The nitty-gritty can be hammered out, remedial suggestions from anyone can be tried, and their rough effects shown (a fuller study is required, if additions to reduce the wind in a given area are suggested and tested, to ensure that the reduction of wind one location has not been achieved at the expense of greater wind at another location where conditions were found formerly to be acceptable).

S.5. Rain and Snow.

S.5.1. The Architect.

This Chapter mainly affects the Architect. A beautiful open vista, and protection from the elements are in conflict and a compromise between the two, which satisfies the brief, has to be achieved.

Section 5.1.5 addresses the approach to protection from the rain in general, and Section 5.1.7.4 gives a lead into the requirements for protection from the rain when not enclosed.

S.5.2. The Engineer.

The responsibility in this area lies with the Architect.

S.6. Ventilation.

S.6.1. The Architect.

This is the preserve of the Mechanical Engineer. Nowadays the Architect should be involved in the ventilation of all Car Parks. This means that Section 6.4 should be understood.

S.6.2. The Engineer.

If a wind tunnel investigation has been carried out, either for the acquisition of wind loading or wind environmental data, then the addition of a Ventilation study can be conducted with very little additional cost, provided that it is agreed before the other two studies are carried out.

Pressure is on designers to use Natural systems wherever possible to save the burning of fossil fuels. It is very difficult to quantify the natural ventilation of a complex building without a wind tunnel investigation. In Sections 6.2 the Ventilation Engineer is presented with the data which can be obtained from a wind tunnel investigation in a format which will allow him to ensure that specifications are met. No only are data on Air Changes per Hour presented, but also velocities through doors, both for the comfort of the users, and as an input to the heat balance calculations on the building.

Should a Forced system be chosen, then the wind tunnel data in Sections 6.3 show where fans should be placed, how they are sized and their modus operandi.

Ventilation of covered Car Parks is becoming a matter of general interest. This is a specialist subject, and even the supply of air from a few fans in a Car Park can still produce stagnation areas where there is very little ventilation. The solution of this problem, either by Natural or Forced means requires a special study which is outlined in Sections 6.4.

S.7. Fire.

S.7.1. The Architect.

The Architect is responsible, but normally uses a Fire Engineer to ensure that the problems are solved satisfactorily.

S.7.2. The Fire Engineer.

This problem is closely akin to that of the Ventilation Engineer, but is more specific.

The fire arrangements have to work in the absence of wind, and all the openings are sized for this situation. It is the job of the Fire Engineer is ensure that the wind does not inhibit their correct working. In particular air must never enter any opening into a smoke reservoir under any wind condition. It is not enough to say that more smoke leaves from a smoke reservoir through some outlets than enters through others, because the entering air is cold, and, mixing with the hot smoke, cools it and creates internal flows which can drive the smoke back towards the people. It is difficult to state that this will not occur without a wind tunnel investigation.

The data available from a wind tunnel investigation are presented in Sections 7.1 and 7.2 with additional comments in the subsequent Sections.

S.8. Emissions from Buildings.

S.8.1. The Architect.

The aesthetics of a building are the responsibility of the Architect, so the provision of chimneys is his province.

This whole Chapter concerns the Architect, some parts such as the efflux velocity in Section 8.2.2 is part of the business of the Mechanical Engineer, but his approach is from a different direction. Thus the Architect and Engineer have to get together on this topic. They both need to understand the implications.

The usual approach is to use tall chimneys, 1.25 times the height of the building, even so efflux velocities are important (see Sections 8.2). On an industrial building there is sometimes the need for many chimneys, and a new alternative approach to manifolding them, which is the use of multiple mini-chimneys, is presented in Section 8.2.8, and should be considered seriously.

S.8.2. The Engineer.

The responsibility in this field is jointly that of the Architect and the Engineer, and the best results will be achieved where a full discussion is undertaken. This means that both should understand all the possible options, including the new ideas in Section 8.2.8; the whole of this Chapter applies to all.

S.9. Sailing.

S.9.1. The Architect.

The problem of inshore sailing is that more often than not sailing time is lost because of lack of wind rather than excess of it. Consequently, if inland water is to be surrounded by buildings, then the form of those buildings should be such as to increase the wind over the water; this is a function of the shape and form of the buildings, and is the responsibility of the Architect.

The problem is laid out in Section 9.1, but the flow patterns explained in Sections 2.2 must be understood if improvements are to be made.

S.9.2. The Engineer.

The responsibility belongs to the Architect.

S.10. Experimental Methods.

S.10.1. The Architect.

This Chapter is of little interest to the Architect.

S.10.2. The Engineer.

This is only of interest to the Engineer when he wants to understand at a deeper level the problems of the Wind Engineer and to understand why he has approached the problem in the way he has.

S.11. Necessary Statistics.

This Chapter has been added in case any of the analysis or discussion in the other Chapters involved terms or operations which were not familiar to the reader. It is not a text on Statistics, but a definition of those items in Statistics whose non-understanding would hinder the following of the arguments in the other Chapters.

1. The Wind

"The wind bloweth where it will" and "The Lord tempereth the wind to the shorn lamb" are two misconceptions. Man can have an effect, but he has to understand the wind and its interactions first.

For a real understanding of the wind, the reader should consult books on Meteorology, in this chapter only the briefest of outlines will be given, sufficient to understand the rest of the book. The application of knowledge about the wind to wind engineering is contained in Section 1.5.

1.1 Global Circulation.

The wind is generated by the differential heating of the atmosphere by the sun. As the sun's rays approach the earth, most of the solar energy of a wavelength which can be absorbed by the atmosphere is absorbed by the air in the mesosphere (between 80 and 50 kilometres from the surface of the earth, and where the assumption that air is a continuum is first tenable). Thereafter (between 50 and 25 km from the surface of the earth) the sun's rays have no energy which can be absorbed by the air and the air temperature decreases towards the ground; this region is called the Stratosphere. Below this altitude (25 to 10 km.) the temperature remains constant, this is called the Tropopause. The sun's rays then continue downwards until they encounter either cloud or the earth's surface, when the remaining energy is absorbed and re-radiated at frequencies which can be absorbed by the air. Consequently, beneath the tropopause, the temperature of the air is highest at the ground, decreasing with height. This explains why, although the sun is the source of our heat, the temperature close to the ground is highest at the ground, decreasing with height to the tropopause. The variation of temperature with

FIG. 1.01 VARIATION OF TEMPERATURE WITH ALTITUDE

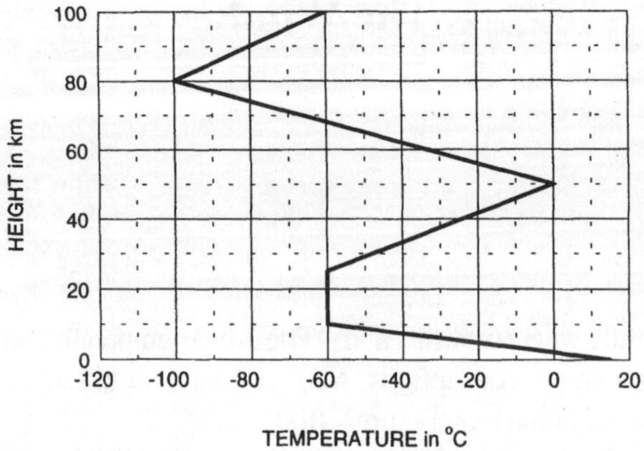

height is shown in Figure 1.01.

Because, for a given land mass, the projected area normal to the sun's rays (adjusted to a minor extent by the inclination of the axis about which the earth rotates) is much greater at the Equator than at the Poles, the equatorial regions become hotter than the polar ones. A temperature gradient thus created produces density and pressure gradients which would create a circulation around a homogeneous earth as shown in Figure 1.02. The rotation of the homogeneous earth, coupled to the surface friction causes this circulation to break up into three separate circulations in each of the Northern and Southern Hemispheres as shown in Figure 1.03. Because the earth is not homogeneous, as it contains large masses of land and sea, these three belts develop a longitudinal rearrangement of pressure called "cells", producing corridors in the prevailing winds. The inclination of the earth's rotation axis causes a seasonal change to these cells: for example, in winter an Icelandic low and a Siberian high which covers most of Europe and much of Asia. In the summer there is a subtropical high over the Azores.

Two types of wind condition are related to these regions of high and low pressure. Winds created around centres of high pressure in winter and low pressure in summer are called "Monsoons", these do not have high wind speeds, but last for many days. The second type of wind condition driven by

FIG 1.02. HOMOGENEOUS GLOBAL CIRCULATION

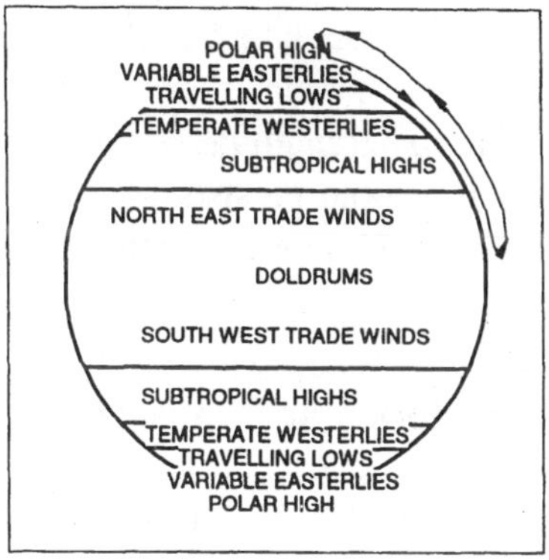

FIG 1.03. HOMOGENEOUS GLOBAL CIRCULATION

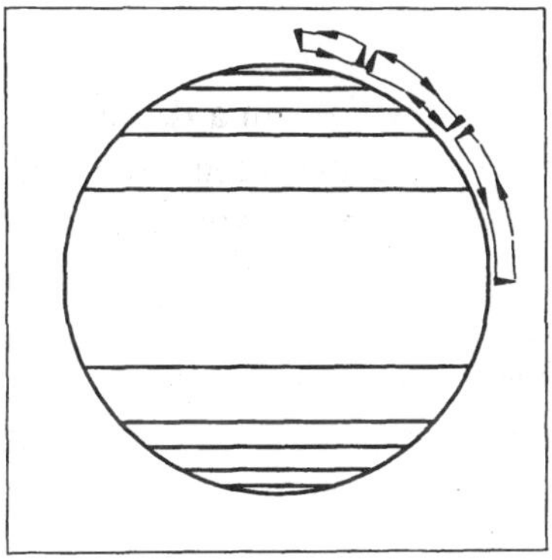

the global circulation is the “Hurricane” or “Tropical Cyclone”.

Warm moist air is carried to high altitude by the vertical velocities in the cell close to the equator (5 to 20 degrees latitude). When conditions are suitable, the warm moist air forms tall convective clouds in which condensation occurs and releases latent heat in immense quantities because the size of the hurricane can be up to 1000 km in diameter. The energy drives the wind in the inner region in a rotary motion (to balance the pressure gradient) causing air to be sucked inwards along the ground into the core, up through the vortex, to be rejected radially at high level (10 to 17 km).

The hurricane contains more energy than other storms and can last for several days, moving all the time. Whilst over the sea it continually gains, or at least maintains, energy from the latent heat of condensation of new water vapour as more and more moist air is drawn into the vortex. When the hurricane passes over land, its strength decreases rapidly as it is cut off from its source of energy, and it seldom persists as a Hurricane beyond 50 km of land travel. Wind speeds of 75 m/s are common in Hurricanes, although values in excess of 140 m/s are not unknown.

1.2. Extratropical Cyclones or Temperate Systems.

No other weather system is directly driven by the global circulation, although all others are consequences of events produced by it.

The other important result of these large high and low pressure regions is that large masses of air tend to move. As these masses travel their water content depends upon their track, and those with a "maritime" track will tend to become saturated, especially in their lower layers. On the other hand, those having a "continental" track will retain a dew point appropriate to the region of their source, because there has been little water to acquire. Polar air moving to lower latitudes is warmed from below and becomes unstable (see section 1.4), and visa versa. This causes vertical movement of the air.

When two air masses meet, the line of discontinuity is called a front (named by V. Bjerkness in 1917); it is called a "warm front" when warm air moves into cold air, and usually rides up over the cold air at a shallow angle. A "cold front" is when cold air moves into warm air and causes the warm air to rise abruptly. An "occlusion" is when a cold front has caught up with a warm one and has pushed all the warm air up, leaving continuous cold air at ground level.

In temperate zones winds are usually created by the movement of air masses which provide long term (up to 4 days) prevailing conditions over large areas; the presence of mountain ranges affecting conditions locally. At fronts rapid changes occur and fast vertical movements of air are possible, especially when kinks occur in a front. This can lead to extratropical cyclones, and the active manifestation is a "thunderstorm".

The description of a Thunderstorm is similar to that of a Hurricane, with two important differences: the thunderstorm is small, related to the front, whilst the hurricane is large (about 1000 km). The second difference is that the upflows and downflows are reversed. In a thunderstorm the wind comes down in the centre and rises around the edge.

Within a thunderstorm it is possible for "tornadoes" to occur. These are small vortices which form within the thunderstorm, and because of the principle of conservation of momentum tend to reduce their diameter to about 300 m, thus increasing their tangential velocity, and wind speeds of more than 100 m/s are not uncommon within them. Because of the large velocities and small radius, the pressure reduction in the core of a tornado can be very large (of the order of 10^4 N/m^2). This very low pressure can cause objects, such as roofs, in the path of the tornado to be lifted, and the cores of tornadoes are often filled with water, sand, dust or debris, and are consequently visible. The lifetime of a tornado is very short, usually minutes, but it is not unusual for a string of tornadoes to occur in a line, one after another, giving the appearance of a single longer-lasting phenomenon. Because of their small size, it is possible for a tornado to demolish completely the houses down one side of a street, leaving those on the other side undamaged.

It is important to realise that in parts of the world where hurricanes occur, extratropical cyclones also occur, and in this case data from each should be collected separately and be analysed as a Mixed Population (see Section 11.2.3.9).

1.3 Strong Wind Speeds.

High wind speeds result from Extratropical cyclones Tornadoes and Hurricanes and are associated with a neutral atmosphere (no thermal gradients). This is because the high turbulence present mixes the layers so that thermal stratification cannot be maintained.

Even so, the velocity patterns are not simple. Records of two storms lasting 22 and 24 seconds are presented in Figure 1.04. These are from data obtained by R.H.Sherlock and M.B.Stout in 1931 and 1933 and were reported in the Journal of Aeronautical Science Vol 5 No 2 pp 53 to 61 December 1937, and subsequently prepared by the Boundary Layer Wind Tunnel Laboratory at the University of Western Ontario, Canada. The measurements defy mathematical representation.

The need to provide mathematical representations of wind speeds is paramount so that calculations can be performed to demonstrate the suitability of a structure or its environment. The data must be sanitised.

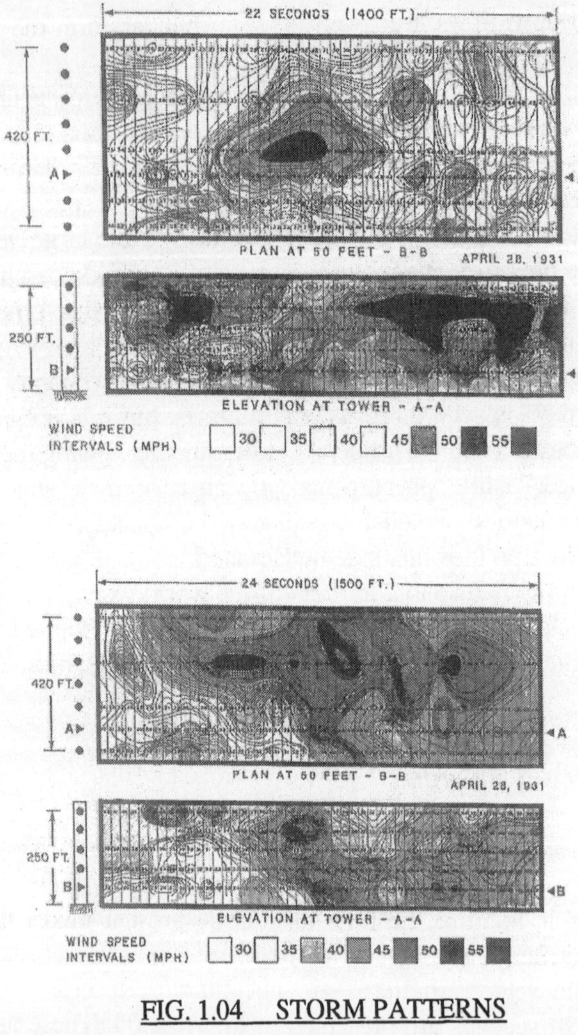

FIG. 1.04 STORM PATTERNS

1.3.1. Mean Velocity Profile.

Recourse was made to Boundary Layer Theory for flow over a rough surface. The mean velocity profile over a surface rough by aeronautical standards was represented empirically by engineers by the seventh power law, viz.

$$V / V_{ref} = (z / z_{ref})^{1/7}$$

where z is height above the surface. This expression was a best-fit to measured data for surfaces covered with sand of different particle sizes. Monin and Oberoff preferred the formulation of the log-law expression

$$V = (U^*/ k) \ln \{(z - d)/z_o)\},$$

where U^* is called the "frictional velocity", and is related to the ground roughness and therefor to the shear stress at the surface (τ_o) which is given by

$$\tau_o = \rho U^{*2} ,$$

k is Von Karman's Constant, equal to 0.4, d is the "displacement height" (see Section 1.5.1)and z_o is the roughness height. The logarithmic approach has the advantage that it defines constant shear stress close to the surface, found by measurement to be so. In the outer regions of the boundary layer, the log-law was found to be unrepresentative, the law of the wake was found to be more suitable. Work by Deaves and Harris established the composite expression

$$V = (U^*/k) [\ln\{(z-d)/z_o\} + 5.75(z/H)]$$

where H is the height of the boundary layer, or the gradient height of the atmospheric boundary layer, which varies with ground roughness but is usually considered to be about 1 km.

For many years this expression was used, with the value for d and z_o being appropriate to the conditions at the site with no reference to the fetch. More recently, with the arrival of computers, it has been possible to compute transitional boundary layers for the wind as it passes from a surface of one roughness to a surface of another roughness. The new part-boundary layer appropriate to the second roughness must grow from the ground upwards underneath the original layer and integrate with it. If the second roughness lasts long enough, then the second equilibrium layer will be established: this rarely happens in practice.

In the recent UK Code of Practice, this "fetch" approach has been incorporated, and data for a profile within the change can be determined approximately. For a more rigorous treatment the reader is advised to use the computer programme produced by ESDU (A9232), or other similar programmes, for the purpose.

1.3.2. Turbulence Profile.

A measurement of wind speed in the vicinity of the ground, as shown in Figure 1.05, contains much turbulence, which is usually expressed as a

FIG 1.05 VARIATION OF WIND SPEED WITH TIME

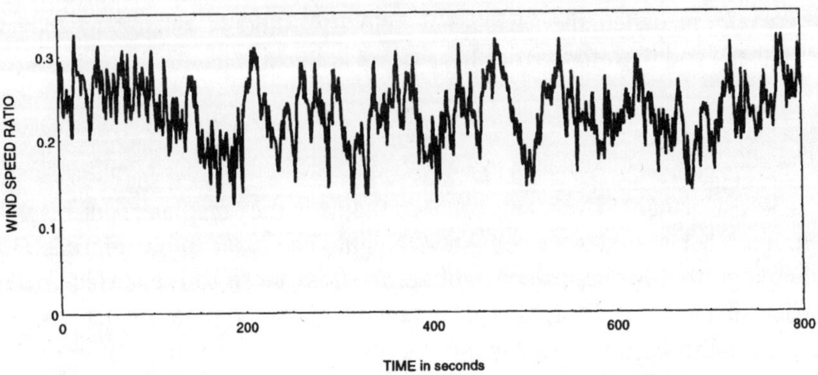

"Turbulence Intensity" (I) defined by

$$I_u = \sigma_u / V$$

where V is the mean wind speed, and the suffix u refers to the u-component of turbulence. Expressions for the equilibrium value of σ_u are given in many papers, for instance:

$$\sigma_u / U^* = 2.63(1-z/H)\{0.538 + 0.09 \ln[(z-d)/z_o]\}^p$$

where $p = (1- z/H)^{16}$. Other representations exist, but the reader is recommended to use a computer programme such as the one recommended for the mean velocity profile (ESDU A9232) because these allow the non-equilibrium profiles to be evaluated.

1.3.3. Spectral Density Function.

This is a measure of how the turbulence is distributed among the frequencies.

The classic spectral density function for the wind was presented by Van der Hoven. He combined the measurements at Brookhaven NY from many investigators to cover the range of frequencies from 5 Hz to 1/(11 years).

To open up the lower frequency end of the spectrum it is often plotted as n S(n) against log(n). The mathematician would have plotted the spectrum as nS(n) against ln(n) because

$$\int_0^{\infty} S(n)\, dn = \int_{-\infty}^{\infty} nS(n)\, d\{ln(n)\} = \sigma^2$$

but the engineer prefers the orders of 10. The curve "after" Van der Hoven, which was measured at a height of 100m, is presented in Figure 1.06.

FIG 1.06 SPECTRUM OF WIND AFTER VAN DER HOVEN

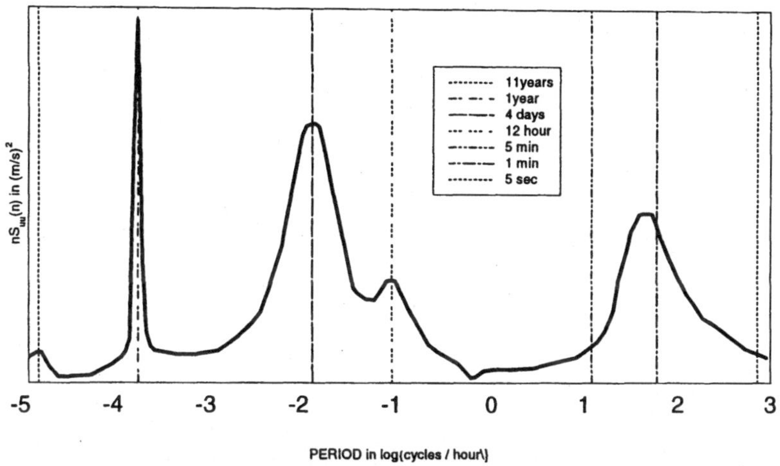

This is a very important presentation because there is an obvious dip in the curve between periods of 20 minutes and 2 hours. The reason for this is that all the turbulence with periods greater than 2 hours are generated by "weather systems" and is called the Macrometeorological range, whereas that part of the curve with periods less than 20 minutes is generated by the friction with the ground and is called the Micrometeorological range. The gap between is called the "Spectral Gap" and is important to the Wind Engineer because he can simulate the Micrometeorological range in his wind tunnel, and treat the

Macrometeorological range as "Met Data". And most important of all, because of the Spectral Gap, there is no correlation between the two. The Wind Engineer can take all the statistical descriptions of the "Hourly-Average Wind Speed" from Meteorological Offices around the world, and simulate the turbulence associated with the Micrometeorological range in his wind tunnel, the statistical effects of these fluctuations appearing in his values of Pressure Coefficient, for example, and he can combine the two without duplication of any fluctuations. The choice of the "Hourly-Average Wind Speed" as the reference value in wind tunnel work is not because it is a nice round number, but is because it is in the centre of the Spectral Gap.

The spectra are often presented in a "Normalised" form in which the Spectral Density Function is divided by the variance. This has the advantage that the area under the curve is unity. The same applies if $nS(n)/\sigma^2$ is plotted against ln(n): in a $nS(n)/\sigma^2$ against log(n) presentation the area under the curve is always 2.303.

A typical Normalised Spectral Density Function for the wind simulation in a wind tunnel is presented in Figure 1.07.

FIG 1.07 SPECTRUM OF REFERENCE WIND SPEED

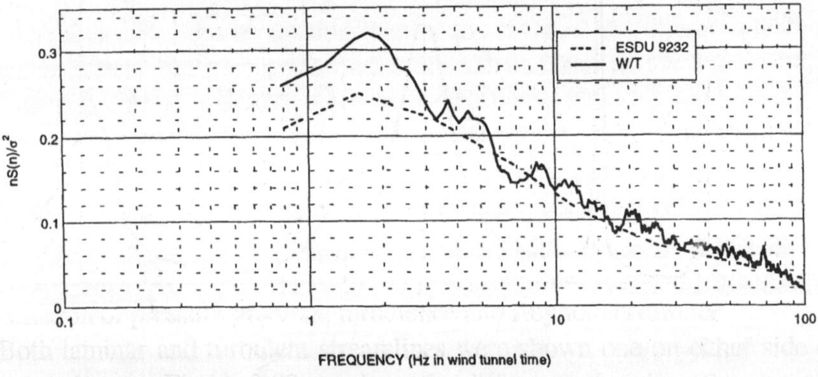

1.3.4. Length Scales of Turbulence.

There are nine integral length scales (three components of velocity in three dimensions), and they are used to give a single measure of the frequency content of atmospheric winds. They are defined in Section 11.1.2.

They are related to the Spectral Density Functions in a very complex way, which is only of interest to the research worker, and such a reader is advised to consult ESDU Data Item 85020 ("Characteristics of Atmospheric Turbulence Near the Ground: Part ii Single Point data for Strong Winds (neutral atmosphere)") or a book on Meteorology.

For the Wind Engineer, their values can be obtained from computer programmes such as ESDU A9232. They are used in calculating values of Equivalent Reynolds Number.

1.4. Stability of the Atmosphere.

1.4.1. Definition.

A system is described as stable when, if it is disturbed from its equilibrium position, forces or moments are set up, due to its disturbance, to restore it to its original equilibrium position.

The atmosphere is described as stable when, if a parcel of air at one height is moved to another height, its density relative to the surrounding air is such as to return it to its original height.

The physical properties of the atmosphere are its pressure, density and temperature. They are related by the equation of state:

$$p = \rho RT$$

where p is the pressure in N/m2 , ρ is the density in kg/m^3 ,T is temperature in degrees Kelvin and R is the Gas Constant and equal to 287 Nm/kg° K for air.

The pressure in the atmosphere is equal to the weight of all the air above, thus

$$p = p_o - \rho gh$$

where p_o is the pressure at ground level, and if the temperature change is defined in terms of a lapse rate (λ) so that, below the tropopause of the standard atmosphere,

$$T = T_o - \lambda h$$

where T_o is the temperature at ground level. By eliminating ρ between the three equations and integrating, the properties of the standard atmosphere are defined as

$$p = p_o\{1-\lambda h/T_o\}^{g/\lambda R},$$

$$T = T_o\{1-\lambda h/T_o\}, \quad \text{and}$$

$$\rho = \rho_o\{1-\lambda h/T_o\}^{(g/\lambda R)-1}.$$

If a parcel of air is lifted from a height with condition suffix o by a height h, and no heat is added to the parcel then

$$p/\rho^{\gamma} = p_o/\rho_o{}^{\gamma}\,[1-\lambda h/T_o]^{(g/\lambda R)-(\gamma g/\lambda R)+\gamma} = p_o/\rho_o{}^{\gamma}$$

which means that

$$\lambda_a = (g/R)\,[(\gamma-1)/\gamma]$$

and λ_a is called the adiabatic lapse rate. For the atmosphere the value of the adiabatic lapse rate is 9.8° C per km.

If the lapse rate at any height in the atmosphere is greater than the adiabatic lapse rate, then the atmosphere at that height is stable, and vice versa.

1.4.2. Implications.

1.4.2.1. Inversions.

A special case of a stable layer in the atmosphere is called an "Inversion". This is a stable layer in the atmosphere, often very thin, which can hang over an area, and can persist for a long time. Any plume emitted below it will rise up to it and then spread out along its underside, often cooling and subsequently dropping towards the ground. Penetration only occurs if the plume has sufficient vertical momentum on reaching the inversion to overcome the stability forces.

When a town or city is in a bowl, inversions occur often in the early morning of a clear day, when the smoke from the chimneys can be seen rising to the layer and being contained by the inversion. Soon the inversion disappears as the town warms up and begins to emit heat, and the pollution disperses.

1.4.2.2. Stable and Unstable Atmospheres.

Neutral atmospheres are assumed to occur for wind speeds in excess of 10 m/s, when sufficient turbulence is present to mix the layers and prevent temperature gradients. Below 10 m/s temperature gradients can exist and should be considered.

In a stable atmosphere turbulence is reduced and visa versa. Because the vertical motions tend to be augmented or suppressed by the buoyancy forces which are brought into play, velocity profiles and spectra are affected by the stability. It is impossible to predict "a velocity profile for a stable atmosphere" because the stability will affect the profile. Singer and Smith at Brookhaven in 1953 published five degrees of stability (called A, B_2, B_1, C and D in that order) and diffusion studies are often based on these classes. Each has a range of velocity profiles and spectra associated with it.

For this reason it is very difficult to achieve agreement about wind conditions in these atmospheres.

1.4.2.3. Application to Wind Tunnels.

In strong winds the atmosphere is neutrally stable because of the mixing due to the turbulence. In weak winds stability is important. The only field of study where light winds are important concerns the removal of effluent from chimneys and the like. These are discussed in Chapter 8.

Atmospheric Diffusion is a complete subject in itself, and students of the topic should read books specialising in the subject such as Frank Pasquill's "Atmospheric Diffusion". Therein stability receives its due weight.

The wind tunnel studies discussed in Chapter 8 are all near field studies, and are involved with the breaking cleanly of the plume from the chimney top and the subsequent motion of the plume around the surrounding buildings: for this study the stability of the atmosphere is unimportant. If the study is to be taken any further downwind, then it is recommended that the wind tunnel is not used. Apart from the difficulty of providing a temperature gradient in a wind tunnel, which we devised at one time at Bristol and is available in other wind tunnels, the question of the velocity profile arises. All the profiles used at present derive from Strong Wind measurements, and it is uncertain how applicable they are to other stabilities of atmosphere.

1.5. Application to the Wind Engineer.

Wind patterns can be very complex, as shown in Figure 1.04. For practical purposes the Wind Engineer has to produce expressions for the parameters which affect his results, expressions which are representations of those real conditions which are liable to produce least conservative results, and expressions which can be simulated by workers around the world. Mathematical representations for the *velocity profile* and *spectrum of turbulence* for normal locations have to be agreed (if a site is in the lea of the Rock of Gibraltar or the peak at Hong Kong , or in a quarry, special profiles and spectra will be required).

The original work in Wind Engineering related to wind loads, the extreme values of which occur in strong winds. The velocity profiles and spectra for this type of analysis must refer to strong winds. It is fortunate that unique data can be provided for neutrally stable atmospheres; different workers provide different expressions, but the neutrality of the atmospheres is in common. Several approved computer programmes have been written which supply these data, and one of these should be used. Not only do they conform to the latest theories, but they allow for fetch on the velocity profiles and spectra. A set of velocity profiles are presented in Figure 1.08, and spectra in Figure 1.09.

FIG 1.08a VELOCITY PROFILE FOR HOURLY AVERAGE WIND SPEED

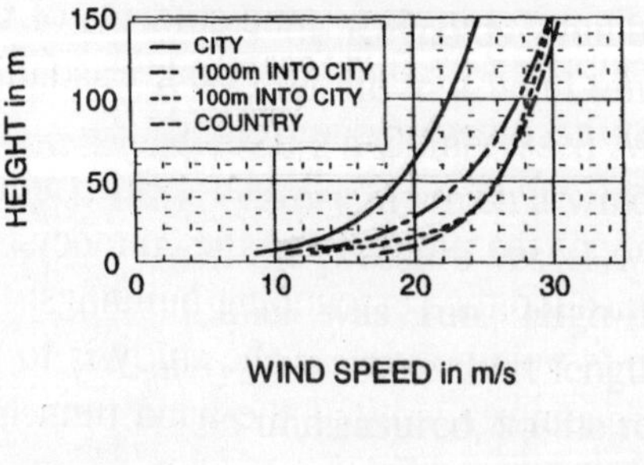

FIG 1.08b VELOCITY PROFILES FOR 1-SECOND AVERAGE WIND SPEEDS

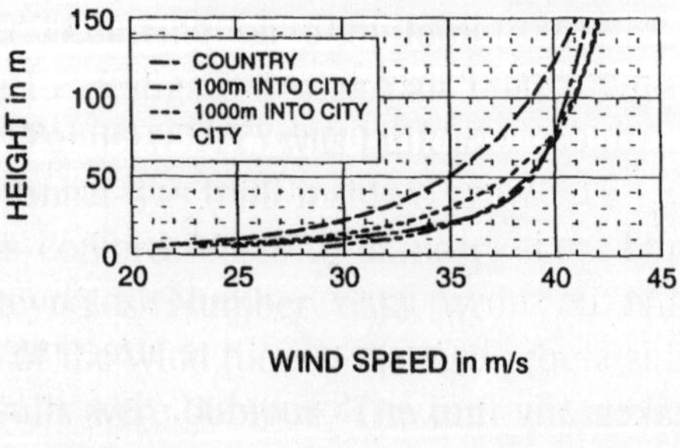

FIG 1.09a NORMALISED SPECTRAL DENSITY FUNCTION FOR COUNTRY

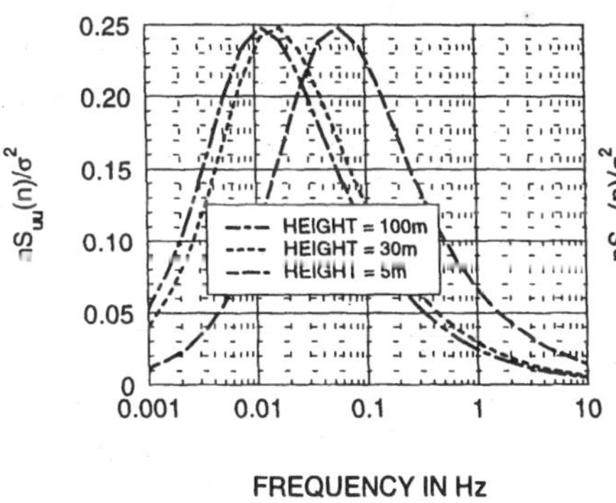

FIG 1.09b NORMALISED SPECTRAL DENSITY FUNCTION FOR CITY

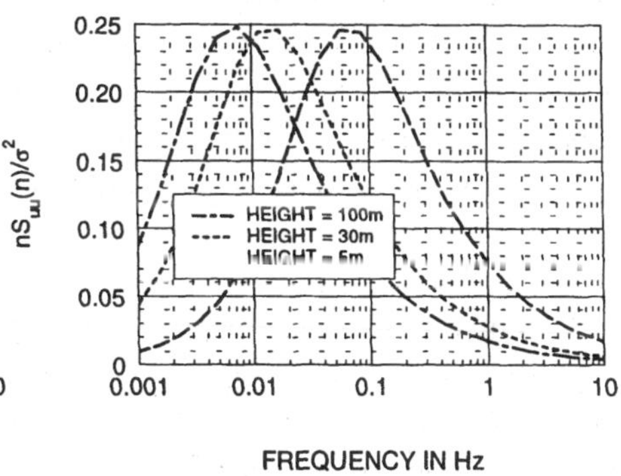

The change from country to city velocity profile is clearly shown on Figures 1.08; it is also clear from a comparison between Figures 1.08a and b that the change in hourly-average wind speed is greater than for the 1 second average values. This is because the extra friction in the city both decreases the average wind speed and increases the turbulence. It should be noted that zero displacement height was specified for both country and city data, whereas in reality the displacement height (see Section 1.5.1) for the city would be about 20m.

The spectra in Figures 1.09a and b show that there is not so much difference between country and city as with height above ground

If the location is exceptional, then a model should be made of the site at a large enough scale so that it extends far enough to reach standard conditions at its edges, and this model should be tested to obtain site conditions. These conditions should then be modelled at an acceptable scale to allow both the atmosphere to be represented and the details of the model to be significant.

Over the years the work of Wind Engineers has spread to other fields, such as Environmental conditions around buildings, ventilation of buildings, the removal of smoke in the case of fire, and emissions from buildings. The study of emissions splits into near field and far field. The applicability of using high speed data is discussed in Section 1.5.3.

1.5.1. Displacement Height and Ground Roughness.

The surface roughness met in Aeronautical Engineering is small and is represented in model experiments by gluing sand to the surface. The ground roughness encountered by the Wind Engineer is very large, and there is a flow within the elements constituting the roughness (the buildings). When measurements of the velocity profile are made above a complex of buildings, and the profile is extrapolated to zero velocity, the height for zero velocity is found to be about 1.5m to 2m below the average height of the buildings: below that height any velocity profile is possible.

The expression assumed for the velocity profile starts a distance above the ground, and that distance is called "the displacement height".

When this displacement height is applied, the ground, or surface, roughness for the buildings in the centre of a city is 0.7m. This is much smaller than the size of the buildings, but represents the size of roughness which generates the scales of turbulence present.

When the boundary is considered to start 1.5m below the average height of the buildings, the roughness height of 0.7m makes sense; the roughness height for the Aeronautical Engineer is less than the diameter of the sand he uses.

1.5.2. Reference Wind Speed.

The only information the Wind Engineer **needs** to know is the reference wind speed at the site.

For wind loading studies this is always the Hourly-Average value of wind speed measured 10m above flat open level ground. This specification applies around the whole world, and I have called it the "Meteorological Standard Wind Speed". However the way its value has been obtained in some parts of the world is open to doubt. Some guidance on the accuracy of the data is given in the Cookbook (N.J.Cook "The Designer's Guide to Wind Loading of Building Structures. Part 1 Background, damage survey, wind data and structural classification" Butterworths 1985). If in doubt, advice can be obtained from the Meteorological Office.

Values of the reference wind speed are usually available superimposed on maps, so that local values for the site can be interpolated. These apply to open flat level sites. For other sorts of sites corrections must be made, and this might involve the making and testing of a model of the local countryside, the results from which are then applied to the model of the building on its site.

For environmental wind, ventilation and fire studies the required data should be in the form of "Tables of Frequency and Direction for winds at

		JAN	FEB	MAR	APR	MAY	JUNE	JULY	AUG	SEPT	OCT	NOV	DEC	YEAR
0	c	5.89	6.53	4.95	5.08	4.69	3.78	4.72	3.68	3.87	3.90	5.53	4.67	5.03
	k	2.50	2.57	2.26	2.29	1.96	2.14	2.06	1.62	1.93	1.88	2.19	2.04	1.99
	p	5.01	6.31	3.79	5.25	6.46	4.37	6.50	3.36	2.28	5.25	5.15	3.77	4.74
30	c	5.62	5.55	4.80	4.50	5.30	3.73	3.79	4.38	4.20	3.41	5.39	5.02	4.60
	k	2.43	2.17	1.93	1.89	2.16	2.19	2.15	1.76	2.13	2.00	2.20	2.08	1.98
	p	4.04	7.36	7.91	5.82	14.01	9.36	5.21	2.61	4.33	8.49	6.19	5.33	6.72
60	c	5.61	5.46	5.02	4.38	4.80	3.95	3.56	3.18	4.30	3.81	5.78	4.29	4.59
	k	2.50	2.09	2.14	1.90	2.16	2.08	2.06	1.66	2.07	1.88	2.27	2.09	1.99
	p	7.19	8.68	13.99	11.07	15.04	11.35	5.00	1.47	6.58	8.73	4.40	7.01	8.45
90	c	5.93	4.82	4.63	4.78	4.66	4.55	4.63	3.47	4.20	3.93	4.56	4.50	4.65
	k	2.79	1.94	1.95	2.00	1.90	2.19	2.09	1.84	2.02	2.19	1.73	2.13	1.98
	p	4.57	6.76	14.56	12.02	11.59	6.78	5.69	2.94	6.80	6.56	2.72	5.33	7.22
120	c	5.02	4.55	4.86	4.33	4.02	4.57	4.72	3.87	3.86	4.59	5.29	4.61	4.64
	k	2.22	2.05	2.06	1.90	1.95	2.14	2.12	1.81	1.84	1.77	2.01	1.92	1.94
	p	2.63	2.98	4.73	3.57	5.79	1.93	1.53	2.83	2.60	4.32	4.79	4.12	3.52
150	c	4.59	4.42	3.98	3.51	3.50	4.25	3.10	3.48	3.96	3.57	3.64	4.52	4.23
	k	1.98	1.62	2.11	1.84	1.86	2.03	2.19	1.84	1.75	1.80	1.75	1.75	1.65
	p	2.52	2.36	2.37	1.84	2.07	1.01	.62	2.94	1.65	3.41	5.29	3.47	2.59
180	c	4.52	5.15	4.51	4.81	3.81	3.85	3.94	3.99	4.55	4.08	4.38	4.78	4.63
	k	1.54	2.15	1.88	1.71	1.76	2.13	2.30	1.92	2.12	1.83	1.96	1.79	1.71
	p	3.83	6.73	3.39	2.69	3.81	1.52	2.23	5.93	4.10	6.45	8.63	7.41	4.64
210	c	6.91	7.03	6.34	6.86	5.74	5.93	5.84	6.02	5.96	5.64	6.02	6.34	6.29
	k	2.64	2.11	2.08	1.87	2.24	2.36	2.29	2.21	2.16	2.15	2.18	2.16	2.14
	p	12.41	14.45	9.78	9.19	7.85	5.95	5.67	15.43	15.43	14.95	14.94	13.92	11.59
240	c	7.79	7.59	6.96	7.33	5.84	6.13	6.04	5.54	6.15	5.98	6.58	6.61	6.65
	k	2.64	2.31	2.13	2.38	2.30	2.22	2.45	2.08	2.13	2.20	2.19	2.17	2.14
	p	25.22	19.51	17.30	17.57	11.93	19.67	17.69	27.97	24.40	22.02	23.83	23.47	20.70
270	c	7.60	7.55	6.36	7.48	5.74	6.58	6.35	5.82	6.03	5.58	5.97	6.68	6.53
	k	2.35	2.36	2.06	2.23	2.24	2.37	2.32	1.98	2.05	2.02	1.81	2.00	2.10
	p	18.73	13.02	10.92	15.99	8.38	21.17	25.49	21.30	17.52	10.30	13.40	15.83	16.02
300	c	6.07	5.01	6.14	5.30	5.00	5.38	4.91	4.16	5.06	4.81	5.84	6.28	5.36
	k	2.18	2.15	1.87	2.10	2.05	2.32	2.07	1.66	1.91	1.90	1.84	2.20	1.88
	p	9.82	7.16	6.64	9.43	7.27	8.79	14.73	7.95	9.76	4.91	6.42	7.41	8.34
330	c	5.42	4.45	4.41	4.68	4.13	4.10	3.96	2.92	3.89	3.78	5.16	4.85	4.49
	k	1.84	2.35	1.87	2.25	2.23	2.09	2.14	1.85	1.92	1.86	1.77	1.89	1.73
	p	4.04	4.70	4.62	5.57	5.02	8.10	9.66	5.26	4.54	4.62	4.24	2.92	5.47
ALL	c	6.57	6.24	5.59	5.78	5.07	5.16	5.15	4.92	5.26	4.80	5.65	5.72	5.57
	k	2.30	2.09	1.96	1.96	2.06	2.09	2.14	1.88	1.99	1.91	1.98	1.99	1.95

FIG 1.10 METEOROLOGICAL DATA FOR

SITE SPECIFIED HERE

ONCE IN 50 YEARS WINDSPEED = 20.8 m/s

UV =SQRT(305.00 + K*32.73)

k= 1.946 MODEK= 261.54 DISPK= 27.10

P(V,WD)=p[1-exp{-(V/c)**k}]/100

specified sites" These divide the year up into either Months or Seasons, and for all, present values of the frequency that the wind is from a range of directions (usually in 30° sectors, although other intervals apply to some data) and of magnitude in the ranges of the Beaufort Scale (or ranges specified by hourly-average limiting wind speeds).

The easiest way to handle these data is to convert the tables of frequencies into Weibull Distributions, so that values of p, c and k specify each distribution. Such a presentation is given in Figure 1.10. To allow for any obstacles close to the anemometer which could affect the results, the data for the whole year can be corrected to give the "Once in 50 Years" value from the map, with the Directional Corrections for the different Wind Directions when these are known. In the rubric the value of the Omnidirectional "Once in 50 Years" wind speed is quoted, together with the Mode and Dispersion of the Square of the Reference Omnidirectional Extreme wind speed (this is to assist the Monte Carlo study described in Section 3.1.7).

1.5.3. Justification for Using Strong Wind Data.

1.5.3.1. Wind Loading.

As maximum values of wind loading are required, critical conditions occur in high winds, so the neutral atmosphere is appropriate.

1.5.3.2. Wind Environment.

Most acceptability criteria are based on the exceedence of stated wind speeds for a stated percentage of the time. The wind speeds used are, for comfort, less than 10 m/s. But these are local wind speeds, the highest local wind speeds within a complex of buildings will occur when the winds above the complex are strong, so that the use of neutral atmospheric winds in the wind tunnel is correct.

1.5.3.3. Ventilation Studies.

1.5.3.3.1. Natural Ventilation.

In natural ventilation studies the volume flows and velocities throughout the building depend, in a linear fashion, on the reference wind speed. For the majority of the time the reference wind speed is less than 10 m/s, so that use of strong wind data are inappropriate. Minimum ventilation will be provided in the lowest of wind conditions. Calm conditions do occur for hours at a stretch, so any ventilation in these conditions will result from buoyancy forces only.

Stable atmospheres reduce turbulence, and therefor the penetration of wind into the building complex: unstable conditions do the opposite. Neutral atmospheric conditions produce penetrations between the two extremes. There are no data about the relative time when stable and unstable conditions occur in towns and cities, and less still about the degree of stability, so the use of neutral data throughout is a compromise, and supplies results which are repeatable. As results from ventilation studies are all expressed in statistical terms, they are as accurate as possible without additional data which are not available. It is not expected that, were those data to be available, the final results would be much altered.

1.5.3.3.2. Forced Ventilation.

In forced ventilation systems, the fans provide the ventilation when the wind is absent, and the purpose of a wind tunnel study is to demonstrate that the wind does not destroy the ventilation when it is strong. For this reason strong wind data are required for the wind tunnel studies of forced ventilation and, these occur in a neutral atmosphere.

1.5.3.4. Smoke Dispersion in Case of Fire.

The basic study carried out by the Fire Engineer is one in the absence of wind. All areas of openings are designed in this study. All that is required of the Wind Engineer is to show that the wind does not inhibit the no-wind performance of the system. For this the greatest effect would be in the strongest winds, so the strong wind study is appropriate.

1.5.3.5. Removal of Effluent from Buildings.

1.5.3.5.1. Near Field.

The questions to be asked in the immediate vicinity of the buildings are two-fold

i) does the effluent break cleanly from its emission point,

ii) is the effluent entrained into the wake of the building.

The critical conditions for both of these questions is the highest wind conditions. It is then appropriate that the wind tunnel study should be conducted in strong wind conditions.

1.5.3.5.2. Far Field.

Once released into the atmosphere, a successful outcome of the near field study, the subsequent path resulting in a maximum ground level concentration will depend upon the stability of the atmosphere, and normal wind tunnel studies have nothing to offer.

Special wind tunnels which have simulated stable or unstable atmospheres can be used, but specification of the velocity profiles and spectra to be used is an open question.

2. Flow Around Bluff Bodies in Turbulent Flow

This book is about buildings, which are bluff bodies, that is to say, they have thickness. The opposite to a bluff body is a plate. There is a version of a plate which has a little thickness, this is called an aerofoil, and this behaves as a plate. It is worth spending a line or two on aerofoils.

The essential for an aerofoil is that it shall have a sharp trailing edge (rear end): it also has a rounded leading edge (front end). The requirement of the sharp trailing edge is that the flows over the top and bottom surfaces of the aerofoil meet at the trailing edge and flow off tangentially: this is called the "Kutta-Jowkoski Hypothesis". The implication of this is that, when the aerofoil is placed at a small incidence to an airstream, the flow over the lower surface would want to turn round the trailing edge to flow up the tail end of the upper surface to a separation point on the upper surface, equating the length of path on upper and lower surfaces. Because the trailing edge is sharp, a shear stress, which is caused because of the viscosity of the air, prevents this sharp turning, so the flow on the lower surface separates from the lower surface at the trailing edge and continues in the windward direction. This in turn creates a suction at the tail of the upper surface which draws the would-be separation point down to the trailing edge. The rounded leading edge helps the flow around the nose to flow from the lower to upper surface without separating, but, even with a sharp edge here, which would cause a separation, the separated flow would turn and flow in the windward direction, reattaching to the upper surface, so the rounded front is not essential.

In mathematical terms in potential flow (assuming zero viscosity) a flow over a flat plate at incidence can be represented by "u" and "v" flows in the x and y directions: these will give the rear stagnation point on the upper surface, as discussed above. The movement of the rear stagnation point to the trailing edge can be achieved by adding a "circulation" to the flow around the aerofoil. It is easily shown that a body with a circulation around it in a uniform flow generates a cross-wind force, called "lift", which is a linear function of the circulation. This is the foundation of aerofoil theory.

On the other hand, a roughly horizontal bluff body at small incidence in a horizontal air stream has a wide wake, and generates no circulation because it has not the same requirement at its tail. However, a bluff body at small incidence does generate a cross-wind force because of the different separations of the boundary layer on the front face at its junction with the upper and lower faces. The pressures in these separations create a cross wind force in the opposite direction to that created by the aerofoil, and it is these separations which we will discuss later in this Chapter, and again in Chapter 4.

A great deal of aircraft aerodynamics is in smooth flow, and is two dimensional. The atmosphere in which buildings are placed is turbulent and three dimensional. The discussion below will be taken in two parts, in the first the flow will be assumed to be two dimensional, and we will study the effects of turbulence. Then we will look at the changes which shear will make on the results.

Much of what follows is about the flow around single buildings in an open space. In practice this rarely occurs. There are nearly always other buildings around, and these will affect the flow around the new building. The first question in the assessment of the wind flow in a complex of buildings, is to try to resolve the flow field in which the new building is to be situated and then the mutual effect of the new on the old, and visa versa. The descriptions of flow given here for individual buildings define how the presence of a new building will affect its neighbours, and then the effect of the neighbourhood on the new building. In most branches of engineering the "Principle of Minimum Energy" applies; this also applies to the wind, and it can be expressed in layman's terms as "Wind is lazy, and will always take the easiest path". As we are all lazy, put yourself it the position of the wind and decide what you would do with the alternatives. It is never "all the wind will go this way and none the other", but, if there are two possible paths, the proportion of wind going one way is inversely proportional to the ratio of difficulty (pressure or friction losses) of following that path rather than the other. With many alternatives it becomes a multi-choice problem, but the principles are the same. This idea is taken up again in the introduction to Chapter 4.

2.1. Shear-free Flow (Two Dimensional).

2.1.1. Dynamic Similarity.

If we are to study the flow around a building at model scale, as this is the only way to proceed before the building is completed, we have to establish the criteria which will ensure that the two flows, the model and the full scale, are similar.

The Buckingham Pi Theorem states that, for dynamic similarity to exist between two systems, if the two systems depend upon n independent variables, then all dependent variables, made "non-dimensional" using some of the independent variables, shall be functions of (n - 3) non-dimensional groups of the independent variables; all the independent variables being used. The reason for the "3" is that the three dimensions of "Mass", "Length" and "Time" shall be satisfied, thus eliminating three variables.

To summarise, if the values of the (n - 3) non-dimensional groups are the same, then the two systems will be dynamically similar.

For instance, consider the pressure (p) on a part of a building as the dependant variable. This will depend upon the independent variables, which are

The shape of the Building
The incidence (orientation to the wind direction) of the Building (α)
The scale of the Building (L)
The wind speed (V)
The turbulence Intensity of the wind speed ($I_u = \sigma_u/V$)
The scale of the Turbulence (${}^xL_u$)
The density of the air (ρ)
The viscosity of the air (μ)
The compressibility of the air ($d\rho/dp$)
The effect of gravity (g)

The frequency of oscillation (n).

In this list we only consider one intensity of turbulence and one integral scale of turbulence; in fact there are three intensities and nine integral scale lengths, but we will assume that all will be treated as the one illustrated.

We would then write Buckingham's Theorem for the pressure on a part of the building as

$$p/(\rho V^2) = f(\,shape,\ \alpha,\ \rho VL/\mu,\ \sigma_u/V,\ {}^xL_u/L,\ V^2/(dp/d\rho),\ V^2/gL,\ nL/V).$$

This is simplified by giving names to the various non-dimensional groups, thus

$$C_p = f(\,shape,\ \alpha,\ Re,\ I_u,\ {}^xL_u/L,\ M,\ F,\ S_t\,),$$

where C_p is the Pressure Coefficient (note the introduction of the 1/2, because $1/2\rho V^2$ is the dynamic pressure, which is a quantity in its own right), Re is the Reynolds Number, $I_u = \sigma_u/V$ is the Intensity of Turbulence in the u component of velocity, ${}^xL_u/L$ is the Integral Scale Length Ratio of the u component of velocity in the x direction, M is the Mach Number, F is the Froude Number, and S_t is the Strouhal Number.

Each of the "Numbers" has a different effect upon the flow, and, as it is never possible to satisfy all the Numbers simultaneously, which is the requirement for complete dynamic similarity, the relative importance of each has to be established, and, when several conflict, then the important ones in the circumstances under consideration must be satisfied. Each will be studied in turn.

2.1.1.1. Reynolds Number.

The major effect of the Reynolds Number, in the form of $\rho VL/\mu$, or VL/ν, where ν is called the "kinematic viscosity", is on "Transition", the change from "Laminar" to "Turbulent" flow. Flow can either be laminar, when layers of flow are assumed to flow as laminae, one over the other, or not, and the "not" state is called Turbulent. It was originally thought that laminar flow had little turbulence, but this has been shown not to be true: the fluctuations are generally of a lower frequency than in turbulent flow, although the intensity can be almost as large. The main difference is that in turbulent flow there is an energy transfer from one lamina or layer to another. This is very important in "Separation and Reattachment", which is discussed in Section 2.1.2 .

In physical terms the Reynolds Number is the ratio of "Inertia Forces" to "Viscous Forces", so that it is of importance where viscous forces are important.

$$Re = \rho VL/\mu \approx (\rho L^3 V / time)/(L^2 \mu / time) \approx (\rho L^3 V / time) / (L^2 \mu V/L)$$

$$\approx inertia\ force / viscous\ force.$$

2.1.1.2. Mach Number.

Mach Number is a measure of the compressibility of the air.

$$M^2 = V^2 / dp/d\rho = V^2 / a^2,$$

where a is the speed of sound.

$$M^2 \approx V^2\ \rho / p \approx (V^2 \rho^2 L^6 / time^2) / (p\rho L^4 V^2) \approx (V^2 \rho^2 L^6 / time^2) / p^2 L^4)$$

$$\approx (inertia\ force)^2 / (pressure\ force)^2.$$

The significance of Mach Number can be seen when compressibility is introduced into Bernoulli's Equation. The incompressible form of Bernoulli's Equation is written as

$$p_o - p_s = 1/2 \rho V^2$$

where p_o is the total pressure, and p_s is the static pressure. The compressible form can be approximated to by

$$p_o - p_s = 1/2\rho V^2 (1 + M^2/4 + M^4/40 + +),$$

so that, provided that M < 0.2, the error in pressure difference will be less that 1%.

The speed of sound at 15°C and 1000 millibar pressure is 340 m/s, so that the wind speed will need to be greater than 68 m/s for there to be a 1% error if the air is considered incompressible.

It would appear that this error is acceptable for most practical purposes, so Mach Number can be ignored.

2.1.1.3. Froude Number.

The Froude Number is a measure of the effect of gravity upon the flow.

$$F^2 = V^2 /(gL) \approx (\rho^2 V^2 L^6 / time) / (gL\rho^2 L^6 / time^2)$$

$$\approx (\rho^2 V^2 L^6 / time^2) / ([gL/time^2 \; \rho^2 L^6)$$

$$\approx (inertia\ force)^2 / (gravitational\ force)^2.$$

Froude Number is therefor only of significance when gravitational forces are important with respect to wind forces. This usually only occurs at interfaces of fluids of different densities.

2.1.1.4. Strouhal Number.

This is a frequency parameter and appears in many places, the best known is in respect to Vortex Shedding. As a frequency parameter it has the same form as the TVL formula which is discussed in Section 3.1.3.

In some situations the reciprocal of the Strouhal Number is used, and is then called a "Reduced Velocity".

2.1.1.5. Pressure, Force and Moment Coefficients.

The usual non-dimensional form of pressure and always, since World War 1, containing the half, is

$$C_p = (p - p_s) / 1/2\rho V^2,$$

where p_s is the static or ambient pressure, which is the datum relative to which all pressures are measured.

The Force and Moment coefficients are defined in like manner, thus

$$C_F = F / (1/2 \rho V^2 L^2), \text{ and}$$

$$C_m = M / (1/2 \rho V^2 L^3),$$

where L^2 can be xy, and L^3 can be xyz.

2.1.2. Separation and Reattachment.

This is the major difference between Aircraft Aerodynamics and Industrial Aerodynamics. In the aircraft field every endeavour is made to obtain attached flow with no separations. This is impossible in the Industrial field.

To understand separation consider the flow over a surface as a Boundary Layer on the surface and Potential Flow outside. The boundary layer is a thin layer of air adjacent to the surface in which the air speed increases from zero on the surface to its value outside. All the shear is contained within the boundary layer, so the Potential Flow is free of shear. The value of wind speed outside depends upon the potential flow around the body (and thin boundary layer), unless separation takes place. Within the boundary layer the flow experiences a frictional force at the surface which dissipates energy, and the boundary layer is the region containing all the air which has lost energy. This loss in energy is transmitted through the boundary layer by viscosity, and, in the case of turbulent flow, by the movement of elements of fluid from a region of one air speed to another, and so a turbulent boundary layer is thicker than a laminar one but is better able to transmit energy from the potential flow outside to the surface. If the flow outside the boundary layer is accelerating, then the kinetic energy of the air there is increasing, and can usually supply the loss of energy at the surface. If, however, the flow outside is decelerating, then there is less energy to feed back to the surface, and the energy of the air over a finite thickness very close to the surface will ultimately fall to zero. The point at which this occurs is called the "Separation Point" (although its position moves continually with time, and it would be more accurate to talk about a "Separation Zone" which bounds the positions of the Separation Point). The air further out in the boundary layer, which still has velocity, then flows over the stagnant air on the surface leaving the surface. The air beneath the active air is often called a "Separation Bubble", and the flow within this bubble rotates slowly, driven by the inner layers of the active air. Further from the separation point the pressure gradient (called "adverse" in decelerating flow) reduces, and energy is transferred back towards the surface by viscous stresses and turbulent movement, until, if there is sufficient distance along the surface, the flow "reattaches" to the surface and the bubble is closed.

Four variables affect separation; they are Reynolds Number, Turbulence in the wind, the Roughness of the surface, and the Pressure Gradient. These will be considered in turn.

2.1.2.1. Reynolds Number.

Reynolds Number is an enabling quantity in that, below a critical value it is impossible to sustain turbulent flow. This value is about 180 (based on the height of the obstruction), and if transition is to be induced on a model by a transition wire, the Reynolds Number based on the diameter of the wire should be at least 200. There is also an upper critical value of Reynolds Number above which it is impossible to sustain laminar flow. This value, in the absence of turbulence with zero pressure gradient on a smooth surface is 3.85×10^5 based upon length along the surface from the leading edge. The presence of turbulence, roughness of the surface, and pressure gradient will reduce this value considerably, and, with 25% turbulence and a typical surface roughness of building models, but no pressure gradient, the critical value is below 10^4 . The value of Reynolds Number for buildings is much greater than 10^6 , so conditions on buildings are always turbulent. Members on and additions to buildings, for instance flag poles, which are much smaller, experience values of Reynolds Number which could require consideration.

The values of Reynolds Number occurring on a building are almost impossible to simulate in a wind tunnel investigation where air is used as the fluid. In the 1930's a Compressed Air Tunnel (CAT) was built at the National Physical Laboratory in which a wind tunnel was built inside a pressure vessel and the air in the pressure vessel was compressed to 25 atmospheres before the wind tunnel was run. High Reynolds Number data were obtained. Unfortunately, due to the short length of the wind tunnel, the turbulence levels were high and unmeasured, so the results were dubious. The tunnel has since been dismantled. For similarity, in an ordinary wind tunnel, the product of length scale and velocity scale would have to be unity. If the length scale is 1/200, then the velocity scale would need to be 200/1. Thus to represent 10 m/s full scale, the wind tunnel wind speed would need to be 2000 m/s, a Mach Number of about 6!

The effect of Reynolds Number can be ignored if the buildings are sharp-edged because separation will always occur at the sharp corner, and reattachment is chiefly controlled by turbulence, but problems exist for rounded buildings. This will be discussed in the section 2.1.3.

2.1.2.2. Turbulence in the Approaching Air.

The first major effect of turbulence in the approaching air is to increase the transfer of energy through the boundary layer. This, in turn can cause a premature transition from laminar to turbulent flow, hence its inclusion in the "Effective Reynolds Number" (see paragraph 2.1.2.5). Scale as well as intensity of turbulence is important, and must be taken into account.

The second major effect of turbulence is on reattachment. Once the boundary layer has separated, and providing that the Reynolds Number is high enough for turbulent flow to be triggered, turbulence is the chief mechanism which will restore energy to the layers of air adjacent to the surface. This can only happen when there is a favourable pressure gradient, or when the adverse pressure gradient is small. In the reattachment process, the amount of turbulence within the correct range of scales will govern the distance between separation and reattachment, i.e. the length of the separation bubble. This has a major effect on the pressure within the bubble, because the shorter the bubble, the lower the pressure within and the greater the negative pressure on the surface. For this reason it is essential that the correct turbulence should be modelled in a wind tunnel investigation.

2.1.2.3. Surface Roughness.

Increase in surface roughness increases the friction at the surface, and so the rougher the surface, the greater the friction and the sooner the separation. This is not the whole story. The increased roughness also generates turbulence, which increases the energy transference across the boundary layer, and this can cause a former laminar layer to become turbulent. Thus roughness can change the value of Reynolds Number at which a certain flow pattern occurs, and thus the definition of a given flow pattern must be in terms of an Effective Reynolds Number, which is the actual Reynolds Number corrected for surface roughness (also turbulence) effects.

The other major effect of surface roughness on a curved surface is on the value of the Drag Coefficient in turbulent flow. Three values of roughness are presented in Figure 2.01, which presents the Effective Drag Coefficient of a Circular Cylinder as a function of Effective Reynolds Number: the magnitude of the effect is evident.

FIG 2.01 VARIATION WITH EFFECTIVE REYNOLDS NUMBER OF DRAG COEFFICIENT FOR A CIRCULAR CYLINDER

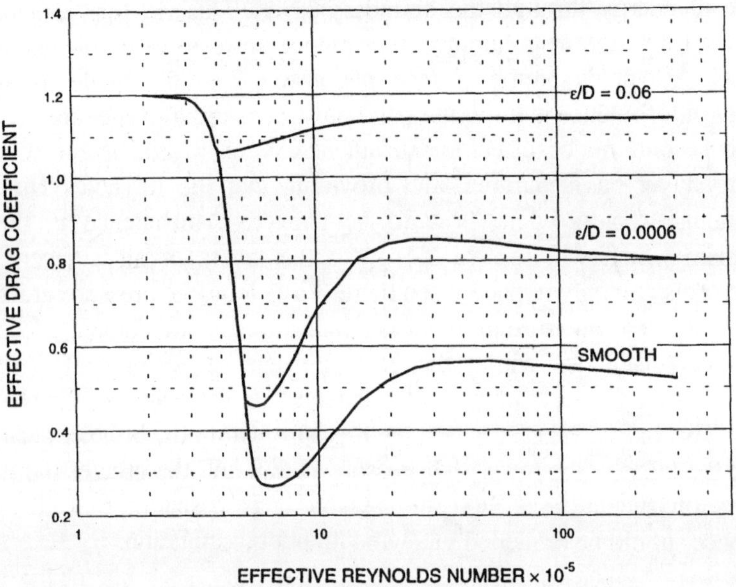

2.1.2.4. Pressure Gradient.

Separation cannot occur in a favourable (*dp/dx* < *0*) pressure gradient, only in an adverse one (*dp/dx* > *0*). The stronger the adverse gradient, the sooner separation will occur (a sharp corner is the ultimate case of an infinite adverse pressure gradient).

2.1.2.5. Effective Reynolds Number.

In their data sheets ESDU presents data for circular cylinders, and other shapes similarly affected, as a function of an "Effective Reynolds Number", which is the value of the basic Reynolds Number with corrections for roughness of the surface and for the scale and intensity of the turbulence. The effect of pressure gradient is contained in the shape of the member for which the data are presented.

2.1.3. Difference between Sharp-Edges and Rounded Buildings.

Because of the shear stresses in the air at a sharp corner, flow will always separate here. In this case Reynolds Number has no importance on separation. Provided that the flow is turbulent, Reynolds Number has negligible effect on rcattachment, which is governed by turbulence and surface roughness.

On a curved surface the pressure gradient changes continually along the surface, and the location of the separation point can have a dramatic effect on the pressures, and therefor the forces, on the member. Consider a circular cylinder as an illustration of this.

The variation of Effective Drag (in the direction of the wind) Coefficient with effective Reynolds Number is presented in Figure 2.01 for three values of surface roughness. The Effective Drag Coefficient presented is given by

$$C_{D,eff} = C_D \,/\, (1+2\,\varepsilon/D)$$

where ε is the effective roughness height of surface and varies from about 10^{-5} m for painted metal to about 3×10^{-3} m for brickwork. In practice this correction is small and can usually be ignored. It can be seen from that Figure that there is a "Laminar" region, and a "Turbulent" region, but there is also a "Transition" region. The laminar region, below an Effective Reynolds Number of 3×10^5 where the value of the Drag Coefficient is 1.2, is sensibly independent of surface roughness, and the turbulent region, above an Effective Reynolds Number of about 3×10^6 , where the value of Drag Coefficient depends mainly on surface roughness. The transition region is very interesting and deserves further explanation. The separation point on a circular cylinder in laminar flow is at an angular position of about 70°, and for the fully turbulent flow at about 120°. This is shown in Figure 2.02. In laminar flow, as the separation is before the maximum width, the separated flow continues to expand and the wake is wider than the cylinder. But in the

FIG 2.02 SEPARATION STREAMLINES AROUND A CIRCULAR CYLINDER

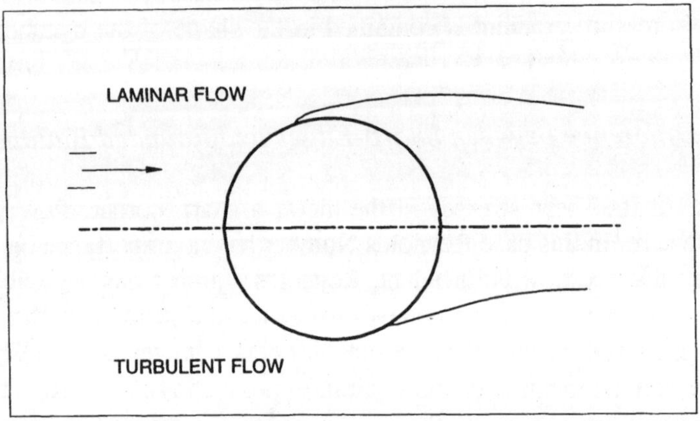

fully turbulent case, the separation is after the point of maximum width, so the wake continues to contract and the wake is narrow. A study of the pressure distribution on a circular cylinder shows that the pressures and suctions on the front face almost balance, and that most of the drag of a circular cylinder comes from pressures on the rear face, so a wide wake means high drag, and visa versa. In the transition region the separation point moves gradually back along the surface to about 130°, and then slowly moves forward a little. This forward movement is due to the effects of a complex combination of pressure gradient, turbulence and Reynolds Number.

Both laminar and turbulent streamlines were shown one on either side of the centre line on Figure 2.02, to show the difference. Laminar flow on one side, and turbulent flow on the other can only happen together in special circumstances, which will be described in Section 2.1.4.1. When they do, the flow downstream is deflected sideways, and not as shown in Figure 2.02, and this produces a cross-wind force on the cylinder.

Other rounded shapes behave in a similar fashion, but the details are different. There arises a difficulty in the wind tunnel testing of members with rounded shapes. The reason is the matching of Reynolds Number and surface roughness between full scale and model. If the member is large, and the full scale Reynolds Number is far in the Turbulent range, then the wind tunnel investigation must also be far in the turbulent range, with a scaled surface roughness. To ensure that the model flow is turbulent, a transition wire, or a strip of sandpaper should be attached to the model upwind of the separation point; but the model surface roughness still has to be scaled.

If the full scale member is small, so that the full scale Reynolds Number is in the transition range, then it is almost impossible to obtain data from a wind tunnel investigation.

2.1.4. Oscillatory Flow Patterns.

There are some shapes of members which produce an oscillatory flow pattern around them, even in smooth shear-free flow. The best known pattern is Vortex shedding, which will be considered in section 2.1.4.1, and many other oscillatory flows, some of which are incorrectly described as vortex shedding.

2.1.4.1. Vortex Shedding.

The flow behind a member of small Aspect Ratio (ratio of the two cross-wind dimensions Height to Width) has an enclosed wake and is stable, this was shown by Calvert (J.R.Calvert "Experiments on the Flow Past an Inclined Disc" J. Fluid Mech Vol 29 pp 691 - 703 1967).

When the aspect ratio increases, the wake opens, and the former boundary layer on the front face separates and travels downstream as two shear layers, each containing vortices of a sign appropriate to their generation, that is to say, the vortices in the two shear layers are of different sign. This system was shown to be unstable by many workers, notably Gerrard (J.R.Gerrard "The Mechanics of the Formation Region of Vortices behind Bluff Bodies" J. Fluid Mech Vol 25 pp 401 - 413. 1966) working in fluids. A mathematical study of two parallel shear layers was undertaken by Abernathy and Kronauer (F.H.Abernathy, R.E.Kronauer "The Formation of Vortex Sheets" J.Fluid Mech Vol 13 pp 1 - 20 1962), and they showed that the flow fields induced by two lines of vortices of opposite sign comprising the shear layers, given a very small initial disturbance (two exactly parallel lines of vortices are neutrally stable) cause the separate vortices to cluster into groups, and eventually, after some time has elapsed from the initial small disturbance, some vortices

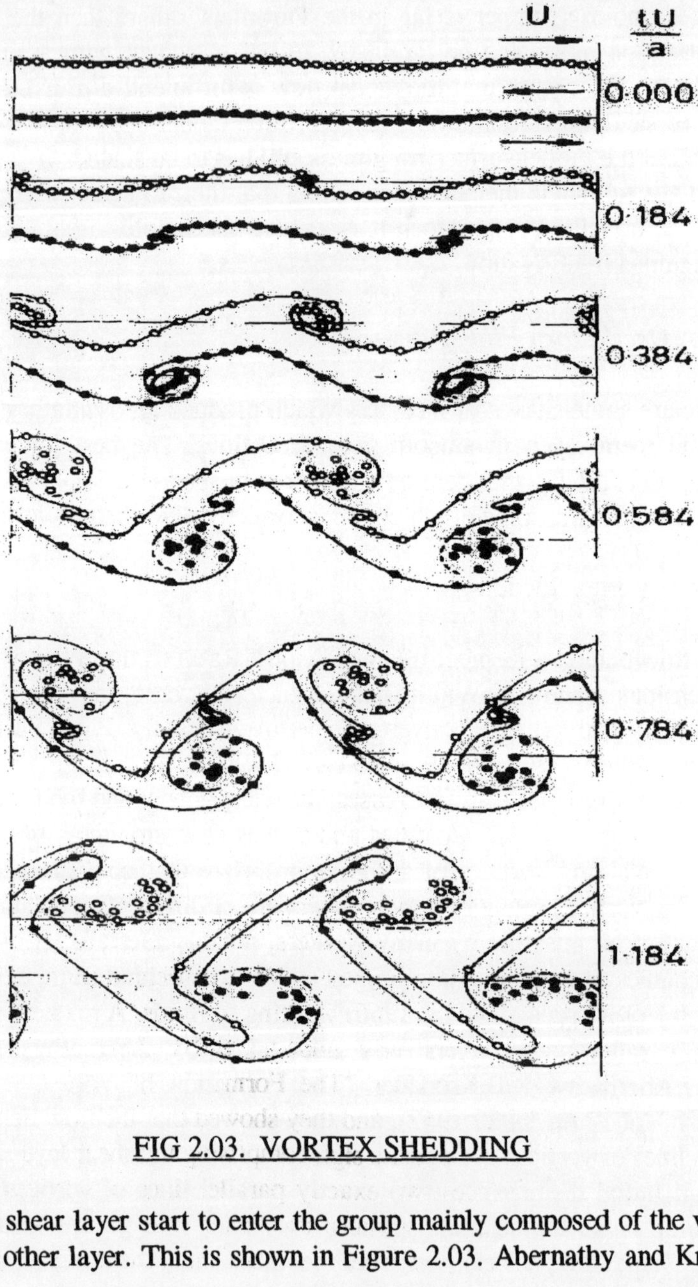

FIG 2.03. VORTEX SHEDDING

from one shear layer start to enter the group mainly composed of the vortices from the other layer. This is shown in Figure 2.03. Abernathy and Kronauer show the vortex sheets to be continuous, but photographs of smoke trails in air showed that the shear layers break up into a series of separate vortices. Because each group of vortices contained a preponderance of one sign of vortices, and because Thompson's Theorem requires that, if there is no circulation around a field containing a member in an airstream, then there can never be a circulation around that field. So, if the member sheds a vortex of strength K, then there must develop a circulation of -K around the member, so that the circulation round the field containing the member and the shed vortex shall still be zero.

This is the crux of the matter, every time a vortex is shed from the member, a circulation is generated around the member. The vortex sheet breaks up into vortices alternatively from each side, and these are of opposite sign to each other. This is called a Karman Street. Kelvin's Theorem states that, if there is a circulation of strength K around a member in an airstream of density ρ and velocity V, there will be a cross-wind force per unit span (L) exerted upon the body given by

$$L = \rho VK.$$

Over time therefor, there will be a cross-wind force of $\pm L / 2$ exerted upon the member, changing every time a vortex is shed. The frequency of change is important. Various theories were put forward by Gerrard et al as to the physics of the mechanism. My favourite is that a vortex grows until it entrains the same number of vortices from each shear layer, so that its strength reaches a maximum , and then it separates. Regardless of the physics, if the frequency of shedding is n, then the Strouhal Number (S_t) given by

$$S_t = n\, L / V,$$

where L is the cross-wind dimension and V is the wind speed. It is shown by ESDU that

$$S_t = f\,(shape, R_e),$$

but that the dependence on Reynolds Number is small. The value of Strouhal Number for a circular cylinder is about 0.20, for a square cylinder is about

0.14, reducing to about 0.08 for a 10:1 rectangle with the flow perpendicular to the longer side.

The frequency of excitation is dependent on wind speed in this case. If the member is flexible, or can move, then a matching of the frequency of excitation to the natural frequency of the member has a dramatic effect on the behaviour of the member; this is considered in section 3.2.1.

The cure for vortex shedding comes from the understanding of its generation: the cure must, as a first approach, prevent the interaction of the two shear layers. This can be done in one of two ways, either by placing a solid sheet between the two shear layers, or bleeding air into the wake between the layers. The former of these cures require knowledge of the wind direction, so that the position of the sheet can be located. In the building context, when wind can come from any direction, this cure is impractical. The second can be achieved by wrapping a porous shroud of slightly larger diameter round the member, so that air can enter the annulus between the shroud and the member where the pressure is positive, leaving where the pressure is negative, i.e. in the wake, this is almost omnidirectional. This shroud can sometimes also reduce the drag of the cylinder.

Not a cure, but an amelioration of the effects can be achieved by spoiling the span wise correlation of the vortex sheets. This can be done by varying the diameter of the member in a cyclic manner along its span by the addition of radial protrusions. A simpler way to achieve this end is to wrap a "strake" around a circular member; a strake is a flat piece attached radially to the member in a helical fashion along the span. The protrusion should be 10% of the diameter, and the helix should be three start and complete one rotation in 5 diameters. The top third only of the member need be covered. This device will increase the drag of the member to which it is fitted.

2.1.4.2. Flow Switching.

When a set of similar buildings are built in a regular pattern and wind blows between them, a stable pattern usually develops, which means that the flow pattern round each building is the same. In some instances a stable pattern can occur with different patterns round each, and the flow pattern about pairs of buildings can "switch" from one to the other. The switching can either be regular with a switching frequency, or it can be random.

The best known example of flow switching is around boiler tubes. The flow around an isolated circular cylinder in laminar and turbulent flow is

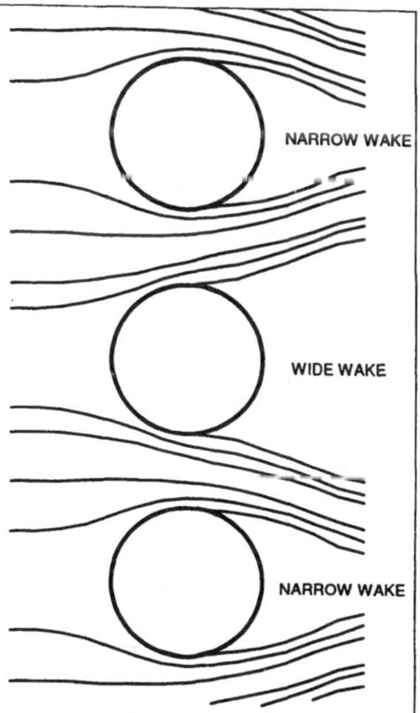

FIG 2.04 STREAMLINES THROUGH BOILER TUBES

shown in Figure 2.02. When there is a line of identical cylinders, the flow round all should be the same. However, providing the Reynolds Number is within a small range of values, it only takes a slight misalignment in either direction for there to develop wide wakes and narrow wakes as the Coanda effect, explained in the next paragraph, causes the flow to stick to one side or another. This is shown in Figure 2.04, although the alternative pattern is not the only one achieved. This pattern can become oscillatory with flexible tubes, because the tubes with wider wakes have a higher drag, and this can cause the tube to deflect further, whilst the ones with the narrow wake will have lower drag and will deflect less. As the tubes deflect fore and aft, the flow pattern can change and an oscillation occur. As flow switching is controlled by the movement of the tubes, and as this will occur at their natural frequency, this oscillation can produce large deflections, and therefor large stresses in the tubes. This is further discussed in Section 3.2.8.

The Coanda Effect was first explained by the Czech scientist Coanda, and describes how a flow impinging on the curved surface of a body will stick to

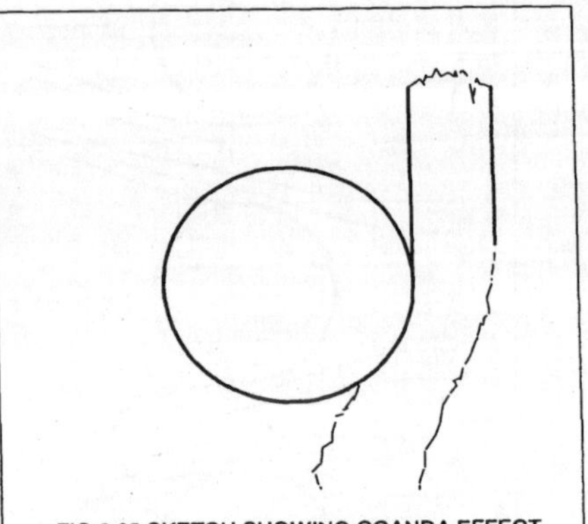

FIG 2.05 SKETCH SHOWING COANDA EFFECT

the surface and enter the wake of the body; this is shown in Figure 2.05. An example of this is when a finger is moved sideways into a stream of water flowing from a tap. As soon as the finger touches the water, it sticks to the finger and turns behind the finger.

2.1.5. Special shapes.

It is possible for some shapes to behave in a special way, and some of these will be considered in this Section.

2.1.5.1. Stranded Cables.

Electricity transmission lines often use stranded cables. This is the cheapest form of manufacture. Special cables were made and have been used, and these will be discussed at the end of this paragraph.

The characteristic which makes stranded cables special is the helical form of the outer strands. The rough cross section of the cable behaves as surface roughness, as described above. However, if the wind direction is inclined at a small angle to the length of the wire, the flow on one side of the cable is more normal to the strands than on the other. Over a small range of Reynolds Numbers the additional effective surface roughness of the strands more normal to the flow can cause transition, whilst the reduced effective roughness of the strands less normal to the flow does not cause transition. It is then possible to have laminar flow over one side of the cable, whilst having turbulent flow over the other. The net result is that the wake is deflected, and this produces a cross wind force on the cable. As the cable is flexible, it is able to move under the wind loads; increase and decrease of drag will allow it to move in a fore and aft movement. When its velocity of movement is added to that of the wind, it is possible that the range of velocities over the cable encompass the critical range, and there will be a change of flow type during the movement, providing the forcing function for the motion. If this is coupled to a periodic lift force, the cable could move it a two dimensional way. This is discussed in Section 3.2.7.

To avoid the critical value of Reynolds Number occurring in the practical range of wind speeds, a cable was produced in which the strands were machined so that they fitted together leaving a surface which had only a 0.15 mm depression between strands, and the outside surface of the strands followed the circular curvature of the whole cable. When made with the same helix angle, the critical wind speed was over 100 m/s, and no problem occurred in practice.

2.1.5.2. Swing of a Cricket Ball.

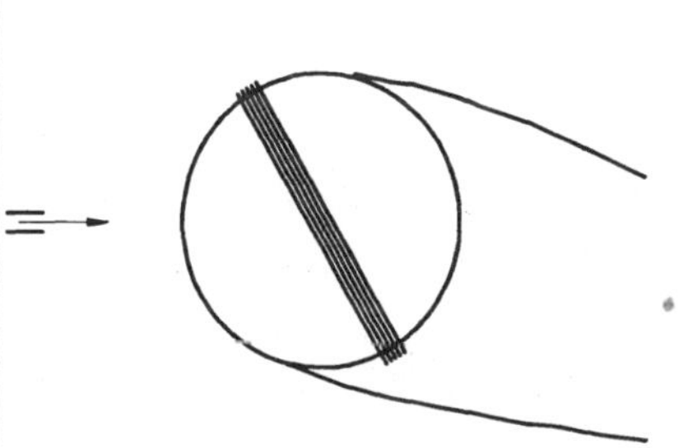

FIG 2.06 FLOW AROUND A CRICKET BALL

Although not an element of a building, the swing of a cricket ball is worthy of mention as an illustration of the same phenomenon. In this case the bowler polishes one side of the ball, and delivers it so that the seam leads on the unpolished side, see Figure 2.06. Over the critical speed range, the seam will trigger turbulent flow when the polished side will not, and the flow described in the last paragraph will occur. The art of the bowler is to vary his speed of delivery so that it can be all turbulent, turbulent/laminar, or all laminar in various parts of the same flight.

2.1.5.3. Electrified Train Overhead Line.

This can behave as a cricket ball. The trigger mechanism is a line of rain drops along the bottom of the cable. The best scenario for their production is for the line to be cooled below zero degrees, the air temperature then rises slightly and a light rain falls, the temperature drops and the rain freezes on the line. Slight melting and freezing will produce a line of drops along the underside of the line, and, within the correct wind speed range, vertical forces can be produced.

The same effect can be produced if a groove is cut along the top of the line to support it. This oscillation does not require rain.

2.2. Shear Flow.

Baines in Canada and Jenson in Denmark were two of the first to realise the importance of Shear in the approaching stream on the flow around bluff members. Shear implies a gradient of velocity perpendicular to a surface, which occurs in any boundary layer, the atmospheric boundary layer being no exception.

The effect of shear is to promote three dimensional flow. No longer can simple two dimensional pictures be presented.

2.2.1. Three Dimensional Flow.

Consider a rectangular block building normal to the flow in two dimensional flow; this is illustrated in Figure 2.07. The wind profile is shown at the left of the elevation. When these wind speeds are brought to rest at the centre of the front face, there will be a pressure gradient down the face of the building on

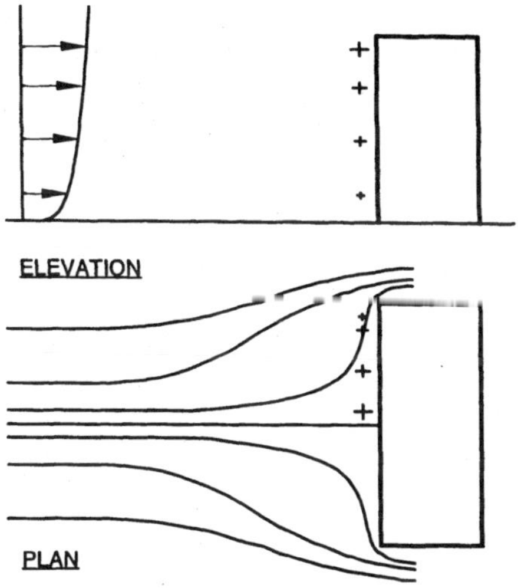

FIG 2.07 TWO DIMENSIONAL STREAMLINES

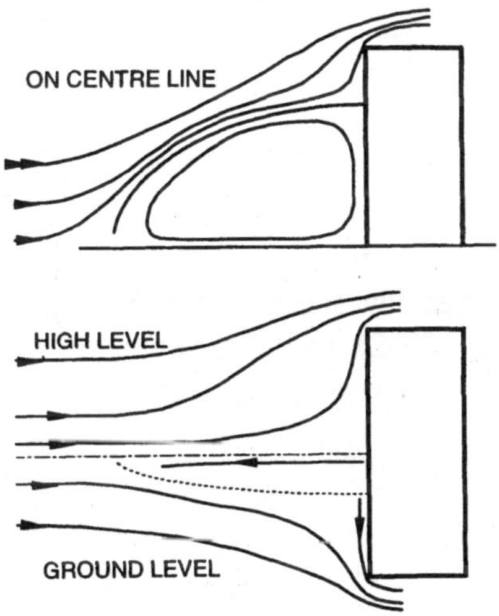

FIG 2.08. FLOW AROUND A BUILDING

the centre line of the plan. This will cause the air to flow down the front face of the building, creating a three dimensional flow, which is shown in Figure 2.08. This is an important change because the building is acting as a scoop, collecting air at height and delivering it at ground level, which means that there is much more wind to distribute at ground level than conceived in the

FIG. 2.09. STREAMLINES ON A 1×1×2 CUBOID. $\alpha = 0^{\circ}$

two dimensional system.

If the stagnation picture shown in Figure 2.07 were to apply strictly, the flow down the face should have started at the top. This is shown in Figure 2.09 not to be so. The reason is that, as the wind approaches the building along the streamline which defines the top of the separation bubble, there is a positive pressure towards the ground, and a large negative pressure over the top of the building. As the flow is subsonic, this information is available to the approaching wind, so the wind which would have impinged at the top of the face has already turned and flowed over the building. This means that there is another stagnation point on the face of the building at some point below the top, which marks the divide between the air flowing up and over, and that flowing down and around. This point is at about 70% of the height of the building. This down flow only occurs near the centre of the building in plan, the wind further away from the centre is turned sideways and flows round the ends of the building with a downward velocity component.

This three dimensional flow is caused entirely by the velocity profile of the approaching wind, and demonstrates the necessity of simulating the shear in the wind when conducting a wind tunnel investigation.

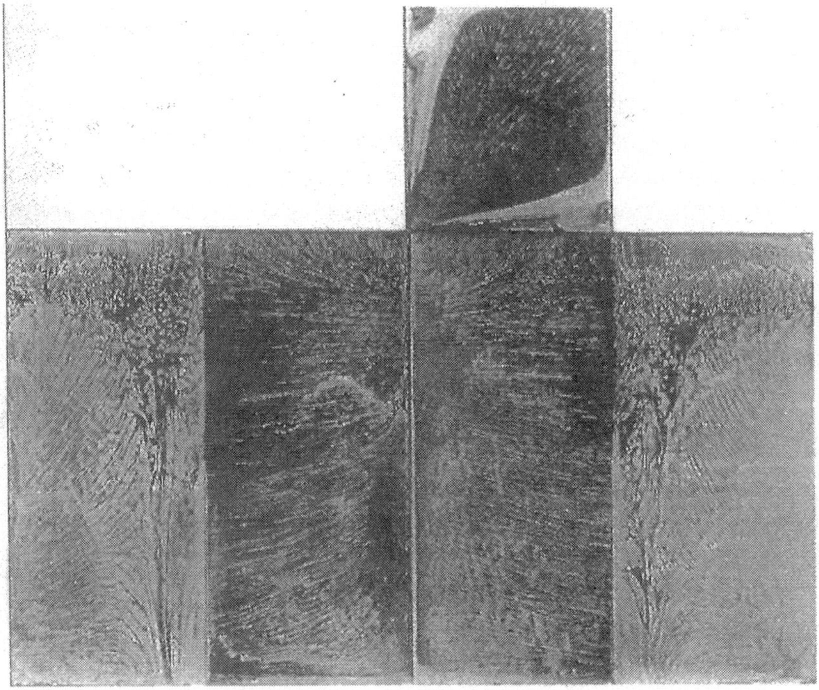

FIG. 2.10 STREAMLINES ON A 1×1×2 CUBOID $\alpha = 45^\circ$

When the wind is inclined at an angle greater than 14° to the front face of a rectangular building, the stagnation line moves to the corner of the building, and there is attached flow along the front two faces, this is shown on Figure 2.10. Between incidences (angles between the wind direction and the normal to the face) of 0° and 14°, the stagnation line moves from the centre to the corner. Downflow only occurs for a restricted range of incidences.

The opposite flow can occur in regions where the pressure is negative, and this produces upflows, but the picture is not that straightforward. An example of such a flow is at the corner formed by the side and rear walls of a building. If garbage is placed against the rear wall here, paper and light rubbish can rise high up this corner of the building. This can be seen in Figure 2.10

2.2.2. *Leading Edge Vortices.*

Another interesting three dimensional effect occurs, but this time when the incidence of the wind to the front face is greater than 14°. This is when the flow is moving sideways and upwards near the top of a front face in attached flow. When the flow reaches the top of the face, it separates in its vertical movement, but still possesses its sideways velocity. This creates a vortex a short distance above the surface of the roof, which starts at the apex, or front corner of the roof, and, as it is above the roof, it is turned into the wind direction by the active wind above the boundary layer on the roof. The same will happen on the other front face with attached flow, so a pair of vortices are formed close to the roof; initially along a line at a small angle to the edge of the roof, but soon being turned into the wind direction, see Figure 2.10. This phenomenon was first observed on the swept wings of aircraft, and the vortices were known as "Leading Edge Vortices": the name has been retained for the pair of vortices on the roof of a building.

The direction of rotation is such as to induce a downward component to the flow over the centre of the roof between the pair of vortices, helping to reattach the boundary layer. The flow on the roof is complicated in that, between the edge of the roof and the line of the vortex, there is a separated region where the pressure is very low (a value of pressure coefficient, based on the hourly-average speed of the approaching wind at the height of the top of the building, of about -2.5), then there is the region under the vortex where the pressure coefficient is of about -1.0, then there is the region in the centre of the roof where the pressure coefficient is of about -0.25. There are therefor extremely large changes of pressure occurring over very short distances in some regions of the roof.

The position of the separated regions and vortices move appreciably with wind direction, and, because the direction of the approaching wind is

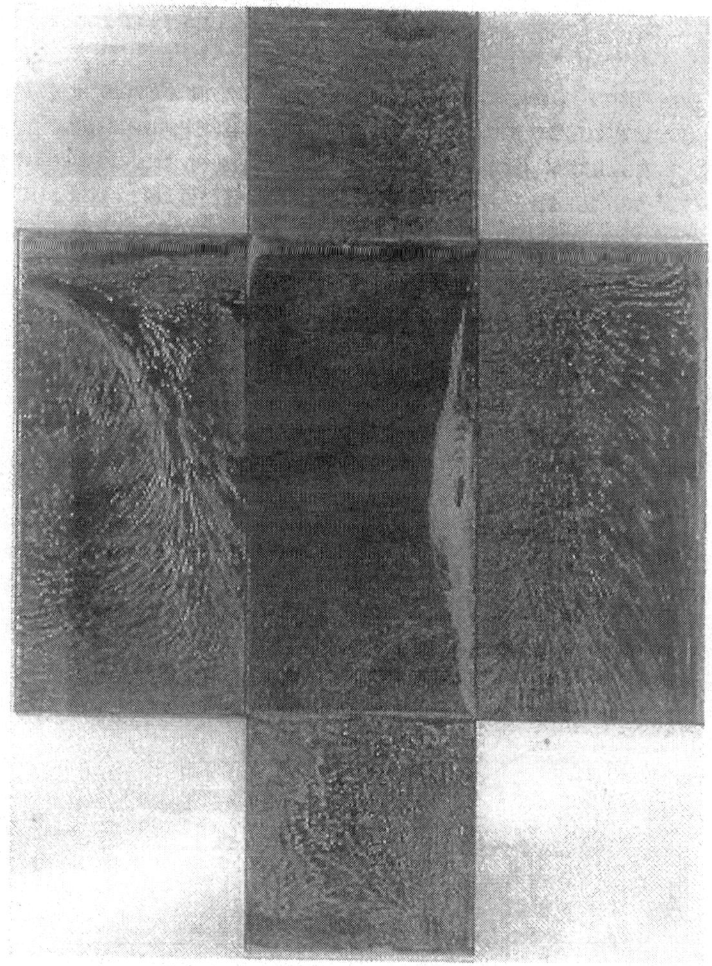

FIG 2.11 STREAMLINES ON A 2×2×1 CUBOID $\alpha = 30°$

continually changing, the positions of these regions of very different pressure also move. It is thus possible to have very large temporal changes of pressure at a fixed location in this region of a roof. If the building has a re-entrant corner in plan, the flow within the corner is oscillatory in that the corner overfills and over-empties in a cyclic fashion with the resulting effect on the roof of a cyclic change of the position of the separated region, the vortices and the attached flow, so some locations on the roof can experience cyclic changes of pressure of considerable magnitude in a very short time. This almost step change in pressure can move along lines on the roof in a cyclic fashion, lines which could represent the joints of roof cladding, causing movement of tiles or the flexing of thin metal sheeting. Some commercial roofing elements employ clever attachment devices to allow rapid installation, and it is possible for the dynamic deflections of the roofing elements to cause these attachments to become detached.

The characteristics of the leading edge vortices are that they are highly structured and small; this means that they persist and are not easily diffused by atmospheric turbulence. Their presence can be felt on adjoining buildings.

2.2.3. Separation Bubble on the Roof.

Apart from the separation bubbles discussed above, a separation bubble can also form on the roof when the wind is normal to a face, see Figure 2.09. The wind blowing up the front face separates at the corner between the wall and the roof. The separated shear layer turns in the wind and ultimately reattaches, or not, to the roof at a location depending upon the length of the roof and its inclination to the horizontal. In this case the separated bubble

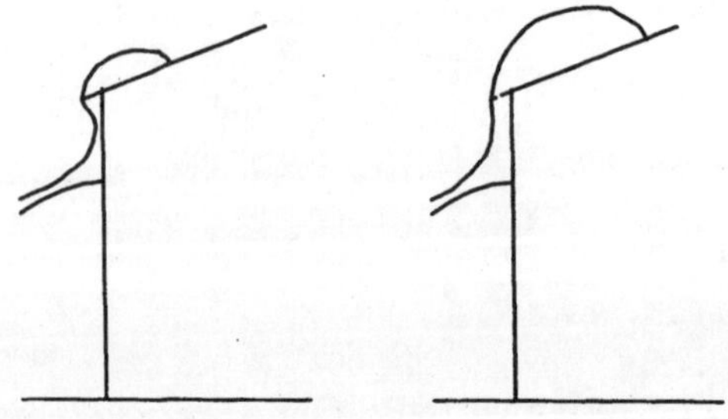

FIG 2.12 STREAMLINES FOR OVERHANG

provides a very high suction on the upper surface of the roof, and, in conjunction with the positive pressure underneath, exerts a very high load on the overhang. The pressure difference across the overhang can be reduced by introducing a hole through the overhang. This has two effects, the first is to reduce the extent of the positive pressure on the undersurface, and the second is to thicken and lengthen the bubble on the top surface, which reduces the negative pressure here: both effects reducing the pressure difference. Work by Melbourne suggests that the optimum length of the hole should be 2.5% of the height of the roof, and it should start at a distance from the front of the roof equal to 2.5% of the height of the roof. These values are only a guidance, the device is effective over a wide range of values.

2.2.4. Effect of the Proximity of Other Buildings.

If there are two buildings side by side, and there is a gap between them, as the volume of wind blowing round the ends of the two buildings through the gap is, in the first instance, the sum of the flow around each building separately, then its velocity must increase above that around the end of a single building. But losses in pressure are proportional to the velocity to some power between 1 and 2, so there will be a build-up of pressure entering the gap. Following the concept that air is lazy, some of the wind will find an easier way than going through the gap, so, although there will be an increase in velocity through the gap, it will not be as large as at first suggested. This is called "Funnelling", and leads to higher wind loads on the sides of the buildings. This is considered in Section 3.1.5.

When the wind blows onto the face of a high rise building, a vortex is created by the downward flow on the front face; this is shown in Figure 2.08. The wind speed near the ground in the reverse direction can reach values in excess of 140% of the reference wind speed. If an existing building is located here, the existing building will experience an increase in its wind loading, especially of its roof. If it is a conventional two storey house, even if it has an overhanging roof, wind loading will most likely not have been considered in its construction, and if nothing is done to strengthen its roof, serious damage could occur.

3. Wind Loading

The original application of Wind Engineering (although it was not called that at the time) to building design was the supply of wind loading data. In the UK the 1952 wind loading code presented an early set of data which were only lightly based upon scientific measurements. These data were found to be wanting, and, in the UK, a new and more scientifically based code was produced, and amended over many years until, under pressure from the enquiry of the Ronan Point disaster, the 1970 edition was published, republished in 1972. These editions are usually referred to as CP3. In them particular effort was expended to get the data on the wind in a more scientific form, and the pressure and force coefficients were, in the 1970 edition, much as in the earlier version, but were improved by amendments over the years as new data became available. As a result of a vast expansion of data, both on wind speeds and loading coefficients, BS 6399 was produced in 1997, and remains the basis for loading calculations in the UK. Around the world national codes were written (an interesting compilation of most was published by the Committee of Wind Loading, Society of Steel Constructors of Japan in 1975 under the heading "Wind Resistant Design Regulations: A World List"). Meanwhile European codes were being written based on the various national codes; this operation is still in progress.

Most codes are of a Quasi-static nature. This infers that the deflection of a building is directly related to the loading by its stiffness. The stresses in the structures are proportional to the deflection of the structure.

$$x = F / K$$

This is easy to understand if F is a static force. But wind speeds fluctuate, so wind forces must also be fluctuating. Even then it is possible to write

$$x(t) = F(t) / K,$$

where the instantaneous deflection is proportional to the instantaneous force. But there are circumstances in which the above equation does not apply, these will occur when the building can move. All buildings can move, so what does this mean? It means either that the movement of the building changes the conditions of the flow, by, for example, changing the incidence of the wind, and therefor the loads on the building, or that the building begins to oscillate and can store energy from one cycle to the next. In both of these cases we have to consider the "Stability" of the building.

A stable building is one in which, when it is distorted from its equilibrium position, forces or moments are produced which will restore it to its original equilibrium position. A building can be either "Statically" or "Dynamically" stable. The difference is that in the dynamic case, the velocity of the building creates additional forces or moments.

Although the term "building" was used in the remarks above, it is not necessary for the whole building to behave dynamically; a part, such as the roof, may behave in a dynamic manner on a building which itself behaves statically. In this context "building" means a building or any part thereof, and sometimes the term "member" or "structure" will be used instead

Consider a flat plate supported by a torsional spring attached to its mid point at both ends of its span, and that the natural frequency of the plate is very low. When placed in an airstream at zero incidence, there will be no moment on the plate. If the plate is give a small angular displacement, a moment will be produced by the wind, which will tend to increase the displacement slowly, this in turn, will increase the moment, which will increase the displacement and so on. The flat plate is "Statically Unstable". A limit state deflection will be reached when the restoring moment of the spring is equal to the disturbing moment due to the wind. This will always occur because the variation of pitching moment with incidence is not positive through the whole range of incidence. In the case of a spring attachment this limit state will be reached, but if the stiffness is provided by the twisting of

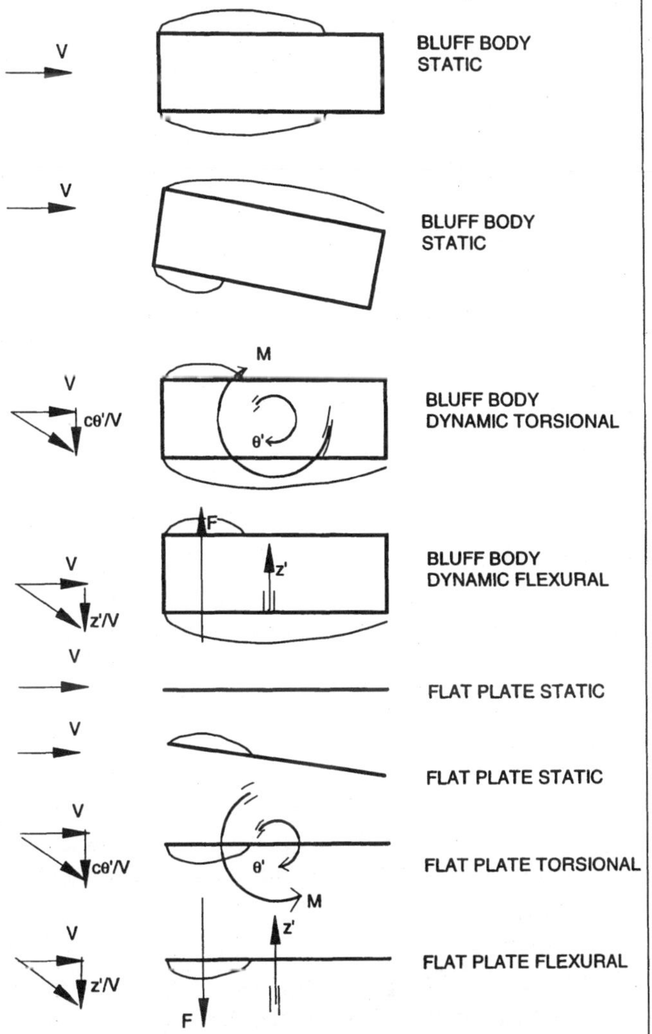

FIG 3.01. STATIC AND DYNAMIC STABILITY.

the member itself, failure of the member might occur before this limit state is reached. This is called "Torsional Divergence" and is a "Static Instability".

If the natural frequency of the same flat plate is high, the rotational velocity would combine with the velocity of the approaching wind as to provide a changing angle of incidence. This is shown on Figure 3.01 . In the case of a flat plate, the velocity produces a reduction of incidence, reducing the moment, so this system is "Dynamically Stable".

The dividing line between these stabilities (static and dynamic) is represented by a "Frequency Parameter". If a member is Statically Stable, it will always be Dynamically Unstable, and vice versa.

A flat plate, and like thin members, must be designed statically, considering possible divergence.

Unfortunately a bluff member, i.e. any member with thickness, behaves in exactly the opposite manner, and is Statically stable, but Dynamically unstable. So, when dealing with buildings or their bluff members, we have to consider the dynamic aspect.

Consider the bluff member shown in plan in Figure 3.01 mounted on springs in an airstream so that it can oscillate laterally. When the member is deflected laterally and released, the lateral velocity of the member towards its equilibrium position will create an effective incidence to the wind which will produce a wind force in addition to the spring force towards the equilibrium position, so that the member will have velocity at the equilibrium position and it will overshoot, the wind and spring forces being now in opposite directions. Eventually the motion of the member will stop, and the spring force will start to return the member to its equilibrium position, the velocity again producing a wind force to assist the spring force once movement starts. The member will then pass the equilibrium position travelling in the opposite direction and an oscillation will have developed. Because the magnitude of the wind force is not linear with incidence, (see Figure 3.02), there will be a limit to the amplitude of oscillation.

If the member has absorbed more energy from the wind in this cycle than it has dissipated in damping, then the second cycle will be larger than the first and the second maximum deflection will be governed not only by the wind and spring forces during the second deflection, but also by the stored energy from the first cycle, and so on.

FIG 3.02 VARIATION OF PITCHING MOMENT WITH INCIDENCE

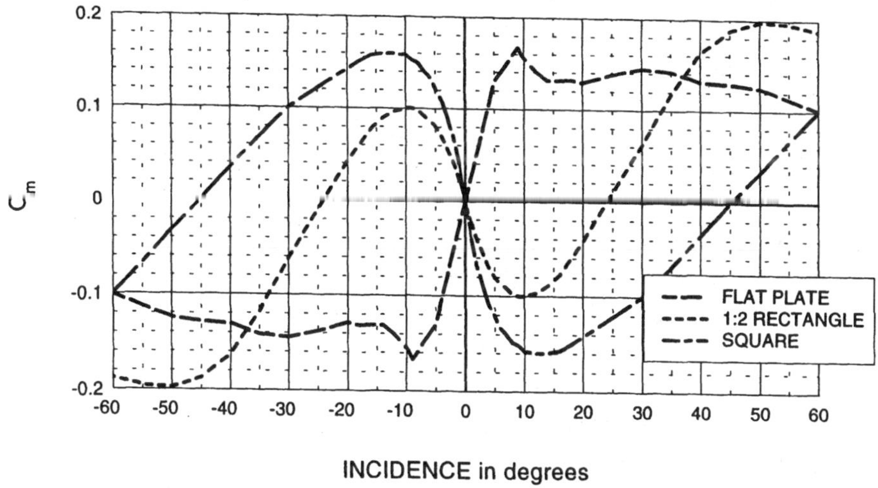

Imagine, for example, a child's swing. A small static load is applied and the swing moves a small distance. If the same small load is applied again and again at the natural frequency of the swing, then the deflection of the swing increases with each application of the load. A limit cycle is reached when the energy supplied per cycle equals the energy dissipated in damping per cycle. If the pivot is replaced by a flexure, and the swing is turned upside down, then the swing becomes a building, and the stresses in the flexure are proportional to the deflection of the swing, and are not proportional to the applied load; although the applied load has its effect on the limit cycle deflection through the damping.

The dividing line between static and dynamic response now depends upon the "Frequency Parameter" and the "Damping".

There are then two ways to approach the loading of a building under a fluctuating force: these are statically (or quasi-statically because all buildings move) and dynamically. The quasi-static approach is simple in that the peak value of the internal stresses is directly related to the peak value of the applied load. In fact the building is designed for the load induced by the strongest gust, of appropriate size, which will occur in the chosen Return Period. This will be considered in Section 3.1.

A fully dynamic approach to the design of a building is long, complicated and therefor expensive and this will be discussed in Section 3.2. The advent of commercial computer programmes has reduced the time and cost aspects dramatically.

Some shapes are unstable, as illustrated above. However, another form of excitation occurs on stable shapes, due to the fluctuating nature of the approaching wind, this is called "buffeting". The forcing function, when considering buffeting, is broad-band, that is to say it contains a wide range of frequencies. The dynamic response of the member is in narrow bands (the fundamental frequency and its harmonics). It could be that, with a building with much damping, there is little energy in the forcing function at frequencies to which the building will respond, and, in doing so, will only amplify the deflections by a small amount, so that the increase in loading due to the movement of the building is small compared to the static loading. This introduces a third type of loading which is called "mildly dynamic". In BS 6399 the term "Dynamic Augmentation Factor" (C_r) was created to account for the increase in dynamic loading over the purely static loading. In that document the building can be designed as Quasi-static if the value of C_r is less than 0.25 or the building is less than 300 m in height. This approach will be discussed in Section 3.3.

Wind loading implies Forces and Moments. Acquisition of data can take the form of direct measurement of Forces and Moments, or it can take the form of measurements of pressure, which can be integrated to produce Forces and Moments. The relative merits of the two paths are discussed in Chapter 10. For most of this chapter pressures will be discussed, although it would have been just as easy to have used forces in some sections.

3.1. Quasi-Static Approach.

The application of Buckingham's Theorem to flow over buildings was explained in Section 2. Here we will be interested in applying it to wind loads and this involves ensuring that the data we use apply the concept of "Dynamic Similarity".

There are two sources of data, from Codes or published data, and from wind tunnel investigations. These sources can supply incompatible data in that reference conditions may be different, and care must be taken when they are mixed.

It will be assumed that, in any wind tunnel investigation the correct velocity profile and turbulence profile will have been installed in the wind tunnel, for the reasons given in Section 2.

3.1.1. Buffeting.

This is the term applied to the fluctuating force produced by a fluctuating wind speed. At first it was assumed that a unique value of Pressure Coefficient applied, and that the pressure was given by the expression

$$p(t) = C_p \times (1/2\rho)\ V(t)^2$$

$$p(t) = C_p \times (1/2\rho) \times \{V_{mean} + u(t)\}^2$$

$$p(t) = C_p \times (1/2\rho) \times (V_{mean}^{\ 2} + 2V_{mean}\ u(t) + u(t)^2)$$

which is sometimes linearised to

$$p(t) = C_p \times (1/2\rho) \times V_{mean}^{\ 2}\ \{1 + 2u(t)\ /\ V_{mean}\}\ ,$$

but, in the era of computers, I would not recommend the linearised form.

In the wind tunnel, where the reference wind speed is the hourly-average and all fluctuations are contained in the value of the Pressure Coefficient, the expression used is

$$p(t) = C_p\ (t) \times (1/2\rho)V_{mean}^{\ 2}.$$

3.1.2. Relation between Peak Values of Wind Speed and Pressure Coefficient.

In real life the time-varying pressure at a point can be written

$$p(t) = C_p\ (t) \times 1/2\ \rho \times V(t)^2.$$

the peak value of p, written as $p\hat{}(t)$, would appear to be given by

$$p\hat{}(t) = C_p\hat{}(t) \times 1/2\rho \times V\hat{}(t)^2,$$

where $V\hat{}(t)$ is the peak value of the wind speed. However, it unreasonable to assume that the peak in the value of the Pressure Coefficient should occur simultaneously with the peak value of wind speed, and practically it is impossible to separate the fluctuations into those caused by the wind and those introduced by the building. In the wind tunnel this difficulty is overcome by representing in the wind tunnel all the fluctuations of wind speed with periods less than one hour which occur in the wind, and which it has been shown in Section 2 to be essential for dynamic similarity of the flow about the building, but to quantify this wind speed by its mean value (almost always the hourly-average value). So now all the fluctuations occur in the value for the pressure coefficient. Thus in the wind tunnel

$$p\hat{}(t) = C_p\hat{}(t) \times 1/2\rho \times V_m^2.$$

This does not work in Codes, where the peak values of wind speed are presented. Their equation would be written

$$p\hat{}(t) = C_{pg} \times 1/2\rho \times V\hat{}(t)^2$$

where C_{pg} is some fictitious value of pressure coefficient which relates the value of peak pressure to the peak value of wind speed and yields a value of pressure which has the required probability of occurrence defined by the value of wind speed used. It is not the mean value of pressure coefficient, a fact which is often misunderstood. It can only be determined by equating the values of $p\hat{}(t)$ in the two equations above.

3.1.3. Effect of Size (TVL Formula).

When evaluating wind forces and moments by the integration of pressure over the surfaces, apart from wanting the peak value of pressure, with respect to time (once in 50 Years for instance), we also want the peak value over the area of the building represented by that pressure. If the turbulence of the wind is considered to be composed of a mixture of all shapes and sizes of eddies flowing over the building, some having been created by the building itself, it is reasonable to suppose that the maximum pressure on the area would occur at the instant when the "best" alignment of all the eddies from the very large down to those of a fixed size occur. The reason for the limiting size is that, with a single eddy, a positive effect would occur within certain boundary around the eddy, but a negative effect would occur outside that boundary. But eddy size in a moving stream of air passing over a surface is synonymous to a time of passage, or an averaging time, this implies that gusts of averaging times longer that a critical value will affect the area in a positive nature and those of a shorter averaging time will have no effect and can be ignored.

When this argument is put in scientific terms, it is stated that the square root of the coherence ($\sqrt{\gamma^2} = \gamma$) of pressure, of a given averaging time, at two points on a building decreases with the distance apart of the points. Measurements of the square root of coherence were made on several full scale buildings, and also on components of buildings and a selection of the results from Maine and Walker (references C.W.Newberry, K.Eaton, J.R.Mayne

FIG 3.03 VARIATION OF γ WITH REDUCED FREQUENCY

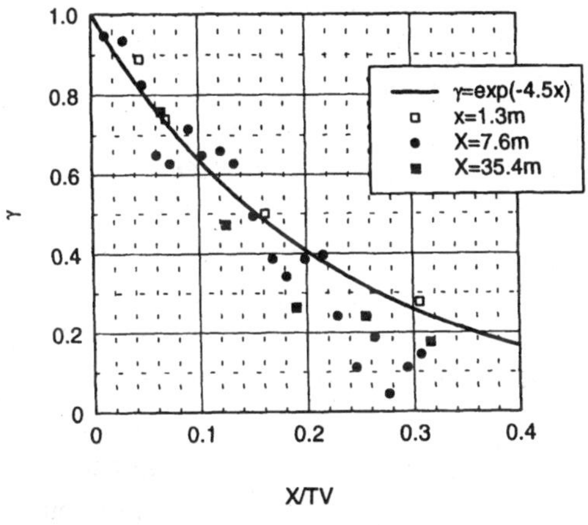

"Wind Loading on Tall Buildings: further results from Roycx House" BRE Current Paper 29/73 HMSO November 1973. and J.R.Mayne, G.R.Walker "The Response of Glazing to Wind Pressure" BRE Current Paper 44/76 HMSO June 1976) are plotted in Figure 3.03. Within quite a wide scatter band, the results of all the results can be approximated by the expression

$$\gamma = exp(-4.5 \times L / TV)$$

A gradual loss of coherence is difficult to deal with, so, for practical reasons, it is assumed that there is complete coherence below a critical value of non-dimensional spacing (L/TV), and zero coherence above that value. The critical value has been chosen to be a value for γ of e^{-1} (0.368). This leads to the well known expression

$$T \times V = L \times 4.5$$

an expression which I derived in the late 1970's, and is so named after my initials. In this equation T is the averaging time in seconds, V is the hourly-average wind speed, and L is the distance (either diagonal of co-ordinate) over which the maximum correlation is to be achieved.

This equation relates "Time" and "Length", and is essential to further calculations of wind loads.

It follows from the TVL equation that values of Pressure are required for a few different values of averaging time, because maximum loading over members of different size are required. This would require a range of values being measured in the wind tunnel. In the Code, this problem is solved by presenting a range of values of wind speed for different averaging times: this has the same problem as mentioned at the end of section 3.1.2. In a wind tunnel study at Bristol it is our custom to present values of pressure for three values of averaging time in our reports, the first is always a 0.5 second average value and relates to Cladding and its fixing, and is the shortest averaging time considered for practical application. The second is the value which will give maximum correlation over the major element in the design, say a roof beam. The third is a long time averaged value which will relate to the value of internal pressure. If more sizes of structural members need to be considered, then data for additional averaging times would be presented.

From a review of wind tunnel investigations on a large number of buildings, in each of which the pressure for a range of averaging time were measured and combined with information obtained from truncating the spectrum of pressure for the location, and when

$$(p_t - p_{300}) / (p_3 - p_{300})$$

was plotted against the log of the averaging time, in the region of

$$1 < t < 50 \; sec,$$

the curve can be approximated by the straight line

$$(p_t - p_{300}) = (p_3 - p_{300}) \times (\log 1000 - \log t) / (\log 1000 - \log 3).$$

This variation is shown in Figure 3.04, and by this expression, the value of the pressure coefficient for any averaging time within this range can be evaluated from the wind tunnel data without having to return to the wind tunnel and re-evaluate the data.

FIG 3.04 STATIC PRESSURES

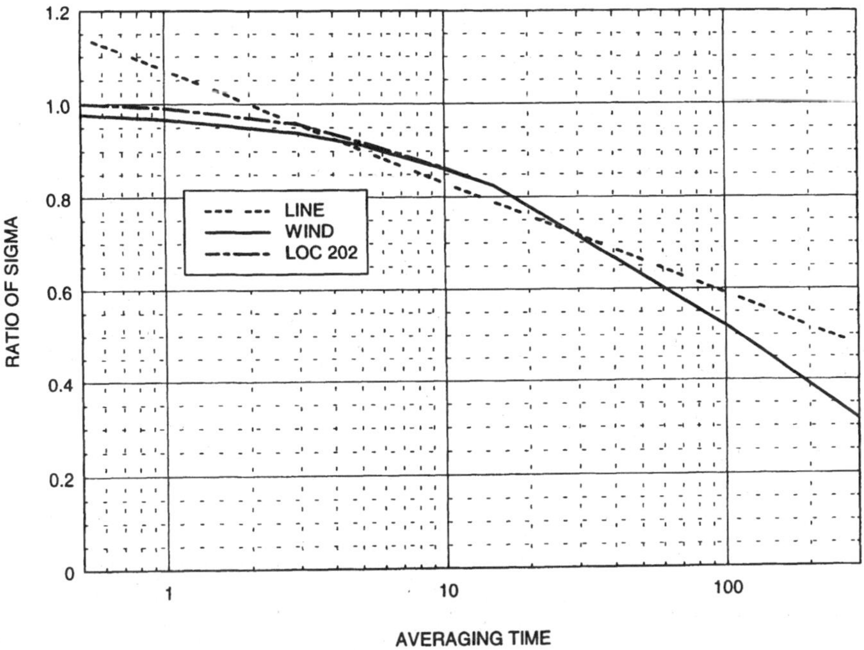

3.1.4. *Correlation Across Faces.*

The TVL formula applies to points on a single face. Where a shear layer separates the flow on the surfaces of two faces, then there is a further loss of correlation. When there is flow onto a corner of a cuboid building, and the flow attaches to two faces, then the TVL formula applies to those two faces with attached flow together and to the other two separately as they are themselves uncorrelated. If the flow is normal to a face, then all four faces are uncorrelated and the TVL formula applies to each face separately.

Measurements conducted at Bristol on a variety of models in the wind tunnel suggested that the peak loads integrated over other faces than the primary should be factored by 0.85 before being aggregated across the whole building. The choice of face which is to be counted as the primary face, or faces, must be chosen to produce the maximum overall load on the building.

3.1.5. Effect of Proximity of Other Buildings (Funnelling).

The problem when two buildings are close together and there is a gap between was mentioned in Section 2.2.4. The reason for the increase in velocity along the facing side walls was explained in that Section. The loading consequence is that the increased velocity produces reduction in pressure (increased suction) on the side walls. This is called "Funnelling".

This effect would be picked up automatically in a wind tunnel investigation. When the building is designed from published data, then some allowance must be made for the effect. The following rules have been written, based on wind tunnel data.

The critical or scaling dimension (d) is either the cross-wind dimension or twice the height of the building, whichever is smaller. If the gap between the buildings is less than d/4 or greater than d there is no effect. The maximum effect occurs when the gap is equal to d/2, when the pressures (suctions) should be increased by about 20%, and partial areas changed. For exact values either conduct a wind tunnel investigation or study Codes of Practice such as BS 6399 sections 2.4.1.4 or 3.3.1.1.3.

This covers the loading of the new building; however, if a new building is constructed close to an existing building, then there will be an increase in loading on the old building, and it is the responsibility of the designers of the new building to ensure that no damage occurs on the existing building..

Another situation in which the construction of a building close to an existing building can affect its loading is when the vortex on the front face extends to the existing building: this is discussed in Section 2.2.4.

3.1.6. Extreme Values of Pressure.

The real way to obtain an "Extreme" value of pressure is to conduct and "Extreme Value Analysis. The procedure would be to measure the maximum value of pressure in a series of samples, each of greater than the stationary length. The maximum values from each sample would then be plotted on extreme value paper (extreme value plotted against the Reduced Variate), a straight line assumed, or fitted with the BLUE, or other, method (see Sections 11.5.2.4 or 11.5.2.5), and a value of Mode and Dispersion obtained. If there was much scatter on the points, then Confidence bands would be fitted and the values of Mode and Dispersion would be obtained therefrom. An example of this type of presentation is shown in Figure 3.05(c). This is a long and slow

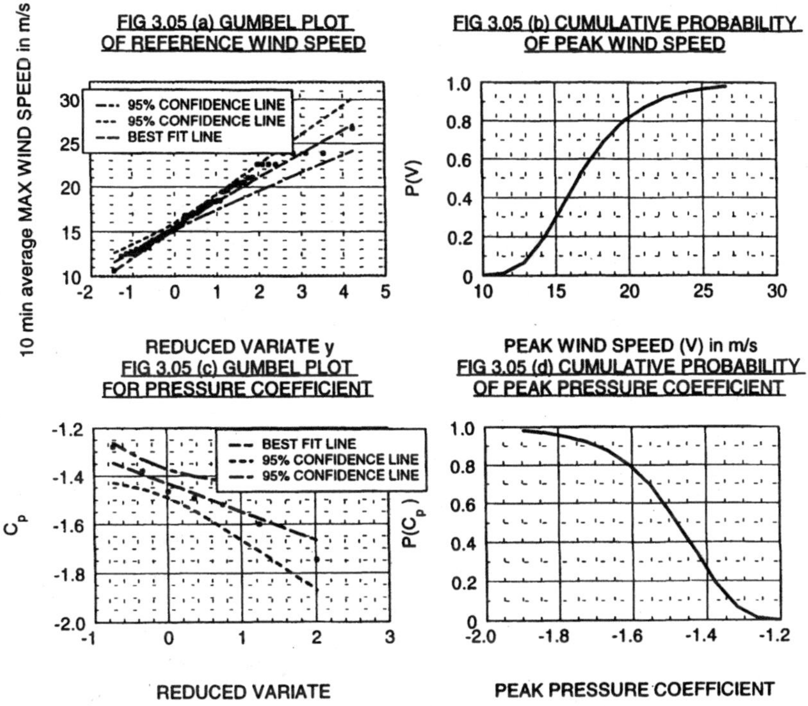

process, and, when it is realised that it has to be repeated for every location studied for every wind direction, the enormity of the undertaking is clear.

This was appreciated at Bristol many years ago.

At Bristol we have always presented data in "Quantile" form rather than presenting values of mean and standard deviation. In the wind tunnel investigation we measure a mean value of pressure coefficient, together with a value of the 3-second average pressure coefficient which is exceeded for 1% of the time. The choice of 1% was made to obtain a value which was repeatable from sample to sample. Obviously the largest value would vary from sample to sample, and the 1% value was the first which showed, for samples from all different kinds of locations, to have a repeatable character.

It was determined from wind tunnel measurements that, if the mean value of pressure coefficient was greater than -0.25, the parent distribution followed a Gaussian Distribution, and that the value of pressure coefficient which equated most closely to the "extreme" value obtained by the full method, was the value which had a probability of occurrence of 0.05% in the parent distribution. Thus for values of pressure coefficient whose mean value was greater than -0.25, the value of pressure coefficient required for further calculations was given by

$$C_{p,\,0.05\%} = C_{p,\,1\%} \times 1.42 - C_{p,\,mean} \times 0.42\,.$$

For values of pressure coefficient less than -0.25, the parent distribution was found to follow a Gaussian core with an exponential tail (see Section 11.2.3.4), so that a better approximation was achieved by the expression

$$C_{p,\,0.05\%} = C_{p,\,1\%} \times 1.73 - C_{p,\,mean} \times 0.73.$$

The value of $C_{p,\,1\%}$ used in this evaluation had been adjusted to the correct averaging time before this calculation.

Originally the Gaussian Distribution was applied to positive values of mean Pressure Coefficient, and that the Gaussian / Exponential Distribution applied to the pressure when the mean value of Pressure Coefficient was less than -0.25. In between these values of Pressure Coefficient, the values in the above equations were calculated by the expression

$$C\,(C\text{-}1) = 1.42\,(0.42) + 0.155\,(\,1\text{-}\cos\,(-4\pi\, C_{p\,mean}\,))\,.$$

However it was decided that this refinement did not justify the complication, as the value of pressure in this range was small, and a step change at the value of Pressure Coefficient of -0.25 was accepted.

If data where the measurements represent the difference of pressure coefficient on either side of a surface, then the latter of the above two expressions was used on the assumption that the exponential tails of the distribution of negative pressure would make the major contribution to the combined value.

Extreme values of pressure are then obtained by multiplying these pressure coefficients by the mean dynamic pressure $(1/2\rho \times V_m^2)$ where V_m is the hourly-average value of wind speed.

3.1.7. Values of Internal Pressure.

For the evaluation of loads across cladding, values of internal pressure arc required. These cannot be obtained directly from a wind tunnel investigation for two reasons. Firstly, any measurement would require complete airtightness of the model, with correct openings modelled. This is an impractical requirement for a model at the end of its time in a wind tunnel. But of greater importance, the value of the internal pressure will depend upon the openings to atmosphere: these can be varied.

To obtain the maximum load on the cladding at a location for a given wind direction, the internal pressure should be the maximum value of (the opposite sign to the external pressure) at any opening which might be open. A combination of openings will always reduce the peak value when only the worst is open. Thus the opening will change with wind direction. It is therefor necessary to measure the pressure at all possible openings, be they doors, make-up air openings, or ventilation inlets.

The averaging time for this pressure needs consideration. Based at work in Bristol, the suggested value for the "Equivalent Dimension" for use in the TVL formula should be

$$L = 10\,(\textit{Volume of Building, or Sealed internal portion})^{1/3}$$

The reason for this is that the internal pressure can only rise if a volume of air is "pumped" into the volume (like a bicycle tyre), and, the greater the volume, the longer, depending upon rate, the pumping will take. This is an empirical expression which appears to give sensible answers. However, for small spaces, for example the space between a tile and the sarking on a roof, this approach is arbitrary. For this case the following analysis might be more appropriate.

3.1.7.1. Analysis for Determination of Internal Pressure in Small Volumes.

This is an order of magnitude calculation, and is based on four assumptions:

i) the value of the external pressure is constant during the averaging time *T*.
ii) the pressure difference across the opening (area *A*) produces a velocity through the opening given by Newton's Second Law of Motion, with a Loss Coefficient.
iii) the volume of internal air in which the kinetic energy of the air is dissipated equals

$$AL = \pi A u_1 T$$

where u_1 satisfies the relationship $\Delta p = 1/2 \rho u_1^2$, and Δp is the original pressure difference $= p_e - p(0)$. This assumption is dubious, but the analysis is only to establish orders of magnitude.

iv) the relation between pressure and density in the volume is isothermal, which means that sufficient time exists during the cycle for the heat exchange between the internal air and that entering to occur.

By assumptions (i) and (iii),

$$\{p_e - p(t)\} A = \rho AL \, du/dt, \text{ or}$$

$$u(t) = (1/\rho L) \int_0^t [p_e - p(t)] \, dt$$

The rate of change of density in the volume can be stated as

$$d\rho / dT = \rho A u / V,$$

where V is the volume of the volume.

By assumption (iv)

$$dp/p_a = d\rho/\rho_a$$

where p_a and ρ_a are atmospheric values, thus

$$dp\,/\,dt = (p_a\,A\,/\rho_a L\,V)\int_0^t [\,p_e - p(t)]\,dt$$

$$= K\int_0^t [p_e - p(t)]\,dt$$

The solution is of the form

$$p_e - p(t) = \Delta p\,exp\,(-i\sqrt{K}t) = \Delta p\,cos\,(\sqrt{K}\,t).$$

For the pressures to equalise across the opening, $p(t) = p_e$, or

$$\sqrt{K}\,T = \pi/2$$

$$K = p_a A/\rho_a\,LV$$

and by assumption (iii)

$$L = \pi\,v_1\,T \;=\; \pi\,(2\,\Delta p\,/\rho)^{1/2}\;T$$

$$T = (\pi\,/\,2)^2\,[\pi\,(2\,\Delta p\,/\,\rho)^{1/2}\,]\,(\rho_a\,/p_a\,)\,(V\,/\,A)$$

$$=1.21\times 10^{-4}\,(\,V\,/\,A\,)\,\sqrt{\Delta p}\;.\text{ in metric units.}$$

This expression can only be used to obtain order of magnitude results because of the assumptions made.

3.1.8. Monte Carlo Simulation.

This is a general technique whereby a situation which is governed by several processes which are uncorrelated can be evaluated in quantitative terms. The pressure on a building is a simple example because there are only two variables.

The pressure at a location can be expressed as

$$p = C_p \times (1/2\rho) \times V_m^{\,2},$$

where V_m is the hourly-average value of wind speed as used in wind tunnel analysis. The van der Hoven spectrum of wind speeds, which extends from a frequency of 1/(11 years) to 10 Hz, was presented in Figure 1.06 and shows several peaks, the causes of which were explained in Section 1.3.3. The important point here is the "Spectral Gap", that portion between periods (the reciprocal of frequency) of 2 hours and 20 minutes, when there is little energy in the wind. Lower frequencies than this Gap are created by the general weather systems, and higher frequencies by the interaction of the wind, so created, rushing over the rough surface of the earth. The two portions of the spectrum are therefor uncorrelated in statistical terms. This is important in the argument which follows.

This decoupling is the reason why wind tunnel engineers use the hourly-average as their reference wind speed. It ensures that all the fluctuations which are present in the approaching wind and those introduced into the wind by the building are only counted once in the fluctuating values of the Pressure Coefficient. The two parts of the above equation for the pressure at a location are uncorrelated. This means that separate extreme value analysis can be conducted on each individually, and the results then combined.

The process is as follows: the Meteorological data for the site of the maximum hourly-average wind speeds in a series of years are plotted as in Figure 3.05(a), and values of Mode and Dispersion derived. These data are then converted into a Cumulative Probability curve, as shown in Figure 3.05(b). The process is repeated for the value of Pressure Coefficient at a location in a stated wind direction based upon samples of one hour duration (shown in Figures 3.05(c) and (d)). Originally a Roulette wheel was spun with numbers from 1 to 100, which was then divided by 100 but now a random number generator is used to produce random numbers from 0 to 1. The argument runs as follows: In Year 1, a random number between 0 and 1 is obtained, and is considered the value of Cumulative Probability for the wind. The value of wind speed with that Cumulative Probability is read from Figure 3.05(b), and is considered the value of the highest hour of wind in Year 1. Another random number is obtained and that is assumed to be the value of the Cumulative Probability for the Pressure Coefficient, from which (Figure 3.05(d)) the highest value of Pressure Coefficient in that hour of wind is obtained. These values are entered into the equation for pressure above and the value of the highest pressure in Year 1 is obtained. The process is repeated for Year 2 and so on.

In a standard investigation at Bristol we present these data for a 50 year period for 5 situations (combinations of location and wind direction) in the order in which they have been derived. We then present the same data in an ordered fashion from the largest to the smallest values of pressure. This is all good fun but it does have its serious side in that it presents the reader with an idea of the range of values which can occur for the largest predicted value for a year. There is a factor of about 2 in nearly every case. We also like to show that the values we have derived by the methods described in Section 3.1.6 do lie in the highest two to five years. An example of our presentation is shown in Figure 3.06 .

3.1.9. Calculation of Loads and Moments from Measurement of Pressure.

A set of xyz axes is set up with the origin at a suitable arbitrary point (see Figure 10.06. The areas over which the pressure at every location is assumed to apply are drawn on the model, and the component of area in the three axis directions are recorded with positive values of area component where a positive pressure would result in a force in the positive direction of that axis. The distances in the three axis directions of the centres of pressure to the origin for every location are also recorded for the calculation of Moments (see Figure 10.05).

The values of pressure (not coefficient) for the correct averaging time for the size of structure considered, have been calculated, but, there are two values for every location and wind direction. One refers to the maximum and the other to the minimum values, that is to say to the two tails of the distribution, a typical example of which is presented in Figure 3.07. The

LOCATION	13	168	185	10	190	PROB	13	168	185	10	190
W.D.	270	270	270	240	300		270	270	270	240	300
UP AP	-1.566	-.992	-1.688	.882	.944		-6.706	-14.562	-8.638	13.537	13.537
1	-801	-607	-957	589	471	.0196	-569	-330	-467	323	424
2	-764	-548	-907	489	424	.0392	-754	-429	-814	305	201
3	-754	-514	-860	476	420	.0588	-454	-514	-463	489	240
4	-705	-513	-814	429	383	.0784	-466	-488	-678	326	307
5	-705	-508	-763	422	383	.0980	-622	-607	-554	316	272
6	-696	-505	-731	419	328	.1176	-433	-328	-397	290	317
7	-691	-488	-728	394	327	.1373	-621	-393	-550	345	230
8	-683	-473	-714	386	326	.1569	-635	-324	-590	429	290
9	-682	-471	-678	384	317	.1765	-673	-373	-499	348	272
10	-681	-441	-675	375	307	.1961	-671	-305	-428	334	239
11	-679	-429	-670	375	302	.2157	-764	-349	-907	394	300
12	-679	-418	-669	374	300	.2353	-434	-401	-462	372	233
13	-673	-411	-665	372	300	.2549	-705	-322	-675	372	383
14	-671	-401	-657	372	290	.2745	-679	-505	-581	287	243
15	-649	-394	-627	372	288	.2941	-649	-471	-602	476	262
16	-636	-393	-625	368	287	.3137	-696	-513	-524	306	238
17	-635	-379	-614	368	276	.3333	-681	-326	-517	294	231
18	-631	-374	-602	348	273	.3529	-553	-285	-514	374	288
19	-622	-373	-595	345	273	.3725	-342	-275	-446	288	383
20	-621	-372	-595	334	272	.3922	-462	-473	-860	589	273
21	-594	-369	-590	326	272	.4118	-563	-374	-419	263	259
22	-590	-364	-581	326	270	.4314	-414	-322	-595	271	254
23	-588	-355	-575	323	266	.4510	-631	-355	-528	299	270
24	-569	-352	-571	323	265	.4706	-508	-379	-494	372	258
25	-566	-349	-555	322	262	.4902	-516	-418	-665	375	193
26	-563	-344	-554	316	260	.5098	-588	-322	-714	386	273
27	-562	-339	-550	316	259	.5294	-682	-344	-506	264	245
28	-553	-339	-550	315	258	.5490	-409	-372	-424	264	231
29	-542	-335	-528	313	257	.5686	-467	-364	-627	242	257
30	-540	-330	-524	306	254	.5882	-679	-252	-763	313	266
31	-535	-328	-517	305	247	.6078	-590	-335	-575	300	420
32	-535	-326	-516	300	247	.6275	-683	-441	-657	244	260
33	-516	-324	-516	299	245	.6471	-691	-508	-550	285	471
34	-508	-322	-514	294	243	.6667	-535	-321	-485	322	302
35	-482	-322	-506	290	240	.6863	-705	-282	-625	269	326
36	-467	-322	-500	288	239	.7059	-442	-288	-516	368	221
37	-466	-321	-499	287	238	.7255	-801	-394	-731	422	234
38	-462	-318	-494	285	234	.7451	-542	-306	-614	316	209
39	-454	-315	-485	280	233	.7647	-540	-315	-555	419	247
40	-452	-306	-483	271	231	.7843	-390	-548	-462	266	328
41	-446	-305	-467	269	231	.8039	-452	-411	-957	384	221
42	-442	-289	-463	266	231	.8235	-562	-229	-728	315	327
43	-437	-288	-462	264	230	.8431	-566	-318	-571	280	287
44	-434	-285	-462	264	221	.8627	-535	-352	-417	326	188
45	-433	-282	-446	263	221	.8824	-594	-339	-483	251	276
46	-414	-276	-428	251	221	.9020	-446	-266	-669	323	231
47	-411	-275	-424	250	209	.9216	-411	-289	-500	375	221
48	-409	-266	-419	248	201	.9412	-482	-276	-516	368	247
49	-390	-252	-417	244	193	.9608	-636	-369	-670	250	265
50	-342	-229	-397	242	188	.9804	-437	-339	-595	248	300

FIG 3.06 MONTE CARLO SIMULATION

AVERAGING TIME = .5 sec

question is which to choose. At first glance the one which gives the larger load over the whole building should be favoured, but this is conservative and incorrect. The choice should be made as follows. To a meteorologist a "gust"

LOC	AVTM SECS	0	30	60	90	120	150	180	210	240	270	300	330	MAX	MIN
							WIND DIRECTION								
400	.5	361	123	-43	76	74	-102	-282	-471	-825	-776	1240	1003	1240	-825
		-15	-28	18	-44	-36	70	49	113	175	749	-280	13	749	-280
	5.0	289	94	-33	56	55	-72	-219	-375	-650	-552	972	813	972	-650
		27	-11	10	-27	-21	48	11	31	47	510	-87	123	510	-87
	30.0	234	71	-24	41	40	-49	-170	-301	-513	-379	764	665	764	-513
		60	1	3	-13	-10	30	-17	-31	-51	324	62	208	324	-51
401	.5	-165	-133	-90	51	-204	-251	-364	-611	-1151	-972	709	397	709	-1151
		69	24	34	-68	71	118	146	242	455	746	-444	-230	746	-444
	5.0	-129	-108	-69	38	-147	-182	-272	-462	-884	-710	542	295	542	-884
		34	1	17	-45	44	76	83	133	236	488	-261	-141	488	-261
	30.0	101	80	62	28	103	127	201	245	-676	-506	413	216	413	-676
		6	-15	4	-26	23	43	34	48	65	286	-119	-73	286	-119
402	.5	-237	-130	-79	-66	-221	-374	-644	-766	-874	-1190	-586	-256	-66	-1190
		76	41	17	53	96	152	122	110	350	476	233	97	476	17
	5.0	-192	-105	-62	-47	-167	-277	-495	-609	-678	-904	-433	-205	-47	-904
		26	14	4	36	54	89	39	1	175	257	138	41	257	1
	30.0	-157	-86	-49	-32	-124	-201	-379	-487	-526	-682	-313	-165	-32	-682
		-12	-6	-4	23	21	41	-25	-83	38	86	64	-2	86	-83
403	.5	-184	-113	-69	-90	-203	-295	-555	-600	-821	-996	-516	-263	-69	-996
		90	45	34	58	79	83	107	119	271	102	271	196	271	34
	5.0	-144	-86	-54	-66	-155	-232	-431	-477	-642	-808	-395	-196	-54	-808
		47	24	17	37	41	31	30	24	120	-42	153	124	153	-42
	30.0	-112	-65	-43	-48	-118	-184	-335	-382	-502	-662	-301	-144	-43	-662
		14	7	4	20	12	-9	-30	-50	2	-155	62	67	67	-155
404	.5	-273	-89	-76	-90	-120	-254	-428	-457	-1064	-1384	-802	-414	-76	-1384
		103	42	20	65	37	42	129	330	306	127	168	230	330	20
	5.0	-208	-70	-59	-66	-97	-204	-331	-337	-800	-1091	-648	-307	-59	-1091
		53	21	7	42	12	2	58	210	154	-36	28	141	210	-36
	30.0	-158	-55	-46	-48	-79	-165	-255	-245	-595	-862	-528	-224	-46	-862
		14	4	-1	23	-6	-28	2	118	36	-164	-81	73	118	-164
405	.5	-193	-96	-112	-108	-178	-207	-239	535	491	-1089	-665	-412	535	-1089
		136	54	32	61	117	179	224	-409	-628	254	154	171	254	-628
	5.0	-148	-73	-81	-85	-132	-149	-170	382	347	-842	-534	-302	382	-842
		81	31	19	33	74	119	152	-276	-432	94	36	104	152	-432
	30.0	-113	-56	-56	-66	-97	-105	-117	262	236	-650	-433	-217	262	-650
		38	14	10	11	39	73	96	-173	-280	-30	-55	52	96	-280
406	.5	-154	-75	-162	-181	161	306	324	684	743	-773	-566	-406	743	-773
		111	63	78	108	-238	-162	-130	-271	-204	480	177	88	480	-271
	5.0	-112	-54	-119	-138	113	234	249	514	572	-581	-458	-301	572	-581
		73	42	49	63	-165	-92	-67	-152	-88	292	59	43	292	-165
	30.0	-78	-37	-84	-105	76	178	191	381	438	-432	-374	-220	438	-432
		44	25	26	28	-108	-38	-17	-59	1	145	-31	7	145	-108
407	.5	340	220	208	358	-533	-629	-517	274	-345	-394	-236	-208	358	-629
		-114	-76	-129	-370	467	687	353	-175	142	83	87	83	687	-370
	5.0	254	168	156	262	-382	-447	-385	193	-261	-312	-177	-152	262	-447
		-62	-38	-79	-246	315	470	221	-120	78	20	48	50	470	-246
	30.0	188	127	115	187	-265	-305	-283	129	-196	-248	-131	-108	188	-305
		-21	-9	-40	-149	196	301	118	-78	28	-28	17	25	301	-149
408	.5	223	162	213	337	441	485	406	-241	-300	251	174	-149	485	-300
		-82	-64	-55	-59	-83	-404	-332	208	134	-304	-116	186	208	-404
	5.0	171	119	163	262	349	347	294	-180	-228	176	128	-106	349	-228
		-41	-39	-24	-14	-16	-272	-220	133	74	-210	-74	127	133	-272
	30.0	130	84	124	203	278	241	207	-132	-172	118	93	-72	278	-172
		-10	-20	0	20	35	-169	-133	75	28	-137	-41	82	82	-169

FIG 3.07 DESIGN PRESSURES IN
NEWTONS PER METER SQUARED

BUILDING AERODYNAMICS

is an increase in speed, a "lull" is a decrease in speed: thus turbulence is a mixture of gusts and lulls.

Consider a steady wind blowing over a building, and that, at the location under consideration, the mean value of the Pressure Coefficient is positive. If the steady wind speed increased, the pressure at that location would become more positive. Back to the original wind speed and the positive pressure, if a "gust" were to occur, the pressure would become more positive. And obviously, if a "lull" were to occur, the pressure would become less positive. As the averaging time for the evaluation of pressures was chosen to give maximum load over the whole integrated area (not the area serviced by an individual tapping), it follows that a "gust" would encompass the whole area at one instant, and a "lull" at another. The integration of pressure into force shall therefor be conducted either in gusts or lulls, and this gives the information for the selection of the values to be used in the integration process. Our practice is to present two values of loads and moments, the one in gusts and the other in lulls. To determine the "gust" value, the value of the mean (hourly average) value of Pressure Coefficient is examined, and, if this value is positive, then the more positive value is chosen as the "gust" value and the least positive for the "lull" value: and vice versa. When the value of the mean Pressure Coefficient is near zero, then the one which would give the greatest overall load should be chosen, but this suggestion is usually ignored as the values involved are small, and the swings and roundabouts argument is invoked.

The appropriate values of pressure for the location are then multiplied by the areas and moment arms to obtain their contribution to values of Force and Moment in the three directions. Every location and averaging time has a value of pressure in both "gusts" and "lulls", so that forces in the three directions are presented for gusts and lulls separately, because it is only in a gust or lull situation that values of pressure can be integrated over a surface. A typical presentation from Bristol is shown in Figure 3.08. In this the nomenclature is as follows: F stands for Force. X, Y and Z stand for directions, with a positive force in the positive direction of the axis. G stands for Gust and L for Lull. Thus, for forces, for example, FXG is the Force in the x direction in gusts. To avoid confusion with Bending, Yawing or Pitching moments, the convention used at Bristol is to present Moments as, for example, FXZG being the Force in the x direction multiplied by the moment arm in the z direction in gusts. Units are stated in the rubric.

It will be seen in Figure 3.08 that the higher loads nearly always occur in gusts.

To obtain values of Bending Moment up a building, the locations for pressure tappings on the model should be in rows at the same height (see Figure 10.04). It is possible to write a computer programme such that all

WIND DIRECTION

	0	15	30	45	60	75	90	105	120	135	150	165
FXG	71.7	70.8	70.6	81.3	64.6	18.5	15.2	9.8	-12.7	-27.5	-33.0	-46.0
FXL	2.2	.8	1.2	-1.7	-1.4	21.5	-1.9	-9.7	-2.2	-7.8	-16.5	-13.9
FYG	20.7	-10.0	00.5	70.0	100.5	117.0	106.6	103.2	02.6	101.7	116.1	03.4
FYL	17.5	-.3	-19.8	-9.9	-11.1	-5.8	-13.7	-15.9	-30.4	-20.1	-1.4	-20.2
FZG	.0	.0	.0	.0	.0	.0	.0	.0	.0	.0	.0	.0
FZL	.0	.0	.0	.0	.0	.0	.0	.0	.0	.0	.0	.0
FXZG	285.9	285.4	286.2	335.8	269.7	97.0	90.3	65.2	-54.5	-116.1	-142.4	-179.7
FXZL	12.2	7.7	10.3	-1.5	-2.7	80.2	-14.7	-49.2	-1.4	-28.4	-63.3	-64.3
FYZG	102.6	-56.4	-186.9	-328.1	-455.9	-524.5	-481.6	-477.0	-380.8	-438.9	-486.0	-379.4
FYZL	62.6	-5.8	-82.3	-46.0	-49.5	-34.9	-59.8	-76.0	-114.9	-96.0	-11.8	-92.0
FXYG	139.6	147.7	153.2	195.5	146.8	66.5	69.7	49.3	-61.1	-103.0	-114.2	-154.2
FXYL	12.8	9.7	12.7	-5.8	-.7	31.8	-15.2	-36.4	5.9	-7.5	-31.2	-7.5
FYXG	75.9	-7.1	-107.1	-143.6	-186.8	-307.3	-269.8	-288.5	-362.7	-542.7	-640.0	-542.0
FYXL	45.5	12.6	-29.5	-55.1	-93.6	-26.2	-69.0	-104.3	-109.3	-13.9	40.7	-66.7
FZYG	.0	.0	.0	.0	.0	.0	.0	.0	.0	.0	.0	.0
FZYL	.0	.0	.0	.0	.0	.0	.0	.0	.0	.0	.0	.0
FZXG	.0	.0	.0	.0	.0	.0	.0	.0	.0	.0	.0	.0
FZXL	.0	.0	.0	.0	.0	.0	.0	.0	.0	.0	.0	.0

FIG 3.08 LOADS AND MOMENTS

Loads in N*1000: Moments in Nm*100000

HEIGHT above Ground 20.00 m.

areas whose upper height limit is z_o or less are equated to zero, and that values for z for the centre of pressure of areas above that value are decreased by z_o .The values of Force and selected Moment calculated by this program are values of Shear Force and Bending Moment above height z_o . As the height from the ground is increased, the averaging time for the values of pressure should be reduced to take account of the smaller area over which correlation is required. The results presented in Figure 3.08 refer to a height of 20m from the ground.

In section 3.1.4 it was stated that there is a loss of correlation across faces if they are separated by a shear layer. This can be allowed for by having a separate file of Areas and Moment arms for each face, so that the whole process is carried out for each face separately, and the addition to obtain a total Load or Moment, using the 0.85 factor for each appropriate face for that wind direction. The choice of different faces for "primary" face often requires that several different runs must be made to obtain the maximum Load or Moment.

The use of pneumatic averagers to obtain forces, and sometimes moments, directly is described in Section 10.1.4.5.

3.1.10. Divergence.

In the introduction to this Chapter we discussed Stability. The static form of instability is Divergence, either linear or torsional. This instability requires movement of the member and it might therefor be considered dynamic. This is not so because dynamic systems refer to those when the "velocity" of the member plays a part. However, to save duplication of part of the analysis, the approach to Divergence will be described in the dynamic section 3.2.6.

3.2. Fully Dynamic.

The fully dynamic approach is different from the Quasi-static in that the deflections are no longer directly related to the load, but are such that the damping at that limit cycle deflection will absorb per cycle the energy which the wind will supply per cycle.

This state of affairs can occur for one of three reasons: the first is the result of the fluctuating nature of the wind speed, this is called "Buffeting". Only when a natural frequency of the member corresponds to high energy in the spectrum of loading might this lead to sufficient deflection to become fully-dynamic. This has therefor been considered in Section 3.1.1 as part of Quasi-Static loading, and in most of the mildly-dynamic approach in Section 3.3.

The second reason is that the particular shape generates an oscillatory flow pattern about it even in a uniform steady stream of air. These types of flow have been discussed in Section 2.1.4. Because the oscillation is wind generated, it usually occurs at a frequency which is wind speed related. It also usually occurs, in practice, in combination with buffeting.. Also in this category are those members with curved rather than sharp edged corners (see Section 2.1.3) or those which have two possible flow patterns around them (see Section 2.1.4.2). The change over might be of a switching nature (a bank of tubes in a cooler, see sections 2.1.4.2 and 3.2.8), or there might be a transition from Laminar to Turbulent flow which is wind speed controlled: these are discussed in Section 3.2.7.

The third reason is that the oscillating force is generated by the movement of the member; these are "Aeroelastic" excitations which usually occur at the natural frequencies of the member. It is with these types of problem that this section is mainly concerned.

Although very few whole buildings need a Fully-dynamic analysis, parts of a building might, so the basic approach to a dynamic building is presented in this Section. Here the description of the oscillating building will be called a "member" rather than a "building" because so few buildings oscillate.

It is suggested in practice that the Mildly-dynamic approach is first followed, and only if the Dynamic Augmentation Factor exceeds 0.25 is the full dynamic analysis undertaken.

The starting point for a fully-dynamic study is an evaluation of the Mode Shapes and Frequencies of vibration. This is a routine analysis nowadays, many computer programmes are commercially available, so the analysis will not be discussed here. It will be assumed that data on Mode Shapes and Frequencies are available from the Structural Engineer. Following the early structural work on dynamic structures carried out in the aeronautical industry, the Generalised Mode Displacement method will be presented here. This is a very important procedure because it separates the different modes of oscillation in which a member can oscillate into the single modes and treats them individually.

Problems occur with the Mode Generalised Deflection method when the frequencies in two different modes are very close, the frequencies are then called "Confluent Frequencies" (within a few percent). If these occur energy can transfer from one mode to another. An instance of this is a circular cylinder, which has the same frequencies in two directions at right angles (in-wind and cross-wind). It also occurs in some street lighting columns when a lateral and a torsional mode can have very close frequencies. Combined mode shapes occur, such as elliptic deflection in the case of the circular cylinder. If both motions are driven, then the combined motion can be assumed. If only one motion is driven, the second motion increases the damping in the first, and the energy extracted from the wind in the first motion has to equate to the energy dissipated in both motions. Neglecting this damping in the second mode leads to conservative results.

3.2.1. Equation of Motion.

All members can be divided into one or many Mass/Spring/Damper systems, so the starting point is to analyse the simplest, a mass supported by a spring and damper; this is shown in Figure 3.09.

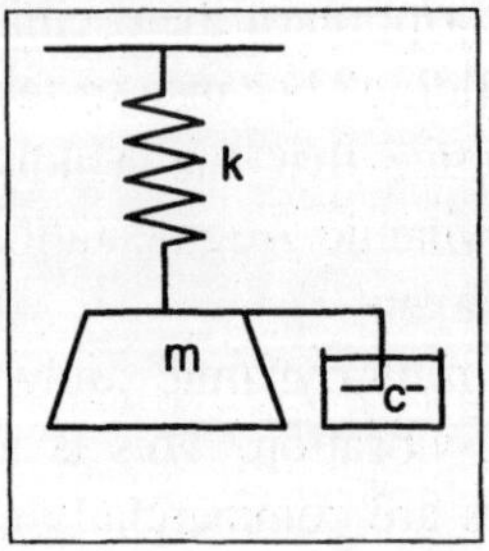

FIG 3.09. MASS SPRING DAMPER SYSTEM

The equation of motion is

$$mx(t)'' + cx(t)' + kx(t) = f(t)$$

where x is the deflection of the mass, x'' is the second differential of x with respect to time, i.e. the acceleration, x' is the first differential with respect to time, i.e. the velocity, and f is the applied force.

Oscillation frequencies are derived when the applied force is zero, so

$$mx(t)'' + cx(t)' + kx(t) = 0.$$

this has a solution

$$x = A\ exp\ (\lambda t).$$

When this is inserted into the equation, it becomes an equation for λ, thus

$$m\lambda^2 + c\lambda + k = 0$$

which has the solution

$$\lambda = -(c/2m) \pm \{(c/2m)^2 - (k/m)\}^{1/2}$$

if $(c/2m)^2$ is greater than (k/m), then the terms under the square root are positive and the square root is real, and, even with the positive sign of the $\pm$; the value of λ is negative which means a dying oscillation. The interesting case is when (k/m) is greater than $(c/2m)^2$ because the terms under the square root become negative and the value of λ becomes complex demonstrating an oscillation; in this case the equation becomes

$$\lambda = -(c/2m) \pm i\,\{(k/m) - (c/2m)^2\}^{1/2} = \mu \pm i\omega$$

$$x = A\, exp\{(\mu \pm i\omega)t\}$$

and the motion is oscillatory with a circular frequency of ω. This is the case upon which we will concentrate.

However, before leaving this stage of the argument, it is worth pursuing the case when

$$(c/2m)^2 = (k/m)$$

$$or \quad c_{crit} = 2(km)^{1/2}.$$

This is called the "Critical" value of Damping, and, as in many other studies, it is useful to know the value of Damping as a ratio to its Critical value; thus

$$\zeta = c / c_{crit}.$$

where ζ is the "Damping Ratio". Another relationship can now be derived; if there is no damping,

$$\omega_o^2 = k/m$$

where ω_o is the Natural Frequency. The equation of motion for a forced motion can be written

$$m\,x'' + 2\zeta\, m\, \omega_o\, x' + m\, \omega_o^2\, x = f(t)$$

with the stiffness *k* and damping *c* replaced . The equation has the solution

$$x = x_o \cos(\omega t - \phi),$$

which, on substitution into the equation of motion, gives

$$-\omega^2 x_o\ m \cos(\omega t - \phi) - 2\zeta m\omega_o \omega x_o \sin(\omega t - \phi) + m\omega^2 x_o \cos(\omega t - \phi) = f_o \cos \omega t.$$

Solving this equation, it is easiest using the Argand diagram, yields the result

$$x_o/(f/k) = \{1 - (\omega/\omega_o)^2\}^2 + 4\zeta^2(\omega/\omega^2)^2\}^{-1/2} \ ,$$

The term $x_o / (f/k)$ would be unity in a static situation, because it is the equation which started this chapter; deflection equals force divided by stiffness. The ratio of this quantity in the dynamic system to that for a static one is defined as the "Mechanical Admittance Factor" and is given the symbol $|H(n)|$, where the frequency n replaces the circular frequency ω. Thus

$$|H(n)| = [\ \{1 - (n/n_o)^2\}^2 + 4\zeta^2(n/n_o)^2\ ]^{-1/2}.$$

If required, the Phase Shift between the deflection and the force can be derived as

$$\phi = \tan^{-1} \{[\ 2\zeta(n/n_o)] / [1 - (n/n_o)^2\ ]\}.$$

Note that the two variables which have come out of this study are the Natural Frequency and the Damping Ratio; these will appear many times in the future

3.2.2. *Measurement of Damping.*

Damping is usually defined in terms of the Damping Ratio. But there is another value of damping which is easy to measure. Consider a series of oscillations wherein the amplitude of the first cycle (arbitrary start) is

$$x_1 = A,$$

the amplitude of the second cycle is

$$x_2 = A\ exp(-\ 2\pi\zeta\ n_o\ /n),$$

or, as

$$n^2 = n_o^{\ 2}(1 - \zeta^2\ )$$

$$x_2\ = exp\ (\ -2\pi\zeta / \{1 - \zeta^2\ \}^{1/2})\ ,$$

as $t\ = 2\pi/\omega_o$ and $c = \zeta \times c_{crit}\ = \zeta \times 2(mk)^{1/2}$. The ratio of the amplitude of the first cycle to the amplitude of the second cycle is

$$x_1 / x_2 = exp\ (2\pi\zeta / \{1 - \zeta^2\ \}^{1/2}), \quad or$$

$$ln\ (x_1 / x_2) = 2\pi\zeta / \{1 - \zeta^2\ \}^{1/2}\ = \delta$$

where δ is called the Logarithmic Decrement or "log dec" for short. If $\zeta < 0.2$ then this expression can be simplified to

$$\delta = 2\pi\zeta.$$

This means that the damping ratio can be estimated by measuring the amplitudes of two consecutive oscillations in an un-forced oscillation (deflect the structure, and leave go, letting the structure oscillate freely).

3.2.3. Equation of Motion for a Whole Member: Generalised Mode Displacement.

The basis of the method is the assumption that the oscillation of a structure in one mode is independent of its oscillation in another. This is true provided that the modes are separated in frequencies. Each mode is treated separately and given a number.

The deflection is divided into two parts, thus, for the first mode;

$$x(l,\ t) = X_1(t) \times \mu_1(l)$$

where l is a position on the member, $\mu_1(l)$ is called the "Mode Shape" of the first mode and defines the shape in which the member deflects and has a maximum value of unity, and $X_1(t)$ is called the "Generalised Mode Displacement" in the first mode and is the deflection of the part of the structure which deflects the most and which varies with time.

The equation of motion can be written for the i th mode thus;

$$M_iX_i(t)'' + 2\zeta(M_iK_i)^{1/2}\,X_i(t)' + K_iX_i(t) = F_i(t),$$

where $X_i(t)''$ is the second differential of $X_i(t)$ with time, and $X_i(t)'$ is the differential of $X_i(T)$ with time, and $F_i(t)$ is the "Generalised Force" in the i th mode.

It follows from the earlier analysis that the natural frequency in the i th mode is given by

$$\omega_i^2 = K_i/M_i.$$

3.2.3.1. Generalised Mass (M_i).

The work done by the Generalised Inertia Force $(M_i\,X_i'')$ in a generalised displacement δX_i in the i th mode is equal to the integration up the member of work done by the strip of the member (mx'') moving through a virtual displacement δx_i in the i th mode. Thus

$$\int_0^L (mx'')_i\,dx_i\,dl = \int_0^L m(l)\,\mu_i(l)^2\,X_i''\,dX_i\,dl = M_i\,X_i''\,dX_i$$

or

$$M_i = \int_0^L m(l)\,\mu_i^{\,2}(l)\,dl$$

where $m(l)$ is the mass per unit length at l.

3.2.3.2. Generalised Stiffness (K_i).

The generalised stiffness is defined as the generalised inertia force divided by the generalised displacement. Thus, for a strip in the i th mode

$$K_i = M_i X_i'' / X_i = \int_0^L m(l)\, \mu_i^2 (l)\, \omega_i^2 X_i / X_i \, dl \qquad or$$

$$K_i = \omega_I^{\ 2} \int_0^L m(l)\, \mu_i^{\ 2}(l)\, dl = \omega_i^{\ 2} M_i$$

3.2.3.3. Generalised Force $F_i(t)$.

The work done by the generalised Force $F_i\ (t)$ in a virtual displacement δX_i in the i th mode is equal to the integration up the member of the work done by the applied force $f(t)$ in a virtual displacement $\delta\, x_i$. Thus

$$\int_0^L f(t)\ \delta x_i\ dl = F_i(t)\ \delta X_i \qquad or$$

$$F_i\ (t) = \int_0^L \mu_i(l)\, f(t)\ dl.$$

3.2.3.4. Aerodynamic Damping.

The wind speed approaching the building can be considered as a mean velocity V_{mean} which will be referred to here as U, and a fluctuating component $v(t)$. If the member is moving in the wind direction, then there will be an additional term

$$V(t) = U + u(t) - dx/dt.$$

On the assumption that dx/dt is small with respect to the wind speed, the square of the wind speed can be written

$$V^2\ (t) = \{U + u(t)\}^2\ -2\ \{U + u(t)\} \times dx/dt$$

and the force can be written

$$D(t) = C_D(t) \times (1/2\rho) \times [U + u(t)]^2 - C_D(t) \times (1/2\rho) \times 2\{U + u(t)\} \times dx/dt$$

where the first term is the force as for the stationary member, and the second term is the "Aerodynamic Damping" and is added to the Structural Damping term because it is related to *dx/dt*, the velocity of the member. When data are obtained from a wind tunnel investigation, where the reference wind speed is the hourly-average and all the fluctuations are contained in the value of C_D, the damping term simplifies to

$$Aerodynamic\ Damping = C_D(t) \times \rho \times U \times dx/dt$$

and this is treated exactly as *f(t)* was in section 3.2.3.3 as it is a force, and it also is divided by $2(M_iK_i)^{1/2}$ to form a "Damping Ratio".

3.2.4. Lateral (or Cross Wind) Galloping.

Galloping is an "Aeroelastic" phenomena in which the excitation is produced by the movement of the member. It is a motion in "One Degree of Freedom", and applies to members which can only move in one direction (or rotation). It arises when the Aerodynamic Damping is negative over part of the cycle of oscillation, and so becomes a forcing function.

Consider the case of a bluff sharp edged member free to move across a wind stream. If the Force Coefficients are in wind axes, the Coefficient of the Cross Wind Force can be written

$$C_F(\alpha) = -C_L(\alpha) \cos \alpha - C_D(\alpha) \sin \alpha$$

$$\approx -[C_L(\alpha) + C_D(\alpha) \times \alpha]$$

$$\approx -\alpha\, [dC_L(\alpha)/d\alpha + C_D(\alpha)]$$

if α is small. For the extraction of energy the value of $C_F(\alpha)$ must be positive over part of the cycle; this means that

$$C_L(\alpha)/d\alpha + C_D(\alpha) < 0.$$

This is the well known "Den Hartog Criterion" (J.P.Den Hartog "Mechanical Vibrations" 4th Edition McGraw Hill, New York 1956) for the onset of this form of galloping. Simpson has shown (A.Simpson "On the Flutter of a Smooth Circular Cylinder". Aero Quart. Vol 22(1) February 1971, and A.Simpson "Wake Induced Flutter of Circular Cylinders - Mechanical Aspects" Aero Quart Vol 22(2) Mar 1971) that, whereas this is a requirement for galloping, its satisfaction does not automatically produce galloping.

The work done by the exciting force per cycle is the integration, over the cycle, of the component of force in the direction of motion multiplied by the distance travelled.

In mathematical terms this can be written

$$\text{Work done by the wind per cycle} = \int_{cycle} F\,dx$$

$$= \int_{cycle} F\,(dx/dt)\,dt$$

If we refer this to the Generalised notation we get

$$\text{Work done by Generalised Force per cycle} = \int_0^{2\pi/\omega_i} F_i(t)\,(dX_i/dt)\,dt$$

$$= \int_0^L \int_0^{2\pi/\omega_i} f_i(t)\mu_i(l)(dX_i/dt)\,dt\,dl$$

If only the first mode is considered and it can be represented by

$$X_1(t) = X_{1o} \sin(\omega_1 t)$$

then the work done by the generalised force in the first cycle is given by

$$WD_{force} = \int_0^L \int_0^{2\pi} f_1(t)\,\mu_1(l)\,X_{1o} \cos(\omega_1 t)\,d(\omega_1 t)\,dl$$

the work done by the generalised damping in the first cycle is given by

$$WD_{damping} = -\int_0^{2\pi} 2\,(M_1 K_1)^{1/2}\,\zeta_{s,1}\,(dX_1 / dt)^2\,dt$$

$$= -2\,(M_1 K_1)^{1/2}\,\zeta_{s,1} \int_0^{2\pi} \omega_1 X_{1o} \cos^2(\omega_1 t)\,d(\omega_1 t)$$

$$= -2\pi\omega_1 (M_1 K_1)^{1/2} \zeta_{s,1} X_{1o}^2.$$

The onset of oscillations will occur when the total work done by the applied force and damping is zero. This is defined by

$$2\pi\omega_1 (M_1 K_1)^{1/2}\,\zeta_{s,1} X_{1o}^2 = X_{1o} \int_0^L \mu_1(l) \int_0^{2\pi} f(t) \cos(\omega_1 t)\,d(\omega_1 t)\,dl$$

and because

$$f(t) = C_f(t)\;1/2\rho V_{mean}^2\,B$$

$$X_{1o} = (\rho V_{mean}^2 B) / (4\pi K_1 \zeta_{s,1}) \times \int_0^L \mu_1(l) \int_0^{2\pi} C_f(t) \cos(\omega_1 t)\,d(\omega_1 t)\,dl$$

or

$$(4\pi\omega_1^2 M_1\zeta_{s,1})/(\rho V_{mean}^2 B) = \int_0^L \mu_1(l)/X_{1o} \int_0^{2\pi} C_f(t)\cos(\omega_1 t)\, d(\omega_1 t)\, dl$$

Call this equation A.

Because this is an unusual procedure, the method of calculation will be described. First derive the normal force (the component of force normal to the body) coefficient in a wind tunnel investigation as a function of incidence. If Drag (in the direction of the wind) and Lift (normal to the wind) Forces are measured, these can be converted into Normal Force Coefficient (note that this is based on a "Body" axis and not a "Wind" axis).

Because, in the oscillating case, the approaching wind speed is composed of the actual wind speed and the velocity of the member, care must be taken to identify the appropriate wind speed. In the wind tunnel the model is rotated so that the wind speed is at an angle α to the face of the member, thus, with the wind tunnel data in bold

$$f(\alpha) = \mathbf{C_f(\alpha)\ 1/2\rho\,(V\sec\alpha)^2 B} = C_f(x'/V)\ 1/2\rho\, V^2 B$$

where, for the calculation

$$\alpha = x'/V = \tan^{-1}\{\omega_1 \mu_1(l) X_{1o}\cos(\omega_1 t)/V\}$$

Novak and Tanaka (M.Novak, H.Tanaka "The Effect of Turbulence on Galloping Instability" Boundary Layer Wind Tunnel Laboratory Report 2-73 Faculty of Engineering Science, University of Western Ontario, Canada. May 1973) suggest that the Force Coefficient is presented as a Fourrier series in terms of x'/V, thus

$$C_f(\tan\alpha) = \sum_{r=1}^{N} A_r (x'/V)^r$$

Notice that the coefficients refer to $\tan\alpha$ and not to α.

The right hand side of equation A can be written

$$\int_0^L \{\mu_1(l)/X_{1o}\} \sum_{r=1}^{N} A_r [\omega_1 \mu_1(l) X_{1o} / V]^r \int_0^{2\pi} \cos^{r+1}(\omega_1 t)\, d(\omega_1 t)\, dl$$

for odd values of n

$$\int_0^{2\pi} \cos^n(\omega_1 t)\, d(\omega_1 t) = P_n = (4) \times (2/3) \times (4/5) \times (6/7) \times\times\times\times (\{n-1\}/n)$$

and for even values of n

$$\int_0^{2\pi} \cos^n(\omega_1 t)\, d(\omega_1 t) = P_n = (2\pi) \times (1/2) \times (3/4) \times (5/6) \times\times\times\times (\{n-1\}/n\}$$

so that the right hand side of the equation becomes

$$(\omega_1 /V) \times \int_0^L \mu_1^2(l) \sum_{r=1}^{N} A_r [\omega_1 \mu_1(l) X_{1o} / V]^{r-1} P_{r+1}\, dl,$$

and, as K is difficult to measure, it will be eliminated so that the full equation becomes

$$(4\pi\omega_1 M_1 \zeta_{s,1})/(\rho BV) = \int_0^L \mu_1^2(l) \sum_{r=1}^{N} A_r \{\omega_1 \mu_1(l) X_{1o} /V\}^{r-1} P_{r+1}\, dl$$

$$= \sum_{r=1}^{N} A_r (\omega_1 X_{1o} /V)^{r-1} \times P_{r+1} \times L \int_0^1 \mu_1^{r+1}(\eta)\, d\eta.$$

The LHS of this equation can be written

$$(\omega_1 X_{1o} / V) \times [(4\pi M_1 \zeta_{s,1}) / (\rho B)] \times (1/X_{1o}).$$

The RHS of the equation can be evaluated for an assumed value for $(\omega_1 X_{1o} / V)$. The procedure is to assume a value for $(\omega_1 X_{1o} / V)$, calculate the appropriate value of X_{1o}, obtain the corresponding value of V by substitution into the assumed value for $(\omega_1 X_{1o} / V)$. This gives one point on the response curve. A second value for $(\omega_1 X_{1o} / V)$ is assumed and the process repeated. An example of a response curve is given in Figures 3.10. Choice of steps in $(\omega_1 X_{1o} / V)$ is made to produce a smooth curve.

FIG 3.10(a) GALLOPING PERFORMANCE uniform

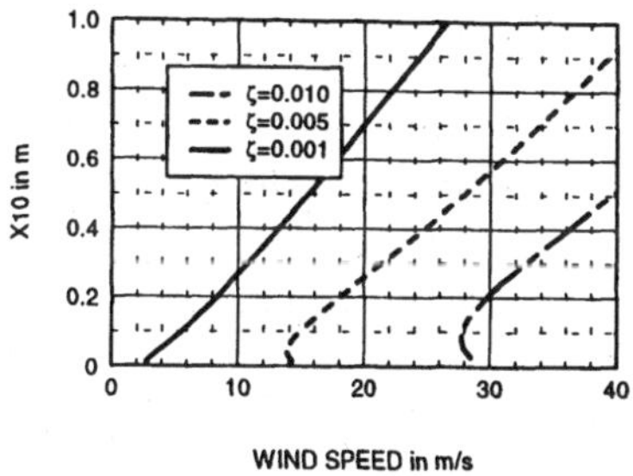

FIG 3.10(b) GALLOPING PERFORMANCE tapered

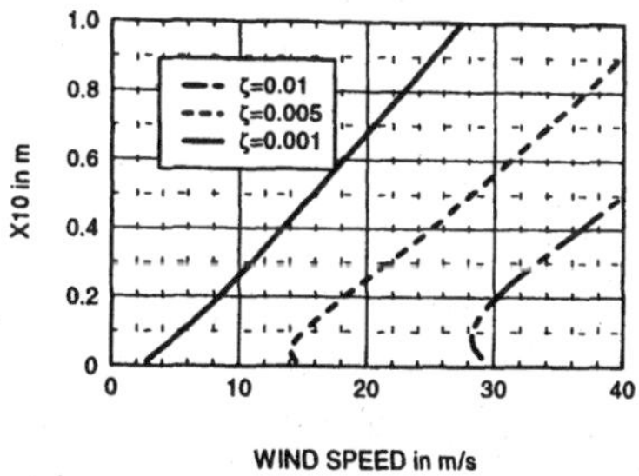

FIG 3.10(c) GALLOPING PERFORMANCE guyed

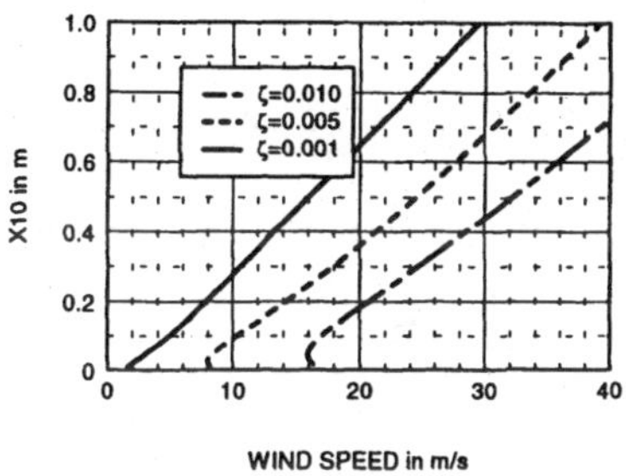

Several expressions for $\mu_1 (l)$ can be assumed,

For a member which moves as a whole

$$\mu_1 (l) = 1.0.$$

For a rigid member hinged at its base

$$\mu_1 (l) = l / L.$$

For a uniform cantilever under uniform loading

$$\mu_1 (\eta) = 1/3 \times (6\eta^2 - 4\eta^3 + \eta^4)$$

and for a uniform cantilever guyed at its free end by

$$\mu_1(\eta) = 3.847 \times (3\eta^2 - 5\eta^3 + 2\eta^4),$$

with a maximum value at $\eta = 0.578$.

However, the oscillatory loading is not uniform, the highest inertia forces are where the structure moves most, so, to see what effect this has upon the shape, a tapered loading of a cantilever was considered. This gives a Mode Shape of

$$\mu_1(\eta) = 0.0909 \times (20\eta^2 - 10\eta^3 + \eta^5).$$

These three mode shapes were fed into a Galloping calculation and the results are presented in Figures 3.10 . It can be seen that changing the cantilever from uniform to tapered loading has no noticeable effect on the results, but that the guyed cantilever is different in that, there is little difference at the lower damping, but at higher values of damping, the guyed cantilever galloped more.

The galloping calculation needs values of

$$\int_0^1 \mu_1{}^n(\eta)\, d\eta,$$

and values for this integral for the three cases above are presented in Figure 3.11.

A very simple computer programme can be written to evaluate these integrals for any mode shape which has been fitted by a polynomial expression.

The coefficients of the expression for Force Coefficient vary with section shape, they also vary from laminar to turbulent flow. They can easily be measured in a wind tunnel investigation.

A soft oscillator, as opposed to a hard one, is described as one which will start to oscillate from zero (or rather a very small) amplitude ($X_{1o} = \varepsilon$). For this case, the above equation simplifies to an expression for the wind speed which defines the onset of galloping;

POWER n	CANTILEVER uniform	CANTILEVER tapered	GUYED uniform
1	0.4000	0.3939	0.5771
2	0.2568	0.2520	0.4463
3	0.1901	0.1863	0.3768
4	0.1512	0.1481	0.3321
5	0.1257	0.1230	0.3002
6	0.1075	0.1052	0.2761
7	0.0940	0.0919	0.2569
8	0.0835	0.0816	0.2413
9	0.0751	0.0734	0.2282
10	0.0682	0.0667	0.2171
11	0.0625	0.0611	0.2074

FIG 3.11. VALUES OF THE INTEGRAL FOR GALLOPING CALCULATIONS

$$V_{crit} = (4\omega_1 M_1 \zeta_{s,1}) / \{\rho B A_1 L \int_0^1 \mu_1 (l/L)\, d(l/L)\} .$$

and depends only upon the first coefficient in the series to define the Cross Wind Force Coefficient.

3.2.5. Wake Galloping.

In the above section an oscillation was possible because, over some part of the cycle, the forces on the member were in the direction of motion, so that the structure could extract energy from the wind. The generation of the force resulted from the motion of the member producing a change of incidence of the wind onto the structure. This is only possible with bluff members which have a range of incidence over which the Force is in the correct direction.

If a member is in the close wake of another, its movement can bring it into regions of different wind speed and direction, so, even if the aerodynamics of the flow round an individual member will not allow a lateral gallop, we must consider whether the velocity field behind one member will allow the second member to oscillate: if so, this would be called a "Wake Gallop". To clarify the argument, think of two cables of an electricity transmission line which are spaced several diameters apart.

A gallop, by definition, can only occur for one degree of freedom, i.e. a deflection in one direction.

If the transverse deflection of a member, in the wake of a second member is given by

$$Y = Y_{1o}\ sin\ (\omega_1 t)\ ,$$

and using static aerodynamic data for force coefficients relative to its position in the wake, it can be shown that it is impossible to extract energy from the wind.

In a similar way if the motion is entirely in the wind direction, then the energy extraction is zero or negative.

It would therefor appear that Wake Galloping does not occur. This is not strictly true. Wake Galloping can occur, especially on sharp edged bluff members, if there is a phase shift between the position of the rear member and the forces thereon. This can happen because it takes a finite time for the flow pattern appropriate to the new conditions to establish itself around the member. In this case the actual flow pattern around the member, and therefor the force thereon, is appropriate to the static value of the force at an earlier time, i.e. an earlier position. Thus, if the lateral position of the rear member is

$$Y = Y_{1o}\ sin\ (\omega_1\ t)$$

and the Lateral Force on it is

$$F = F_{1o}\ sin\ (\omega_1\ t - \phi)$$

then a gallop is possible when the rear member is constrained to move in only one direction. The value of ϕ depends upon the "Frequency Parameter". This is further discussed in Section 3.2.9.2 .

3.2.6. Torsional Galloping and Divergence.

The term "Divergence" has been introduced in the introduction to this Chapter. This is a static form of instability which can occur when a member is flexible. In the torsional application (it is also possible for linear divergence to occur), torsional divergence is the state of affairs when a member in equilibrium between wind and restraining forces (a spring) is given a small disturbance, and the moments so produced cause the disturbance to increase.

Consider a member which is pivoted about its mid-point and held in an equilibrium position along the wind direction by a torsion spring. If M is the Pitching Moment, positive in the direction of increasing incidence, this type of divergence is possible if

$$C_m(\alpha) \times 1/2\ \rho V^2\ B\ W^2 > k\ \alpha$$

where $C_m(\alpha)$ is the Pitching Moment about the pivot, B is the width of the member, W is the chord of the member and k is the stiffness of the torsional spring.

FIG 3.12 VARIATION OF PITCHING MOMENT WITH INCIDENCE

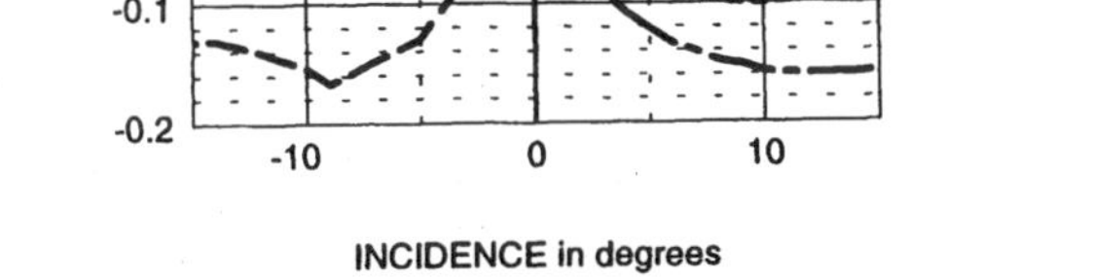

Over a small range of incidences, the Pitching Moment Coefficient can be assumed linear with respect to incidence (see Figure 3.12), so that

$$C_m(\alpha) = C_{mo} + \alpha \times dC_m / d\alpha$$

and the equation becomes

$$C_{mo}\, qBW^2 + dC_m(\alpha)/d\alpha\, qBW^2 \times\alpha = k\,\alpha$$

where $q = 1/2\rho V^2$. Thus

$$\alpha = (C_{mo}\, qBW^2) / [k - (dC_m(\alpha)/d\alpha)\, qBW^2\,]$$

and α will become infinite when

$$k - (dC_m(\alpha)/d\alpha)\, qBW^2 = 0$$

which gives a divergence wind speed of

$$V_d = \{2k/[(dC_m(\alpha)/d\alpha)\,\rho BW^2\,\}^{1/2}.$$

This is a torsional divergence and occurs when $dC_m/d\alpha$ is positive over sufficient range to cause failure. In practice the range of incidence over which $dC_m/d\alpha$ is positive is restricted, see Figure 3.12.

For the member to be statically stable,

$$dC_m(\alpha)/d\alpha < 0$$

To study "Dynamic" stability, we assume that the member will oscillate and we introduce the velocity of the member. For simplicity assume that $C_{mo} = 0,$

$$C_m(\alpha) = A\,\alpha.$$

Let the incidence of the member at time t be

$$\alpha = \alpha_o \sin\omega t$$

The rate of rotation of the member will be

$$\theta' = d\alpha/dt = \omega\alpha_o \cos(\omega t)$$

The incidence due to motion $= -W\omega\alpha_o \cos(\omega t)/2V$

$$Aerodynamic\ Incidence = \alpha_o \{\sin(\omega t) - W\omega\cos(\omega t)/2V\}$$

$$WD\ by\ wind\ per\ cycle = 1/2\rho V^2 W^2 L \int_0^{2\pi/\omega} C_m\, \theta' dt$$

$$= 1/2\rho V^2 W^2 L \int_0^{2\pi} A\alpha_o \{\sin(\omega t) - W\omega \cos(\omega t)/2V\}\alpha_o \cos(\omega t)d(\omega t)$$

$$= - 1/4\rho VLW^3\ \omega L \int_0^{2\pi} \cos^2(\omega t)d(\omega t)$$

$$= - (\pi/4)\rho VLW^3 \omega A \alpha_o^2 .$$

If the value of A $(dC_m/d\alpha)$ is negative, the member is dynamically unstable: if the sign of A is positive, then it will be dynamically stable.

It is interesting to note that if the member is statically stable, then it is dynamically unstable, and visa versa.

A study of Figure 3.12 shows that a flat plate with an equilibrium incidence of 0° is statically unstable and dynamically stable. It is also clear that a member with finite depth at an equilibrium incidence of 0° is statically stable and dynamically unstable. This is summarised in Figure 3.01.

As wind can approach from any direction, the slope of the Pitching Moment curve over the whole range of values of incidence must be studied: the equilibrium value of α is irrelevant and, in the dynamic situation, the oscillation will occur over a limit cycle amplitude such that the energy extracted from the wind over the central portion of the oscillation (described above) is dissipated by the sum of the energy put into the wind by the member and extracted by damping. The calculation is exactly the same as that presented in Section 3.2.4 for a linear gallop, with Moment replacing Force and Rotation replacing Displacement.

3.2.7. Reynolds Number Excitation (Drag Saddles).

This is an example of a transition phenomenon. The drag of a circular member varies with Reynolds Number, Turbulence in the approaching wind, and the Roughness of the surface. The variation of Drag with wind speed is shown in Figure 3.13 (a). The three curves are for laminar, turbulent and transitional flow, the position and shape of the transitional curve depends upon the factors mentioned above. The region of the curve where *dD/dV* is negative is unstable for a member which can move in the wind direction.

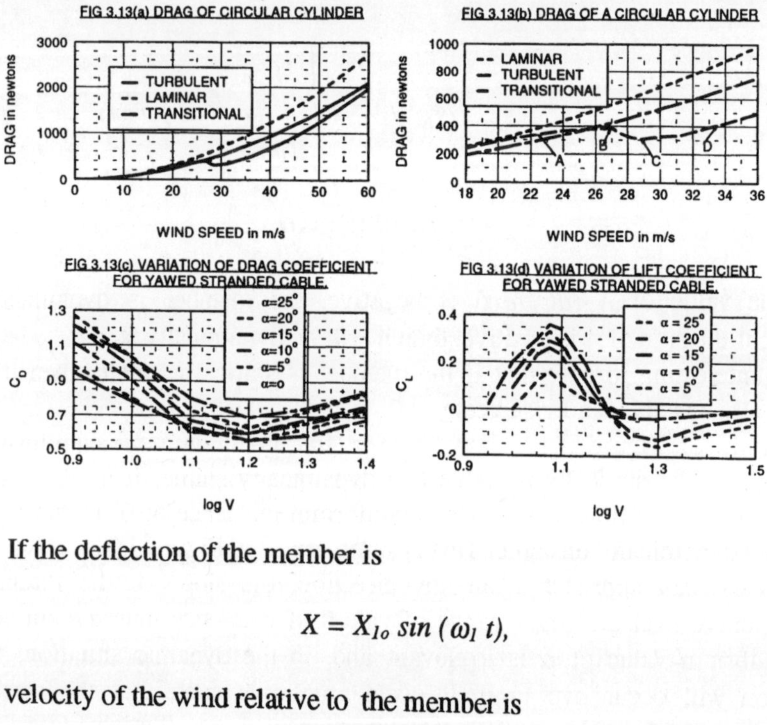

If the deflection of the member is

$$X = X_{1o} \sin(\omega_1 t),$$

the velocity of the wind relative to the member is

$$V = V_{wind} - dX/dt.$$

If the wind speed is as shown on Figure 3.13(b), then there is a possible oscillation between points A and D on Figure 3.13(b), where the energy extracted from the wind between points B and C is dissipated by the wind in regions A to B and C to D. The calculation is exactly the same as derived in

Section 3.2.4, with the curve from A to D represented by a Fourrier series in terms of tan α.

The exact shape of the force in this region depends upon the turbulence in the wind and the surface roughness of the member. A special case occurs if the member is a stranded cable, because the strands are wound on a helix, there will be a different separation point on the upper surface (for a horizontal cable) to that on the lower when the wind is yawed (the wind is at an angle to the normal to the cable). A Reynolds Number oscillation will occur with a slight change in the variation of Drag with wind speed, but, and of significance, the value of critical wind speed can be reduced by an order compared with that for a smooth cylinder, and now occurs in a range of wind speeds which occur in nature (Figure 3.13(c)). Of additional importance, the presence of a stranded surface will create a lift force on a stranded cable over the same range of wind speed when the wind is not normal to the cable (Figure 3.13(d)). At first glance, this would suggest that the mechanism has become "flutter" because a second direction of deflection has been introduced. However, this is not so as the lateral deflection, unless in the near wake of another member, extracts no energy from the wind, in fact, it introduces a little aerodynamic damping and the calculation in Section 3.2.4 applies. A typical variation of Lift Coefficient with wind speed is presented in Figure 3.13(d). The real significance of the lift force is that the cable now oscillates in an elliptic shape, and, because electricity cables of different phases are placed one above another, it is possible for arcing to take place between two phases which would not have occurred had the deflection been purely horizontal.

3.2.8. Flow Switching.

Over a range of values of Reynolds Numbers a bank of cylinders placed normal to an airstream can exhibit a phenomena known as flow switching, which has already been discussed in Section 2.1.4.2. The effect is that there can be laminar separation from some cylinders and turbulent separation from others. The cylinders with laminar separation will have a wide wake and high drag, and those with turbulent separation will have narrow wakes and low drag. This pattern can often be alternate along the bank. Under the high and low drags, the tubes will deflect differently, and the new positions can trigger a different arrangement of wide and narrow wakes. It is thus possible to produce an oscillation of the tubes by this continual switching, see Figure 2.04.

This is a specialist subject and a consultant should be approached on this subject.

3.2.9. Flutter.

Classical Flutter is an oscillation in two or more degrees of freedom, with the member stable in each separately. Often a motion is described as Flutter when two or more degrees of freedom are involved even though it is unstable in one degree as well. The purists would describe this as a gallop in the prime motion, aggravated by the second motion.

A bridge structure is the most common civil structure to flutter. This is a very specialist subject, and, as many whole books are devoted to it, it will not be covered in this one.

3.2.9.1. Wake Flutter.

It was stated in Section 3.2.5 that one cable in the wake of another could not gallop in either along-wind or cross wind directions separately unless there was a phase difference between the position and the quasi-static loading. Let us here consider the case when the frequency parameter (see section 3.2.8.2) is low enough so that a gallop cannot take place, then it can flutter when movements in 2 directions are considered.

Consider the rear cable moving sidewards: as it moves away from the line joining the cables (the centreline of the wake), it will experience an increased velocity (and possibly a change of wind direction as well). This will cause its drag to increase, so it starts to move backwards (assuming that the tension in the cable balanced the original drag): its lateral velocity will decrease due to the increased tension in the cable. It will ultimately come to rest laterally while still moving backwards. The tension in the cable now exceeds the drag and the cable will now start it moving towards the centre of the wake again, and, as it moves, the drag will decrease and the tension will slow up the downwind deflection. Eventually, in the wake, the tension forces in the cable will be larger than the drag forces, so the cable will start to move upwind again, and the tension will also slow the lateral movement. The cycle will repeat. The requirement for an oscillation is for the cable to extract energy from the wind, and to do this the integral

$$\int_{cycle} F \times dv$$

must be greater than zero.. This is obviously possible in the above explanation, because the cable moves downwind in the faster stream when Force and velocity are in the same direction and are both larger, than in the return path when the force and motion are in opposite directions and the forces are smaller. The rear cable moves in an elliptic path in the wake of the front cable, the amplitude of the oscillation depending upon the damping in the cable. This oscillation is also possible when the wind direction is not exactly aligned with the centres of the cables.

There is a region very close to the rear of the front cable where the velocity has reversed, if this region is reached, the amplitude of the oscillation increases and impact between the two cables is possible.

3.2.9.2. Frequency Dependant Members.

As mentioned in Section 3.2.5, it is possible for a time to elapse between the arrival at a position or incidence of a moving member, and the full development of the flow pattern appropriate to that position / incidence in a static situation. The faster the deflection, the greater the phase shift. Flower and Simpson studied this for a 5:2;2 rectangular box in an airstream (representing a box slung beneath a helicopter). In their investigation they forced the deflection of the box, and measured the pressure over the box instantaneously during the motion. They found that the phase shift, ϕ, varied with the frequency of oscillation according to the expression

$$\tan \phi = \omega W / V,$$

where W is the length of the body in the wind direction, ω is the frequency and V is the mean wind speed. The main feature of the flow pattern was the variation in size of the separation bubble.

3.2.9.3. Flexure - Torsion Flutter.

If the frequencies of a Flexure mode are very close to that of a Torsional mode, then Flexure - Torsion flutter is the result.

Consider a member which is essentially a flat plate which has a common frequency ω in flexure and torsion. The lateral and rotational motions are given by

$$z = \mu_z(l)\, Zo \sin(\omega t) \qquad z' = \omega\, \mu_z(l)\, Z_o \cos(\omega t)$$

$$\theta = \mu_\theta(l)\, \theta_o \sin(\omega t + \phi) \qquad \theta' = \omega\, \mu_\theta(l)\, \theta_o \cos(\omega t + \phi)$$

the values of Lift and Pitching Moment will be, assuming small deflections,

$$L / unit\ span = 1/2\rho V^2\, W\, (dC_L/d\alpha) \times (\theta - z'/V)$$

$$M / unit\ span = 1/2\rho V^2\, W^2\, (dC_m/d\alpha) \times (\theta - k\, \theta'/V).$$

where k is the location of the twist axis. When these expressions are put into an expression for the extraction of energy from the wind, the resulting expression is

$$E = 1/2\rho VW \int_o^L \{G_1 \mu_1(l)\, \theta_o \mu_z(l) Z_o \sin\phi - (\omega W/V)\, [\, (G_1 \mu_z^2(l)\, Z_o^2 + WG_2 k \mu_\theta^2(l)\, \theta_o^2)/W]\}\, dl,$$

where $G_1 = dC_L/d\alpha$ and $G_2 = dC_m/d\alpha$.

If Z_o or θ_o equal zero, no energy can be extracted from the wind, so the flat plate will not gallop. However, if they both have values, energy can be extracted, the maximum amount of energy is when ϕ tends to 90°. To estimate the limit cycle in the presence of damping, the equation

$$(\omega W/V) \int_o^L \{Z_o^2\, \mu_z^2(l)\, [4(MK)^{1/2} \zeta_{s,z} + G_1/W] + \theta_o^2 \mu_o^2(l) [\, 4(MK)^{1/2} \zeta_{s,\theta} + G_2 k]\} dl$$

$$= \rho V W^2 \int_0^L G_1 \theta_o Z_o \mu_z(l) \sin\phi \, dl$$

must be solved.

3.3. Mildly Dynamic Approach.

The number of "Fully Dynamic" buildings is negligible, the "Mildly Dynamic" ones are more interesting to the Wind Engineer and are also few in number. If there is any doubt whether a building or member is dynamic, the usual approach is to assume that the building is mildly-dynamic, work out the Dynamic Augmentation Factor, and if this is above 0.25, then go back to the beginning and conduct a Fully-dynamic study.

The major parameter is the size of the structure. For maximum correlation over the structure, or that part of the structure under consideration, the minimum averaging time which will contribute to the load is given by the TVL formula, viz.:

$$T \times V = L \times 4.5.$$

For a mean wind speed of 22.5 m/s this expression reduces to

$$T = L / 5.$$

In other words, for maximum correlation over 25 m, an averaging time of 5 seconds is required. The implication of this on the spectrum of loading is that the spectrum should be truncated at 0.2 Hz,. This is the reason for the statement that any member of 25 m or more, shall suffer no dynamic effects providing its natural frequency is over 0.5 Hz (a period of less that 2 seconds). Larger structures are unaffected by even lower natural frequencies. The effect of size is discussed in Section 3.3.7.

However to demonstrate the procedure, it will be explained for the minimum averaging time recommended for wind loading, i.e. 0.5 seconds.

There are three sets of parameters which control the Dynamic Augmentation Factor for the loading at a location. The first are the dynamic characteristics of the member (Natural Frequency and Damping), the second is the spectrum of the loading, and the third is the relationship between the mean (static) and fluctuating (standard deviation) components of the loading. The first two can be taken together.

3.3.1. Mechanical Admittance Factor.

The "Mechanical Admittance Factor" relates the deflection of a structure to the applied load divided by the stiffness. It is presented in the form

$$|H(n)| = \{[1-(n/n_o)^2]^2 + 4\zeta(n/n_o)^2\}^{-1/2},$$

where n_o is the Natural Frequency and ζ is the Damping Ratio.

The Variance of the Deflection will be, omitting the Generalised Mode Number,

$$\sigma^2_x = \int_0^{\infty} [S_{FF}(n)|H(n)|^2 / K^2]\, dn.$$

With computers it is now a simple matter to take the spectrum for the force from either a wind tunnel investigation, or from tables and perform the above augmentation. The spectrum of the wind is shown in Figure 3.14(a) which represents a situation when it is assumed that the fluctuations are due entirely to the turbulence in the wind. Two examples are presented, on Figure 3.14(b) for a Natural Frequency of 0.2 Hz and a Damping Ratio of 5%, and on Figure 3.14(c) for a Natural Frequency of 2 Hz and a Damping Ratio of 30%. On both Figures the curve for the displacement, called "Dynamic", is shown. On Figure 3.14(b) the whole of the spectrum is shown (frequencies from 0.0005 to 6Hz.), but on Figure 3.14(c) only the limited range of frequencies from 0.07 to 5Hz. In most wind tunnel investigations the very low frequencies are absent, and the curves presented are more like Figure 3.14(c).

In all wind tunnels the approach is the same, although the actual values of the constants will be unique to the particular wind tunnel. In the Bristol wind tunnel we estimate that the measurements of pressure in the wind tunnel contain all frequencies between 0.005 and 4 Hz. When we present a spectrum of the pressure at a location, we present it between the frequencies 0.07 and 4 Hz. We measure the ratio of dynamic to static areas on this spectrum (say

R^2), which is not the true ratio of the variances. We correct this ratio by assuming that the spectrum of frequencies lower than 0.07 follow the spectrum of the wind.

FIG 3.14(a) WIND SPECTRUM

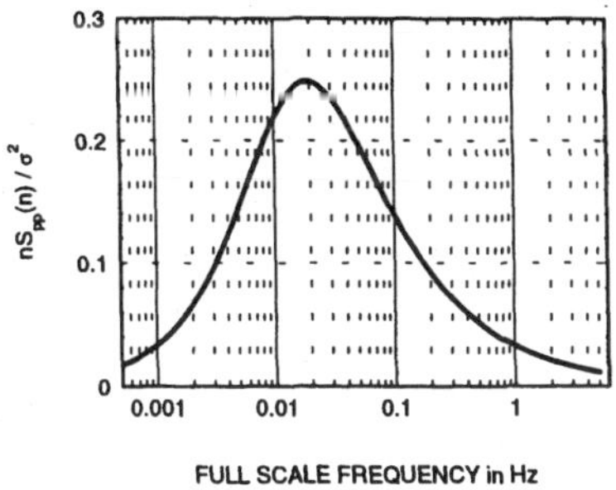

FIG 3.14(b) WIND SPECTRUM N=0.2 ζ=0.05

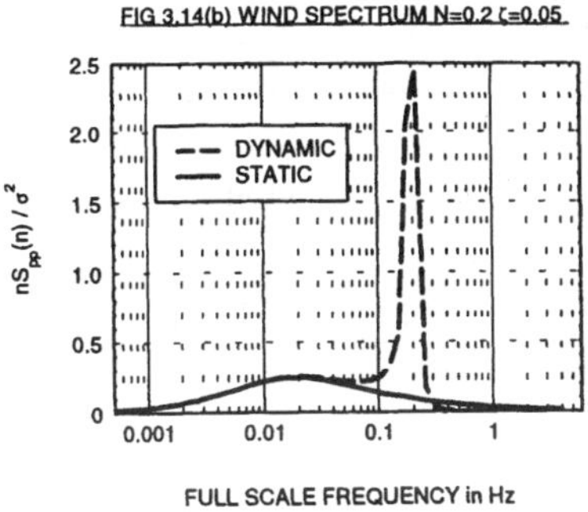

FIG 3.14(c) WIND SPECTRUM N=2.0 ζ=0.3

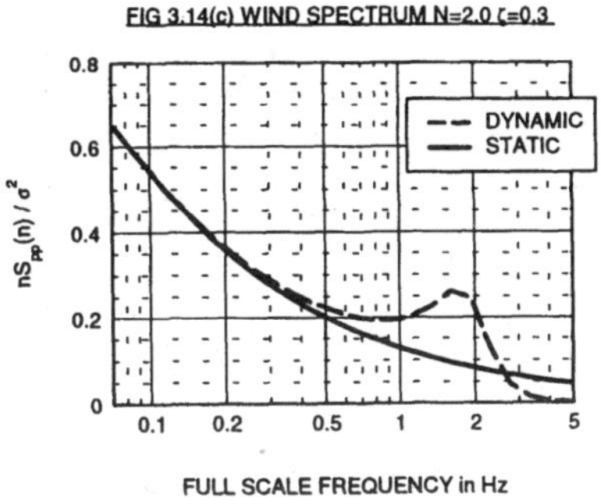

Thus the corrected ratio of variances (R_c^2) is equal to

$$R_c^2 = 0.63 + 0.37\,R^2.$$

This assumes that the spectrum between frequencies of 0.0005 and 0.07 Hz follows the spectrum for the wind, and that the spectrum between 0.07 and 4 Hz is as presented for the particular location and contains, in addition, all the frequencies which the building has introduced to the spectrum.

3.3.2. Dynamic Augmentation Factor.

The decision whether the situation is mildly-dynamic or fully-dynamic depends upon the ratio of the dynamic pressure to the static pressure. This depends upon the mean and fluctuating components of the pressure which have been measured in the wind tunnel investigation. This is why the fluctuating content of the wind tunnel measurement of the loading had to be introduced in the third paragraph above.

In Bristol we assume that the "Once in 50 Years" value of pressure is equal to the mean value plus k times the Standard Deviation. As we present values of short term average and mean pressure in our reports, the value of the standard deviation is back calculated as

$$\sigma_s = |(p_g - p_m)| / k$$

where σ_s is the static standard deviation, p_m is the mean pressure, p_g is the short term average pressure and k is a constant whose value is 4.63 if the mean Pressure Coefficient is less than -0.25, and equals 3.29 for larger values of mean Pressure Coefficient. Therefor the value of the dynamic standard deviation (σ_d) is

$$\sigma_d = \sigma_s \times R_c.$$

The design dynamic pressure is then

$$p_d = p_m + k \times \sigma_d$$

and the critical ratio for the determination of a mildly-dynamic structure becomes

$$p_d / p_s = (p_m \pm k \times R_c \times \sigma_s) / (p_m \pm k \times \sigma_s)$$

A numerical illustration of the calculation of the Dynamic Augmentation Factor is given in Section 3.3.6.

3.3.3. Effect of Natural Frequency.

To illustrate the approach we will consider the case of a constant value of C_p, when the spectrum of the pressure would be identical to that of the wind. Figure 3.14(a) shows the spectrum of the wind as determined by ESDU for a

FIG 3.15(a) VARIATION OF SD RATIO WITH FREQUENCY ζ=0.05

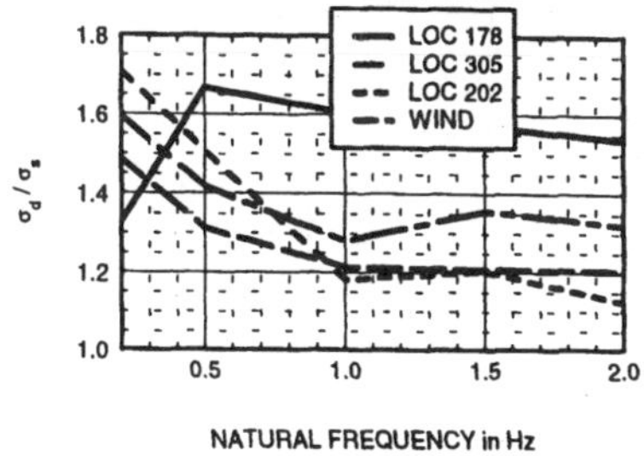

FIG 3.15(b) VARIATION OF SD RATIO WITH FREQUENCY ζ=0.10

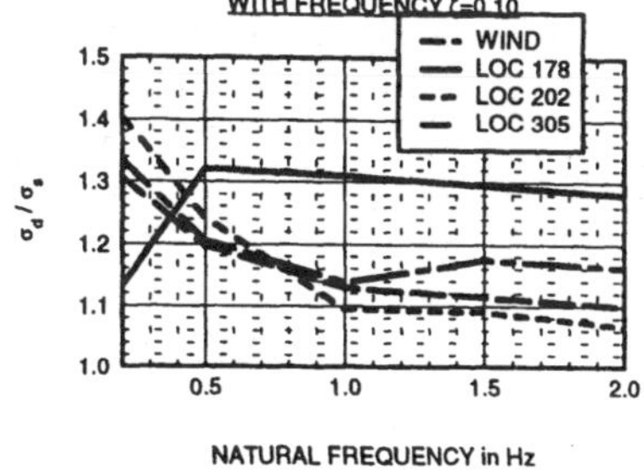

FIG 3.15(c) VARIATION OF SD RATIO WITH FREQUENCY ζ=0.30

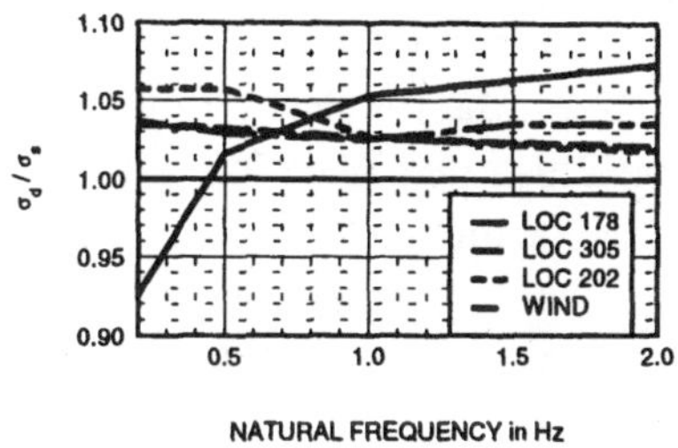

FIG 3.16(a). LOC 178 WD 330 N=0.2 ζ=0.05

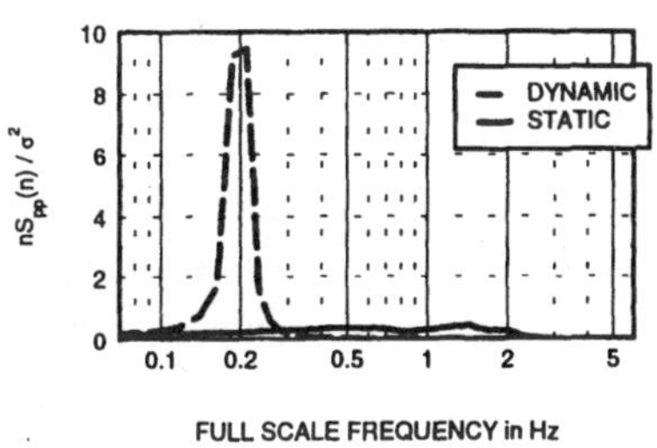

FIG 3.16(b). LOC 178 WD 330 N=0.5 ζ=0.05

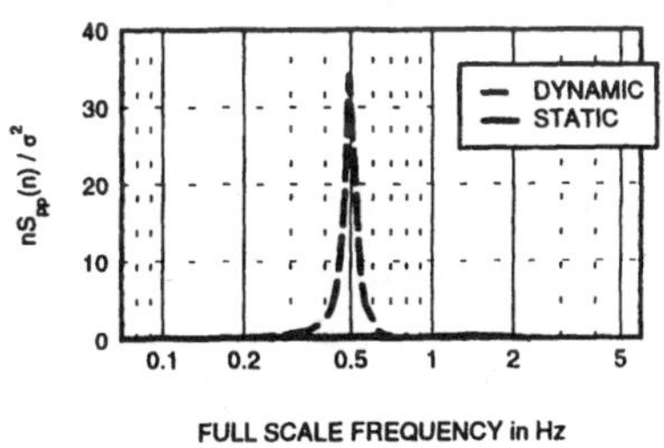

height of 50 m in a city situation. Figures 3.14(b) and (c) show the dynamic spectrum superimposed upon the "static" one. The variation of the corrected values of the standard deviation ratio *($R_c = \sigma_d / \sigma_s$)* with Natural Frequency are presented for the wind in Figure 3.15(a), (b) and (c) are for Damping Ratios of 5%, 10% and 30% respectively. A study of the line for the wind on each shows that the ratio decreases with increasing Natural Frequency.

However, the structure introduces its own frequencies, and, if we make the same comparison of values of R_c, for several spectra from building

FIG 3.17(a) LOC 202 WD 330 N=0.5 ζ=0.1

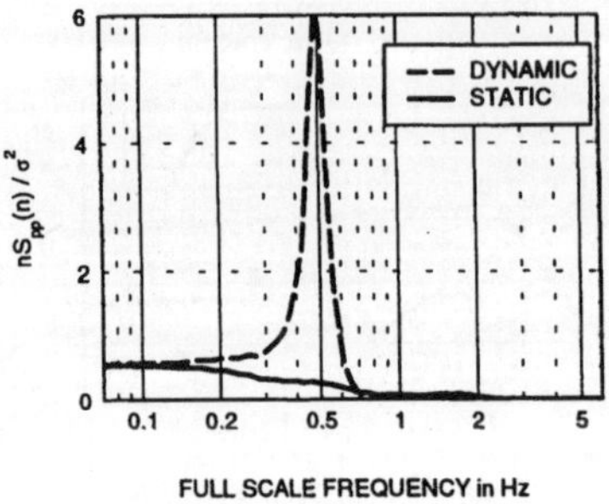

FIG 3.17(b) LOC 202 WD 330 N=2 ζ=0.3

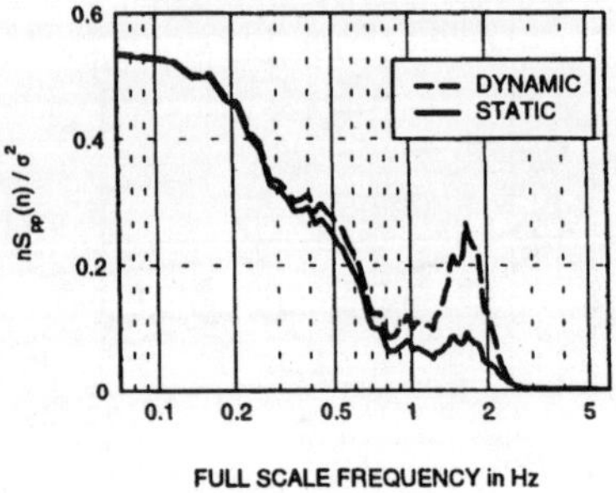

situations, then that rule does not necessarily apply. In some cases the variation is small,

although there is a slight rise in the frequency range about 1.5 Hz in Figures 3,15, but, for one location illustrated (location 178), the curve is altogether different in shape. For this location the value of R_c rises in the frequency range under consideration, to a maximum value at a natural frequency of 0.5 Hz. for the two lower Damping Ratios to fall thereafter, but is still rising at values of natural frequency up to 2 Hz for the higher value of damping ratio studied. The reason for the different shape of the curve for location 178 is shown in Figure 3.16a: the Normalised Spectral Density Function is still rising at these frequencies (to more than 0.5Hz), whereas the usual Normalised Spectral Density Function falls at these frequencies (see Figure 3.17a for location 202). This is emphasised by comparing the peak values of $nS_{pp}(n) / \sigma^2$ in Figures 3.16a and b: for location 178 for a natural frequency of 0.2 Hz the value is about 10 whereas for a natural frequency of 0.5 Hz the value id about 35.

3.3.4. Effect of Damping.

The effect of increasing damping is always to reduce the value of the Dynamic Augmentation Factor. This is shown in Figure 3.18.

3.3.5. Excitation of Harmonics.

The discussion so far has concentrated upon the fundamental frequency, the next question is whether the first harmonic can be excited. Consider the case when the Fundamental Frequency was 0.5 Hz, with a Damping Ratio of 10%, and that the first Harmonic Frequency was 2 Hz with a Damping Ratio of 30%. Because the Generalised Modes occur independently, the two spectra of Figures 3.17(a) and (b) apply separately, the values of σ^2_d / σ_s^2 for the two modes are 1.44 and 1.040. The two are combined by adding their variances, thus

$$\sigma_d^{\ 2} = \sigma_B^{\ 2} + \sigma_1^{\ 2} + \sigma_2^{\ 2}$$

$$\sigma_d^{\ 2} = (1.000 + 0.440 + 0.040) \times \sigma_s^{\ 2}$$

$$\sigma_d^{\ 2} = 1.480\ \sigma_s^{\ 2}$$

$$\sigma_d = 1.217\ \sigma_s.$$

3.3.6. Dynamic Augmentation Factor Calculation.

To calculate the Dynamic Augmentation Factor, we have to introduce values for the pressure in terms of its mean value and its Standard Deviation. For the cases considered above the values are given in the Figure 3.19: the values of Wind Direction are degrees East Of North (EON), and the values of Pressure

FIG 3.18(a) RATIO OF DYNAMIC TO STATIC PRESSURE

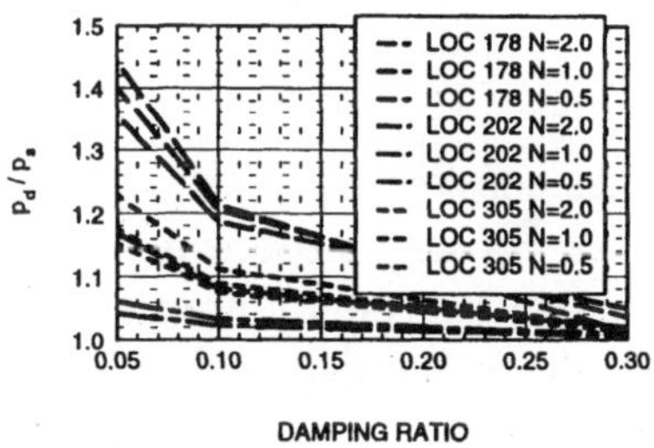

FIG 3.18(b) RATIO OF DYNAMIC TO STATIC PRESSURE

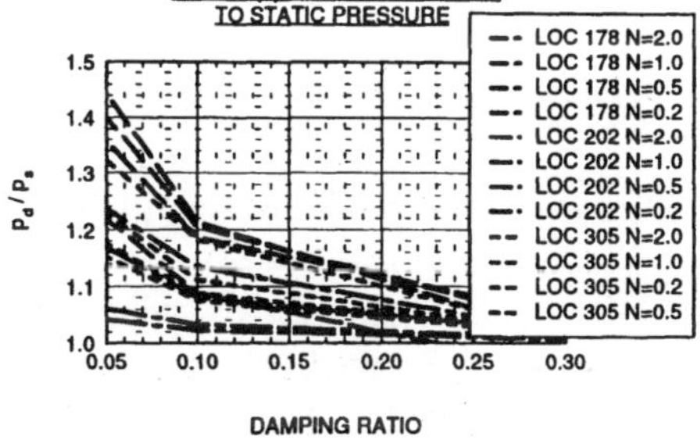

are in Pascals based on a 0.5 second averaging time and the "Once in 50 Years" wind speed.

The ratio of Dynamic to Static Pressure can be evaluated and it is this value which is compared to the 0.25 criterion in BS 6399. This ratio is plotted

LOCATION	WIND DIRECTION	MEAN	STANDARD DEVIATION
178	330	247	148
202	330	-527	57
305	270	-628	163

FIG. 3.19. VALUES OF MEAN AND STANDARD DEVIATION FOR ILLUSTRATED EXAMPLES

in Figures 3.18 ,two examples of this graph are considered, in Figure 3.18(a) Natural Frequencies of 2.0,1.0 and 0.5 Hz are presented, and in Figure 3.18(b) additional curves for a Natural Frequency of 0.2 Hz are added. In Figure 3.18(a) the curves for the three locations are almost separate, whereas they are more intermingled in Figure 3.18(b). With only the data of Figure 3.18(a) the conclusion might be drawn that the location is the overriding factor, but, with the introduction of Figure 3.18(b) it is impossible to make the clear statement that the location spectrum is critical for all values of Natural Frequency, but it has a very important effect.

If the ratio of dynamic pressure to static pressure is greater that 1.25, then a fully-dynamic approach is required according to the requirements of BS6399.

3.3.7. Effect of Size.

Once the process has been explained, let us consider the practical case of a member of size 25m, with a cut-off at 0.2 Hz in the spectrum. In Figure 3.20(a) the spectrum for the wind is presented for a Natural Frequency of 0.2 and Damping Ratio 0.1. The same data for the frequency range $0.07<n< 0.20$ Hz are presented in Figure 3.20(b). The value of R_c (σ_d / σ_s) for the full spectrum is 1.306, which is reduced to 1.177 for the truncated spectrum. For location 202 for the same values of Natural Frequency and Damping Ratio

(Figures 3.20(c) and (d)), the full and truncated values of R_c are 1.316 and 1.232 respectively. To show the importance of the Natural Frequency, the spectra for the wind and location 202 for a value of Natural Frequency of 0.5 Hz are shown on Figures 3.20(e) and (f) respectively, where values of R_c for

FIG 3.20(a) WIND SPECTRUM N=0.2 ζ=0.1

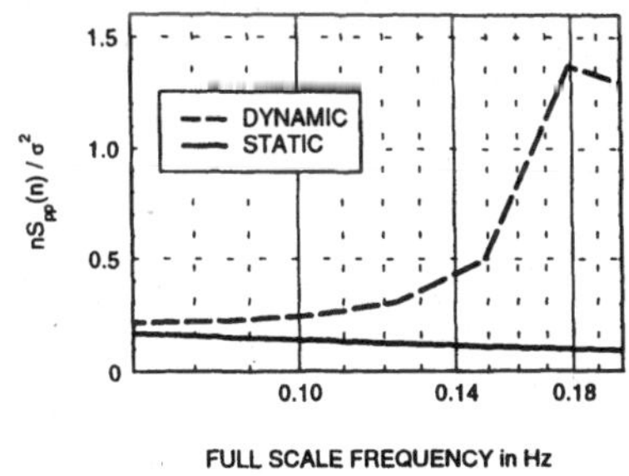

FIG 3.20(b) WIND SPECTRUM N=0.2 ζ=0.1

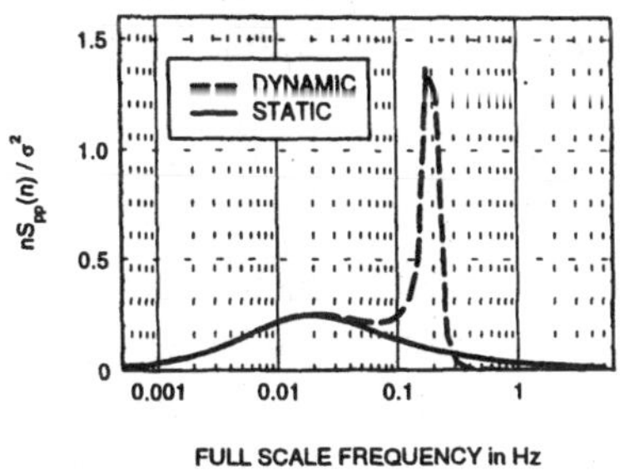

FIG 3.20(c) LOC 202 WD 330 N=0.2 ζ=0.1

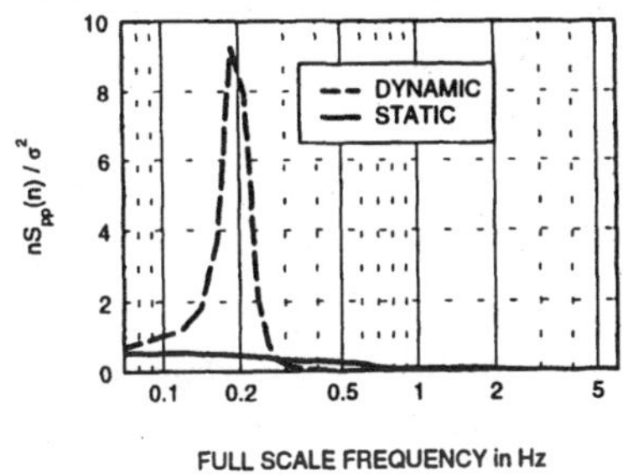

FIG 3.20(d) LOC 202 WD 330 N=0.2 ζ=0.1

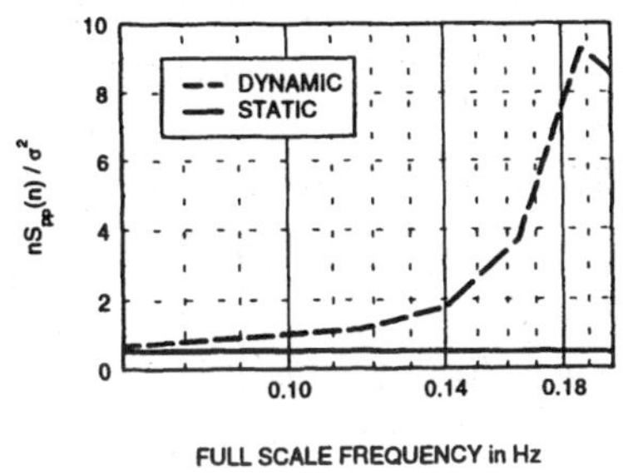

FIG 3.20(e) WIND SPECTRUM N=0.5 ζ=0.1

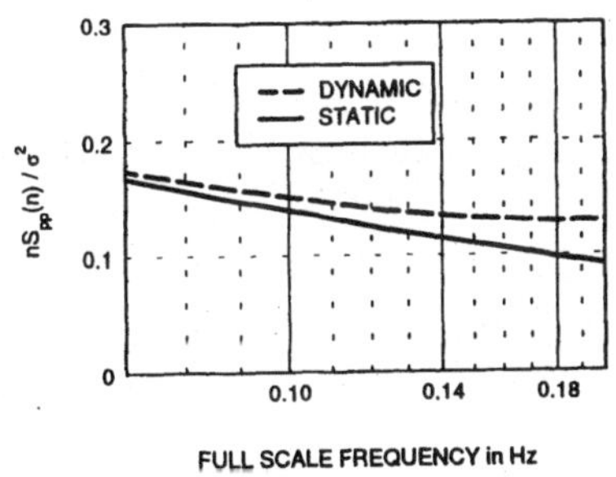

FIG 3.20(f) LOC 202 WD 330 N=0.5 ζ=0.1

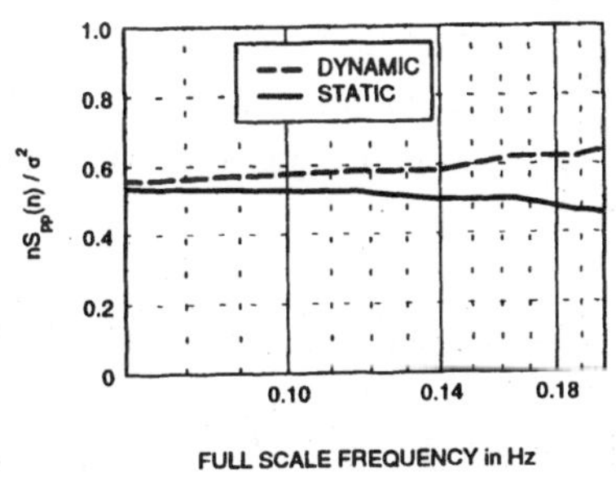

wind and location 202 are 1.011 and 1.012 respectively. For location 202 the value of the Dynamic Augmentation Factor (the ratio of dynamic to static pressure), with the values of natural frequency and damping stated on the Figure is 1.004.

The statement can be made that, for members larger than 25m, there will be negligible dynamic effects providing the Natural Frequency is greater than 0.5 Hz., and it is obvious that the First Harmonic would have no effect.

3.4. Dampers.

A damper is a device which converts movement energy into heat, and in doing so, reduces the energy of the movement. The dissipation of energy occurs in either a solid or liquid component of the damper.

There are two types of damper, the first can be attached to two parts of a structure which have relative movement. The second type is attached to a structure which moves, and the damper has to supply within itself a part which moves differently from the point of attachment.

3.4.1. The Addition of a Damper When There is Relative Movement Between Two Parts of the Structure.

The simplest form of this type of damper is a dash-pot, a porous piston in a cylinder filled with oil. The movement of the piston relative to the cylinder squirts oil through the piston, the velocity of the oil ultimately converting the energy into heat. A wide variety of silicon oils with different viscosities are available commercially.

Some solids, called elastomers, perform the same operation.

The advantage of this type of damper is that it adds little weight to the structure.

3.4.2. Dampers Providing a Reference Point.

3.4.2.1. Simple Form.

In the simplest form of this type of damper, the reference point is a mass. If this mass is attached to the member to be damped by stiffness and damping devices, the result would be a system such as that shown in Figure 3.09. If the natural frequency of the damper is far removed from the excitation (either above or below) then the mass would remain almost stationary. The dampers would dissipate some energy.

The drawback to this scheme is that the mass is almost stationary and the structure, whose movement is to be reduced, performs the greatest movement. It would be advantageous to reverse the roles.

3.4.2.2. Tuned Damper.

If the natural frequency of the damper were the same as that of the structure to be damped, then the mass would move out of phase with the applied oscillation, and would apply to the structure a force reducing the motion. Thus the motion of the structure would have been transferred to the mass, with a great reduction to the movement of the structure. The damping devices between the mass and the structure would absorb energy to limit the amplitude of movement of the mass. A mass of about 4% of the mass of the structure is required for this type of damper.

The simplest example of this type of damper is a "Stockbridge" Damper. This is a mass attached to the member to be damped by a cable which is impregnated with an elastomer; the cable and elastomer providing the stiffness and damping.

3.4.2.3. Multi-frequency Dampers.

The limitation of a tuned damper is that it only damps one frequency effectively, whereas structures can have several frequencies of excitation. To attempt to provide a damper for this situation, several dampers are on the market which have a mass of contorted shape, the distribution of the mass within the shape allows the system to oscillate in several different modes with different frequencies.

The design of these dampers is a specialised art, and the specialist should be approached for further information.

3.4.2.4. Broad Band Dampers.

There is a family of dampers which are not tuned, and therefor do not gain the advantage of the optimum transfer of energy from the structure to the mass. An example of this type is a set of laminae held together by a spring through a clearance hole in their centre. The spring exerts a pressure between the laminae, but the clearance hole allows limited relative movement between them: the friction between the laminae providing the damping.

Commercial manufacturers of dampers should be approached for details of such devices.

4. Wind Environment

The choice of the location for early dwellings was made mindful of the need for water, both for itself and for the transport facilities it afforded, so that early development started in valleys, where shelter from the winds was considerable. Early buildings, except for churches which were usually surrounded by graveyards, were low, because the materials and technology for the plentiful construction of tall buildings were unavailable. In recent years buildings have become taller, and, with the shortage of space in valley sites, have become closer spaced in those sites as well as spilling over on to more elevated and exposed ones. The advent of new stronger and lighter materials, for which the stabilising effect of weight no longer applies, has meant that the designers can build higher for a greater number of structures, and, when these occur among a complex of lower buildings, problems can occur in an area which was previously free of problems.

The importance of producing a pleasant environment to buildings is increasing, and wind engineers are now often asked to look over designs when they are in the formative stage, when serious changes such as orientation, gaps with surrounding buildings and other fundamental ideas are not yet finalised. Design is a compromise, but the best compromise is one in which all aspects have been considered. In the past, wind was often not considered and arbitrary decisions were made which produced serious wind problems, which could have been avoided without compromising any of the other requirements for the building. It is with a view to that form of advice that the following paragraphs are written. Always remember, when looking at a complex design of many buildings, that air is lazy, like yourself, and will always take the easiest path. It is just a matter of defining what is the easiest path, or the proportion of wind which will follow each of several possible paths.

Tall buildings, defined as those which protrude above their neighbours, act as scoops to collect the wind over much of their height and deflect it to ground level. As wind speed increases with height, the taller the building, the faster the wind speed at its top and the greater the wind speeds delivered to ground level around its base. The flow patterns around the buildings, and the locations around the base where wind speeds are critical, have been explained in Chapter 2.

This Chapter has two purposes: firstly to explain some of the guide lines which should be followed, and the pit-falls which should be avoided in the earliest stage of design. Secondly to describe criteria which would allow the wind environment to be quantified, so that it can be compared with other environments, or, better still, could be applied to wind tunnel investigations of buildings in their detail design phase. This would be facilitated if a set of criteria, which would be widely accepted, would form the basis on which approval could be given or withheld. Should modifications be required, it would be advantageous if the criteria were so presented as to suggest where redesign is required and what form it should take to ensure that the wind environment of the final building is acceptable.

The emphasis in this Chapter is on people and the effect of wind on them. Two aspects must be examined separately, their comfort and their safety, and each requires its own set of criteria.

Temperature affects the assessment of comfort, and it is known that wind can affect that assessment. The interaction of wind and temperature is discussed in the first Section.

4.1. Effect of Temperature.

The effect of wind on a person is mainly felt as a force on their body, their clothing or their accessories. The effect of this force is either to make them work harder to walk against the wind (and for this the hourly-average wind speed is the most significant measure), or to make them stagger when hit by a gust. A gust can also affect their clothing and accessories in that it causes coats to flap and umbrellas to turn inside-out. Temperature does not directly affect these phenomena. The temperature has its own effect on the comfort of the person and the presence of wind makes the temperature appear lower and the complaint of the combination is about the temperature rather than the wind: the interaction is called "Chill Factor". The cure for adverse temperature is suitable clothing. The temperature does not vary spatially much so the statement can be made that "if you dress suitably for the temperature when you set out from home, making allowance for the type of area (possible increased windiness) into which you are going, then temperature need not be considered in relation to the building".

Data of simultaneous measurements of wind speed and temperature are insufficient to base a criterion thereon, so the best that can be achieved at present is to present criteria based solely on the wind, but to present that data on a Month-by-Month or Season-by-Season basis, so that the user can apply any allowance he considers necessary for the effect of temperature.

Hereafter the wind will be considered by itself.

4.2. General Points and Typical Pit-falls

Prevailing wind directions should be established at the start. As will be obvious later when criteria are considered, criteria are based upon moderate wind speeds for short percentages of the time, so that winds from the direction of the strongest winds will make a major contribution to this total.

Two rules-of-thumb may be useful.

Consider two lines of buildings of the same height with the wind blowing at right angles to the lines. If the spacing between them is less that the height of the buildings, the space between them is reasonably peaceful. If the spacing is four times the height, then the wind will reach ground level at the downwind building, and it will receive no shelter. If the spacing is between these limits, with the strongest effect for a spacing of 2.5 heights, there will be an oscillatory flow pattern in which the space between the lines of buildings will fill with air and empty in a cyclic fashion. The process is as follows: the description starting at a point in the cycle when the stagnation streamline (the line which separates the air flowing over the building from that circulating between the buildings) impacts at a point, called the stagnation point, at the top of the front face of the downwind building, and the stagnation point is moving down the face. Air will start to be deflected into the space between the buildings, and the pressure there will start to rise, slowing the downward movement of the stagnation point. By the time the stagnation point has stopped moving, the pressure between the buildings will be above ambient and still increasing, so the stagnation point starts to move up the face of the building, all the time the stagnation point is on the building the pressure between the buildings increases slightly. Eventually the stagnation point reaches the top of the face, and air starts to escape from the space between the buildings, thus reducing the pressure. As the stagnation streamline moves higher, more air escapes and the internal pressure drops below ambient, thus slowing the upward movement of the streamline. Eventually the movement of the streamline stops, with the pressure between the buildings below ambient, so the streamline starts its downward path with air still leaving the space between the buildings and the pressure there decreasing. When the streamline reaches the top of the face of the building, the start of the cycle is reached and the cycle repeats. The period is of the order of 20 seconds depending upon the size of the buildings. This oscillatory flow can be annoying as the direction of the wind at ground level between the buildings changes back and forth.

A golden rule for courtyards, defined as having more than three quarters of their perimeters enclosed, is that acceptable conditions will occur within the courtyard, providing the enclosed area is less than five times the square of the average height of the surrounding buildings. Vortices will form in some corners of a courtyard, and leaves and rubbish will collect there.

Planting is often used to improve local conditions, and it must be emphasised that planting (either man-made or natural) only protects a given area for one wind direction. This means that for planting to be most effective, it should be defined after a detailed wind tunnel investigation has been performed (see Section 4.3). Planting can be used in one of two ways, it can be used to move the wind away from one area to another, where it will cause less trouble, or it can be used to extract energy from the wind. If a single tree with all its summer leaves is considered, it forms a solid body in the wind, and the wind will flow around it. At the sides of the tree, the wind speed will be increased and in the wake the speed will be reduced. After some 20 diameters of the tree, the two streams will have mixed and the wind speed will be slightly reduced, leaving an area in the immediate wake where the wind speeds have been reduced significantly, but the turbulence level has been increased. If several trees are planted in a pattern, the wake region can be extended. The result will have been to provide a sheltered region (the region changes with wind direction), behind the tree and other, smaller, regions of increased wind speed. If a tree without leaves , such as a plain tree in winter, is planted, the wind will flow over every twig and branch, each of which will act as a separate body, with local speed-up and retardation, mixing within 20 times the diameter of the twig or branch, so that the mixing is over is a short distance, but also the wind has flowed over many twigs in its passage through the tree and therefor has had much more energy extracted from it. This leads to a rule-of-thumb if you want to move wind, use evergreen trees, and if you want to extract energy in the winter, when the wind speeds are greatest, use deciduous ones.

The most common design pit-fall arises when an passage penetrates the building at ground floor on the centre line of its broad face. The flow pattern for the wind normal to the broad face has been shown in Figure 2.08. At ground level, in front of the opening, the wind travelling down the face of the building is brought to rest and its kinetic energy is converted to pressure, forming a region of positive pressure relative to ambient. From here the wind will move to all regions of lower pressure, the quantity of wind moving in any one direction from a position at ground level at the centre of the building varies with the pressure drop in that direction. Behind the building the pressure will be negative, usually more negative than at the other regions in front of the building. Consequently much of the wind will turn and flow through the opening, some will flow upwind and some will flow sideways and around the corners of the building. This tunnel is an attractive location for Entrance doors, but it is a very windy one. If it is essential to have such an opening, then some amelioration can be achieved by placing a false ceiling to the tunnel, the ceiling (which must be structurally strong) must protrude both front and back. The purpose is to catch the wind flowing down the face and deflect it through the tunnel above the ceiling. On leaving the "duct" the wind will diffuse, and should reach a suitably low speed before it reaches head height. The depth of the duct should be considerable because it is expected to pass a considerable volume of air.

This leads to the more general problem of the wind brought down to ground level by a large tall building. Once the wind has reached ground level, it will flow around the building and its neighbours until its energy is slowly dissipated in friction: this can take some distance. Two solutions are possible; either to stop the wind reaching ground level, or to deal with it when it has reached the ground by "planting" and other means. The first solution would obviously be advantageous because it does not require obstructions on the ground coupled with local windy spots. The first solution is what I have called a "Wind Gutter". Like a rain gutter, the purpose of a wind gutter is to collect the wind and dispose of it where it will cause no trouble. It is placed on the face of a building to collect the flow of air down the surface, so it must be attached to the building at a small distance above the ground, usually determined by aesthetics. It needs to be fairly near the ground so that it collects most of the wind on the face, yet it needs to be high enough so that it does not cause problems when it sheds the wind. About third floor level is ideal, other factors not applying. The gutter must be wide, depending upon the height of the building, a minimum of about 1m for low buildings increasing to about 3m for tall buildings, and it must have an upstand at its front of 600mm to 1000mm. The other essential is that it shall span the building from side to side. The way the gutter works is that it slows the downward movement of the wind, converting kinetic to pressure energy, the particles of air in the gutter at the centre of the building, with raised pressure, look for the lowest pressure region into which to flow. If the gutter spans the building, the wind sees the very low pressures (suctions) at the corners of the building, and flows along the gutter to the corners of the building, where it is discharged at the height of the gutter, thereafter it diffuses upwards and downwards so that its velocity, by the time it reaches head height, is acceptably low. Should the gutter not reach the corners of the building, the slowed air in the gutter sees pressures at the ends of the gutter similar , if not slightly higher than that below the gutter, so that most of the air will flow over the front of the gutter, and carry on down the face of the building to ground level. Wind gutters are not universally acceptable.

When a new building, especially if it is tall, is constructed adjoining an existing building, even if it is low, it can increase the wind speeds around the existing building (see Sections 2.2.4 and 3.1.5).

4.3. Wind Tunnel Investigation.

A full description of wind tunnel investigations is given in Chapter 10. However, to make parts of the next three paragraphs clear, a very brief resume will be given here,

Wind speeds, both gust speeds and mean values, are measured at head height at a series of locations for a range of wind directions as fractions of a reference wind speed in the wind tunnel. For the roughness of the fetch and surrounding buildings, the ratio of the reference wind speed in the wind tunnel to the "Meteorological Wind Speed", the hourly-average value of wind speed measured 10 meters above flat open level ground in the vicinity of the site, is determined. From Meteorological Offices around the world, the statistics of the Meteorological Standard Wind Speed are known, so that the statistics of the gust and mean wind speeds at head height at the chosen locations around the site are determined.

It is these values which will be discussed in the following paragraphs.

4.3.1. Criteria of Acceptability.

There is a need for a set of criteria of acceptability to be established which are approved around the world. Two topics should be addressed in any accepted set; Comfort and Safety.

There are almost as many sets of criteria as there are workers in the field, but differences are often small between them.

The first point of disagreement is the velocity than should be used. Gust wind speeds can either be measured directly, as at Bristol, or be computed as a mean value plus a multiple of the intensity of turbulence, viz.

$$V = \bar{U} + K \times (\sigma / \bar{U})$$

and values for *K* differ from 0 (NPL) , 1 (Gandemer), 1.5 (Western Ontario), 2 (Feis) to 3 to 4 (Hunt). Western Ontario and Bristol express their wind speeds in terms of the Beaufort Scale, but this has problems when it is related to a value of wind speed.

The main part of the operation is to investigate the response of people to wind alone, the subject of temperature has already been considered in Section 4.1. In the Bristol method a series of steps of "Perceived Response to Wind" have been specified. In doing this, recourse has been made to the Beaufort Scale, because Admiral Beaufort in 1805 devised his scale so that any sailor could report wind speeds with sufficient accuracy for log purposes, and most present day sailors know the feel of a Beaufort Scale "n" wind. The Admiral allocated a range of his scale to every different appearance of ship (sail) or sea. However, the Beaufort Scale was found too coarse for landlubbers, only ranges 2 to 6 being appropriate. In consequence two steps were allocated to each range of the scale. The other parameter is a person's reaction to wind, apart from strength, is frequency of occurrence, so that a step in the scale of perception of wind is defined as "Exceedence of Beaufort "n" for "x" percent of the time". Association of frequency and strength of wind allows many combinations to be used.

Some investigators choose one wind speed and define a range of frequencies depending upon designated use of the area: this is acceptable providing that the value of wind speed chosen is one which relates to a person's reaction. This can involve the use of frequencies either so infrequent as to be under-represented by the parent meteorological data, or so frequent as to be meaningless as far as reaction is concerned.

Other investigators choose a single frequency, and associate a different wind speed for each use: this can be more practical and is the basis of the criteria for acceptance by the LDDC (London Docklands Development Corporation) (explained in reference T.V.Lawson "The Determination of the Wind Environment of a Building Complex before Construction" Department of Aerospace Engineering, University of Bristol Report Number TVL 9025 May 1990).

A hybrid system, which has been used at Bristol for the last 30 years, is described below.

A fourth system was defined by Bill Melbourne which uses the probability distribution function to describe the wind. Most readers use the Weibull Distribution, viz.

$$P(V) = 1 - exp\ \{ - (V/c)^k \},$$

with the value of k centred on 1.85. For his formulation Melbourne assumed a value of 2 for "k" (i.e. a Rayleigh Distribution), leaving only a value to be ascribed to c for each use.

A fifth system has been devised in the "Local Wind Effect" section of the BREEAM (Building Research Establishment Environmental Assessment Method, published as a BRE Report) document , although the requirements are not directly comparable as they describe a maximum permissible height for a building, in either a rural or urban setting and in a geographical position (located on a map of the UK), which will automatically receive a "Credit" towards an overall environmental assessment of the building. Because building shape & orientation, and height & location of surrounding buildings are not considered, the requirement is overstrict as it has to apply to the worst combination of parameters. Practical situations are always better. The document does allow for a wind tunnel investigation to be performed, and the credit be awarded if local wind speeds of Beaufort Force 4 are exceeded for less that 10% of the time at every location. This is roughly equal to the Bristol criterion for "Business Walking".

Providing a single specific Probability Distribution could be derived for all cases, the first three criteria could be made identical, and if it were the Rayleigh Distribution, then the first four would be the same once the measurement of wind speed was agreed. Without a specific distribution being applicable, then the use of either large or small values of wind speed or frequency in the criteria could cause meaningless differences in the results.

The Bristol method will be described in the Sections which follow.

4.3.1.1. Comfort Criteria.

These are criteria which quantify a person's annoyance with the wind, in a situation in which his safety is not in question.

At this stage three subjective descriptions of the wind environment will be made:

ACCEPTABLE when the wind will not be noticed.

TOLERABLE when the wind will be noticed but its presence will not prevent the area being used effectively for its designated purpose. In this case remedial measures should be taken providing they are economic and do not adversely alter the aesthetics of the building or complex.

UNACCEPTABLE when the wind is of sufficient strength and frequency as to deter people from using the area for its designated purpose. In this case some remedial alterations should be made.

To illustrate the difference between "Tolerable" and "Unacceptable"; imagine a shopping precinct on which are two supermarkets "A" and "B". Suppose the entrance to supermarket "A" is deemed to be "Unacceptable", whilst that at supermarket "B" is "Tolerable". Then shoppers will say that it is always windy at supermarket "A" and go, if possible, to supermarket "B". Whereas the talk of conditions at supermarket "B" is that it was windy there to-day, with the expectation that the wind would be unnoticeable on the next few visits. The Bristol method is the only one to incorporate the "Tolerable" status: most other systems have only a single value which compares with the "Unacceptable" criterion.

In the choice of wind speed and frequency for the criteria, the Bristol (hybrid) method resorts to the steps in the scale of "Perceived Response to Wind" mentioned above. The set of steps is

4%B6: 2%B6: 6%B5: 2%B5: 4%B4: 2%B4: 6%B3: 1%B3: 6%B2: 4%B2,

Beaufort Force	Hourly-Average Windspeed m/s	Description of Wind	Noticable Effect of Wind
0	<0.45	Calm	Smoke rises vertically
1	0.45 - 1.55	Light	Direction shown by Smoke drift but not by vanes
2	1.55 - 3.35	Light	Wind felt on faces: leaves rustle: wind vane moves
3	3.35 - 5.60	Light	Leaves and twigs in motion: wind extends a flag
4	5.60 - 8.25	Moderate	Raises dust and loose paper: small branches move
5	8.25 - 10.95	Fresh	Small trees in leaf sway
6	10.95 - 14.10	Strong	Large branches begin to move: telephone wires whistle
7	14.10 - 17.20	Strong	Whole trees in motion
8	17.20 - 20.80	Gale	Twigs break off: Personal progress impeded
9	20.80 - 24.35	Gale	Slight structural damage: chimney pots removed
10	24.35 - 28.40	Strong Gale	Trees uprooted: considerable structural damage
11	28.40 - 32.40	Storm	Damage is widespread: unusual in the UK
12	> 32.40	Hurricane	Countryside is devasted: only occurs in tropical countries

FIGURE 4.01. THE BEAUFORT SCALE

where 4%B6 means that there is a probability of 0.04 that Beaufort Force 6 winds will be exceeded. This can be interpreted loosely to mean that Beaufort Force 6 wind speeds will be exceeded for more than 4% of the time.

The use of Beaufort Force has hidden the variable mentioned above as a choice of a value for K. Different phenomena used by the Admiral to define his different ranges were affected by gusts of different sizes. This caused him no problem because he only needed to know the wind speed for a single environment i.e. a ship in the open sea, and an hourly-average value suited his purposes. When applied to comfort purposes, different effects on people occur in gusts of different sizes. Tables defining the ranges of the Beaufort Scale (see Figure 4.01) define them in terms of the hourly average wind speed.

It is well known that a value of the hourly average wind speed could define the energy expended in walking across a large site, but it is the gust of a second or so duration which turns an umbrella inside-out or makes your coat tails flap. If Wind Speed (hourly average) and Gust Speed (say 3 second average) are considered rather than Wind Speed and Turbulence, then a ratio can be defined between the value of Gust Speed, with that averaging time and a low probability of occurrence in an hour of wind, to the hourly-average value of Wind Speed, for a stated value of the Intensity of Turbulence. In the Bristol method the value ascribed to this ratio is 1.85, which relates to a Turbulence Intensity of 30% for a 3-second average gust speed with a 1% probability of exceedence. The value of 30% was chosen as a typical value in a shopping precinct, an area where most different uses will be found, and to which many wind tunnel investigations apply. The reason why consideration of turbulence is necessary is because different building complexes bring wind and gusts down to ground level differently, and even in the same complex, some areas have high turbulence and others low. In a wind tunnel investigation both should be measured. In the Bristol method, the measured Gust Wind Speed is converted into an "Equivalent Hourly-Average Gust Speed" by dividing it by 1.85, and then both Equivalent Hourly-Average Gust Speed and Wind Speed are compared to the same criteria, which then depends only on use. A ratio of 2.0 is used for some areas overlooking water, where people's response to wind is more tolerant.

	USE SYMBOL	UNACCEPTABLE	TOLERABLE	CRITERIA
Roads and Car Parks	A	6% > B5	2% > B5	10 9
People Around Buildings	B	2% > B5	2% > B4	9 7
Pedestrian Walk-through	C	4% > B4	6% > B3	8 6
Pedestrian Standing	D	6% > B3	6% > B2	6 4
Entrance Doors	E	6% > B3	4% > B2	6 3
Sitting	F	1% > B3	4% > B2	5 3

FIG. 4.02 USER DEFINITIONS

LOC	AVTM	BEAUFORT FORCE 1	2	3	4	5	6	7	8	9
1	3	92.99	6.99	.03	.00	.00	.00	.00	.00	.00
	15	98.41	1.59	.00	.00	.00	.00	.00	.00	.00
2	3	33.30	40.39	21.43	4.62	.25	.00	.00	.00	.00
	15	40.55	32.25	18.82	6.97	1.30	.11	.00	.00	.00
3	3	31.27	39.38	21.79	6.75	.78	.03	.00	.00	.00
	15	43.47	31.00	18.63	6.15	.73	.03	.00	.00	.00
4	3	32.39	39.30	21.44	6.19	.67	.02	.00	.00	.00
	15	41.47	31.74	18.88	6.61	1.13	.16	.01	.00	.00
5	3	62.97	27.92	8.03	1.04	.04	.00	.00	.00	.00
	15	65.75	23.29	8.56	2.06	.31	.02	.00	.00	.00
6	3	96.81	3.19	.00	.00	.00	.00	.00	.00	.00
	15	99.56	.44	.00	.00	.00	.00	.00	.00	.00
7	3	37.37	45.54	15.46	1.62	.02	.00	.00	.00	.00
15	3	48.89	38.97	10.69	1.31	.12	.01	.00	.00	.00
	15	64.81	28.74	5.09	1.10	.23	.03	.00	.00	.00
16	3	23.83	48.34	24.96	2.79	.08	.00	.00	.00	.00
	15	24.39	48.32	23.18	3.82	.27	.02	.00	.00	.00
17	3	30.98	47.48	18.87	2.60	.07	.00	.00	.00	.00
	15	42.26	41.58	13.92	2.14	.10	.00	.00	.00	.00
18	3	29.84	33.66	25.77	9.41	1.25	.07	.00	.00	.00
	15	32.52	33.20	23.41	8.80	1.86	.20	.00	.00	.00
19	3	75.87	17.14	5.91	1.03	.05	.00	.00	.00	.00
	15	79.54	13.01	6.22	1.18	.05	.00	.00	.00	.00
24	3	26.50	39.33	24.46	8.60	1.07	.04	.00	.00	.00
	15	31.95	30.55	21.54	11.84	3.46	.62	.04	.00	.00

FIG 4.03 PERCENTAGE OF TIME OF WIND

FOR JANUARY

BUILDING AERODYNAMICS

LOC	USE	UT	YEAR G	YEAR W	JAN G	JAN W	FEB G	FEB W	MAR G	MAR W	APR G	APR W	MAY G	MAY W	JUN G	JUN W	JUL G	JUL W	AUG G	AUG W	SEP G	SEP W	OCT G	OCT W	NOV G	NOV W	DEC G	DEC W
1	E	G G	0	0	0	0	0	0	0	0	0	0	0	0	0	0	0	0	0	0	0	0	0	0	0	0	0	0
2	C	D C	5	5	5	26	5	5	5	5	5	5	5	5	5	5	5	5	5	5	5	5	5	5	5	5	5	26
3	C	D C	5	5	26	26	5	5	5	5	5	5	5	5	5	5	5	5	5	5	5	5	5	5	5	5	26	26
4	C	D C	5	5	26	26	5	26	5	5	5	5	5	5	5	5	5	5	5	5	5	5	5	26	5	26	5	26
12	D	F D	25	25	25	25	25	25	25	25	24	24	24	25	24	24	24	24	24	24	24	25	25	25	25	25	25	25
13	D	G G	0	0	0	0	0	0	0	0	0	0	0	0	0	0	0	0	0	0	0	0	0	0	0	0	0	0
14	D	D C	25	25	46	46	25	25	25	25	25	25	25	25	25	25	25	25	25	25	25	25	25	25	25	25	46	46
18	D	D B	46	46	46	47	46	46	46	46	46	46	25	25	25	25	25	25	25	25	25	25	46	46	25	25	46	46
19	D	F D	3	3	25	25	25	25	24	24	3	3	3	24	0	0	0	0	0	0	0	0	3	25	24	25	25	25
20	C	F D	4	5	5	5	4	5	4	5	4	5	4	5	3	4	3	4	3	4	4	4	5	5	4	5	4	5
21	C	D C	5	5	5	26	5	5	5	5	5	5	5	5	5	5	5	5	5	5	5	5	5	5	5	5	5	26
22	D	F D	24	24	24	25	24	25	24	24	24	24	24	24	3	3	24	3	24	3	24	24	24	24	24	24	24	24
23	D	F D	25	25	25	25	25	25	25	25	25	25	25	25	25	25	25	25	25	25	25	25	25	25	25	25	25	25
24	D	C B	25	47	46	48	25	47	25	47	25	47	25	46	25	46	25	47	25	46	25	46	25	47	25	46	46	47

FIG 4.04 COMFORT CRITERIA

%	4.0	2.0	6.0	2.0	4.0	2.0	6.0	1.0	6.0	4.0	50.0
		B6		B5		B4		B3		B2	B1
	12	11	10	9	8	7	6	5	4	3	2

BUILDING AERODYNAMICS

User areas are defined and the subjective descriptions are associated with a step in the scale of "Perceived Response to Wind": these are described in Figure 4.02.

To see whether exceedence has occurred, tables of Probability of Exceedence of each range of the Beaufort Scale (for example Figure 4.03) would have to be scanned for every location, with different criteria for each location, depending upon its use, in mind: this would be long and tedious. To assist the reader the computer programme, which derived Figures 4.03, has been used to scan the tables and present the first step which has been equalled or exceeded. The "Use Symbol" can be presented opposite the Location Number so that exceedence can easily be seen. Because it is easy to miss one number in a large table, in Bristol, 40 is added to the Criteria Number for every instance when the Unacceptable" criterion has been equalled or exceeded, and 20 is added if the Tolerable criterion has been reached or exceeded. It is then impossible to miss any exceedence of either criteria.

Recently two additional columns have been added to the User Description column; the first additional column, headed "U" for Unacceptable, is the lowest (starting at "Sitting") "Use Symbol" for which conditions would be classified as "Unacceptable", and in the second additional column, headed "T" for "Tolerable" is the Use Symbol for which conditions would first be classified as "Tolerable". If no conditions would exceed the "Unacceptable" or "Tolerable" categories, then the symbol "G" appears in the appropriate column. An example of this presentation is shown in Figure 4.04.

FIG 4.05 OVERLAY FOR FEB

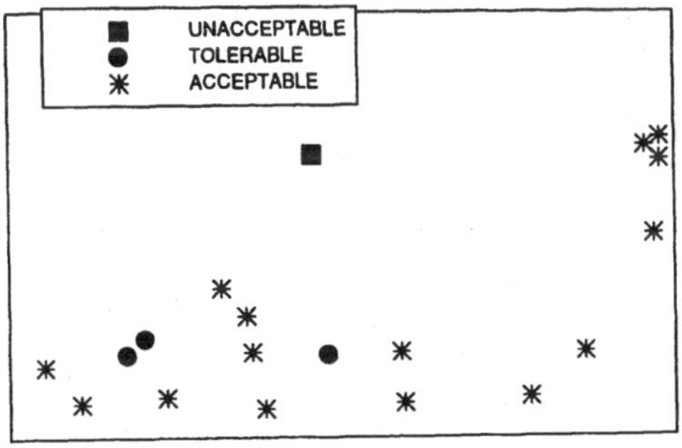

Some of our clients prefer a pictorial presentation to a tabular one, so we superimpose on a photograph of the site an overlay which locates the following symbols at the position of their measurement. For "Unacceptable"

conditions, a solid square symbol is superimposed, for "Tolerable" conditions a solid circular symbol is placed, and for a location which has been found "Acceptable" by measurement, an asterisk is placed. An example of an overlay is shown in Figure 4.05.

It is recommended that the report be studied as follows: firstly the uses attributed to the locations should be checked, and approved. Once the usage has been agreed, any infringements of either criterion is immediately obvious. Should one occur, then two possible remedies are available: the use could be changed, or redesign could be required. To see whether change of use is applicable, a study of the second or third column under use symbol will show the use which first exceeds each description, and its practicality can be considered. If a change of use is not permissible, then some form of redesign is required. This can either consist of changes to the building, or the provision of shielding upwind in the form of planting or the addition of man-made structures. To help in this choice, the probabilities when the wind will be in the Beaufort Ranges 2 to 5 are presented for each wind direction for each month and for the Year: a whole page being devoted to a single location. An example of this presentation is shown in Figure 4.06. The wind direction which contributes to the high wind speeds is identified, and suitable remedial measures can be detailed as explained in Section 4.2.

In the LDDC method, a probability (percentage of the time) exceedence of 5% is chosen, and the values for the wind speed (Equivalent Hourly Average Wind Speed) of 10 m/s for "Business Walking", which is defined as objective walking from A to B or for cycling: 8 m/s for "Pedestrian Walking": 6 m/s for "Pedestrian Standing"; and 4 m/s for "Pedestrian Sitting".

In Melbourne's approach, the values of "c" for "Business Walking" was 6 m/s: for "Pedestrian Walking" was 4 m/s: for "Standing" was 3.2 m/s and for "Sitting" was 2.5 m/s.

A comparison of the criteria from the various methods superimposed on actual probability curves for the various user types from several recent studies at Bristol are shown in Figure 4.07

4.3.1.2. Distress Criteria.

A second criterion must be established to identify those areas where someone could find walking difficult, or could even stumble or fall, this is called the

BF	0	30	60	90	120	150	180	210	240	270	300	330
						W I N D D I R E C T I O N						
JANUARY		CRITERIA 46										
2	1.41	.87	2.00	1.08	1.31	3.15	5.10	.56	7.33	4.18	9.20	.06
3	1.51	.12	.19	.00	.98	.70	.73	.00	4.24	7.34	4.21	.00
4	.36	.00	.00	.00	.12	.01	.01	.00	.77	5.32	.16	.00
5	.01	.00	.00	.00	.00	.00	.00	.00	.04	1.27	.00	.00
FEBRUARY		CRITERIA 25										
2	2.92	2.01	2.15	1.38	2.37	2.02	4.41	.49	6.06	4.03	8.83	.00
3	1.82	.87	.84	.00	1.16	.15	.98	.00	3.35	4.68	3.16	.00
4	.23	.04	.06	.00	.07	.00	.06	.00	.74	2.55	.08	.00
5	.00	.00	.00	.00	.00	.00	.00	.00	.06	.58	.00	.00
MARCH		CRITERIA 25										
2	2.16	1.64	1.98	1.09	6.24	4.73	4.19	.52	4.00	3.30	1.66	.00
3	1.03	.19	.07	.00	1.58	.43	.25	.00	2.90	3.59	1.62	.00
4	.14	.00	.00	.00	.04	.00	.00	.00	.97	2.66	.08	.00
5	.00	.00	.00	.00	.00	.00	.00	.00	.14	.81	.00	.00
APRIL		CRITERIA 25										
2	5.40	2.02	1.43	.13	3.40	1.99	2.98	.55	5.24	3.46	6.19	.00
3	2.19	.18	.18	.00	.28	.08	.18	.00	2.67	5.67	2.09	.00
4	.11	.00	.01	.00	.00	.00	.00	.00	.44	3.41	.07	.00
5	.00	.00	.00	.00	.00	.00	.00	.00	.02	.56	.00	.00
MAY		CRITERIA 25										
2	5.65	4.53	2.20	.19	4.88	2.84	2.87	.57	3.10	2.43	4.16	.00
3	1.55	.56	.22	.00	.56	.20	.22	.00	1.96	3.95	1.16	.00
4	.07	.01	.00	.00	.00	.00	.00	.00	.49	2.48	.03	.00
5	.00	.00	.00	.00	.00	.00	.00	.00	.04	.47	.00	.00
JUNE		CRITERIA 25										
2	5.43	1.54	.51	.01	3.59	1.92	2.45	.25	4.70	3.76	5.95	.04
3	1.35	.05	.01	.00	.26	.06	.18	.00	2.51	4.52	.97	.00
4	.07	.00	.00	.00	.00	.00	.00	.00	.57	2.14	.01	.00
5	.00	.00	.00	.00	.00	.00	.00	.00	.05	.33	.00	.00
JULY		CRITERIA 25										
2	3.69	.63	.19	.00	3.04	1.65	3.00	.30	4.93	4.87	7.55	.00
3	.61	.00	.00	.00	.08	.07	.22	.00	2.58	7.12	1.04	.00
4	.01	.00	.00	.00	.00	.00	.00	.00	.46	4.04	.00	.00
5	.00	.00	.00	.00	.00	.00	.00	.00	.02	.71	.00	.00
AUGUST		CRITERIA 25										
2	3.09	1.12	.54	.03	3.17	2.40	2.98	.26	5.65	5.37	4.24	.01
3	.85	.05	.01	.00	.23	.15	.20	.00	2.78	6.32	.71	.00
4	.07	.00	.00	.00	.00	.00	.00	.00	.59	2.70	.01	.00
5	.00	.00	.00	.00	.00	.00	.00	.00	.05	.33	.00	.00
SEPTEMBER		CRITERIA 25										
2	2.07	2.18	1.33	.12	2.75	2.60	3.97	.52	5.89	5.01	6.42	.00
3	.48	.38	.09	.00	.09	.11	.32	.00	2.95	6.37	1.72	.00
4	.01	.01	.00	.00	.00	.00	.00	.00	.65	3.22	.04	.00
5	.00	.00	.00	.00	.00	.00	.00	.00	.06	.53	.00	.00
OCTOBER		CRITERIA 25										
2	1.27	1.04	.67	.10	1.90	2.74	5.21	.56	7.98	5.18	5.72	.01
3	.79	.43	.02	.00	.65	1.02	.57	.00	4.30	7.29	2.25	.00
4	.18	.04	.00	.00	.08	.17	.01	.00	.65	3.76	.09	.00
5	.01	.00	.00	.00	.00	.01	.00	.00	.02	.55	.00	.00
NOVEMBER		CRITERIA 25										
2	1.92	1.56	2.10	.90	1.91	3.71	6.53	.13	6.58	4.51	6.50	.00
3	.74	.57	.27	.00	.99	1.28	.47	.00	2.64	6.17	1.68	.00
4	.02	.02	.00	.00	.08	.10	.00	.00	.22	3.25	.01	.00
5	.00	.00	.00	.00	.00	.00	.00	.00	.00	.53	.00	.00
DECEMBER		CRITERIA 46										
2	1.19	1.08	.86	1.20	1.52	3.97	5.60	.71	7.59	3.06	7.12	.00
3	1.13	.31	.15	.01	1.30	.89	.21	.00	5.41	5.86	2.52	.00
4	.10	.00	.00	.00	.27	.03	.00	.00	1.50	4.74	.03	.00
5	.00	.00	.00	.00	.01	.00	.00	.00	.14	1.27	.00	.00
YEAR		CRITERIA 25										
2	2.92	1.75	1.29	.47	3.08	2.88	4.13	.45	5.90	4.09	6.32	.03
3	1.24	.28	.12	.00	.72	.32	.37	.00	3.22	5.82	2.00	.00
4	.14	.01	.00	.00	.03	.00	.00	.00	.64	3.35	.06	.00
5	.00	.00	.00	.00	.00	.00	.00	.00	.04	.63	.00	.00

FIG 4.06 BREAKDOWN OF PERCENT OF TIME

FOR LOCATION 14
AVERAGING TIME IS 15 MNS

BUILDING AERODYNAMICS

FIG 4.07 (a) BUSINESS

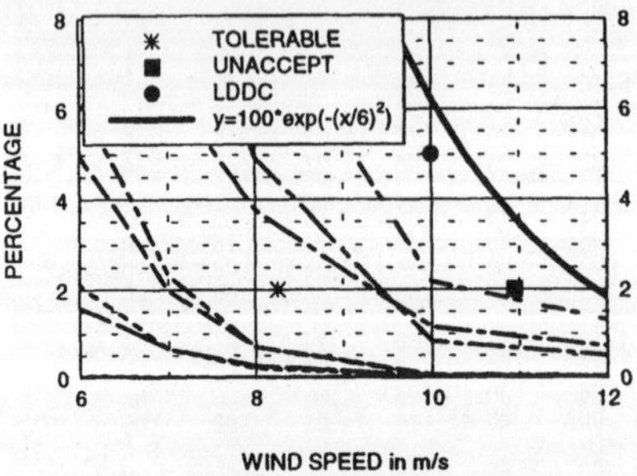

FIG 4.07 (b) WALKING

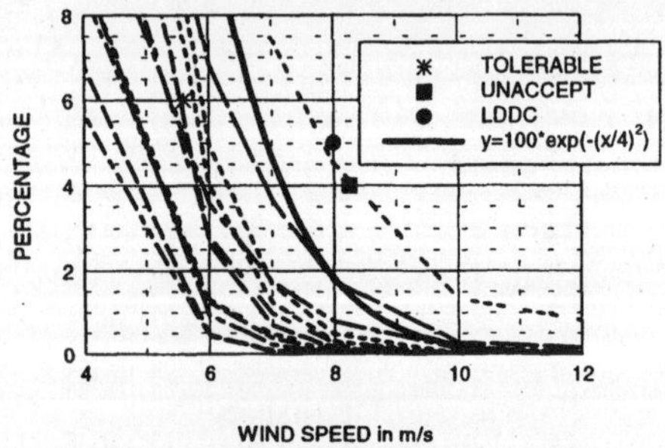

FIG 4.07 (c) STANDING

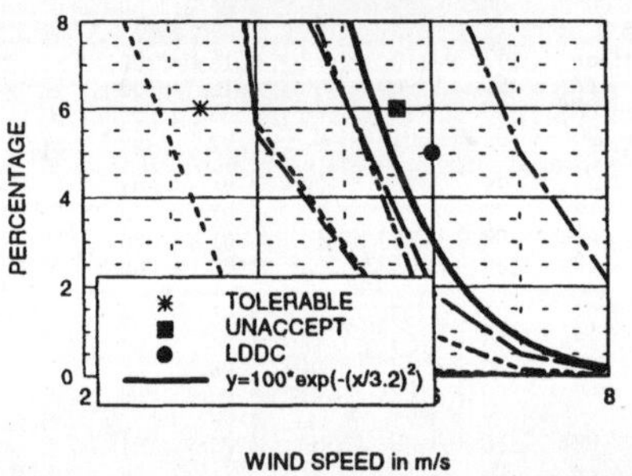

FIG 4.07 (d) SITTING

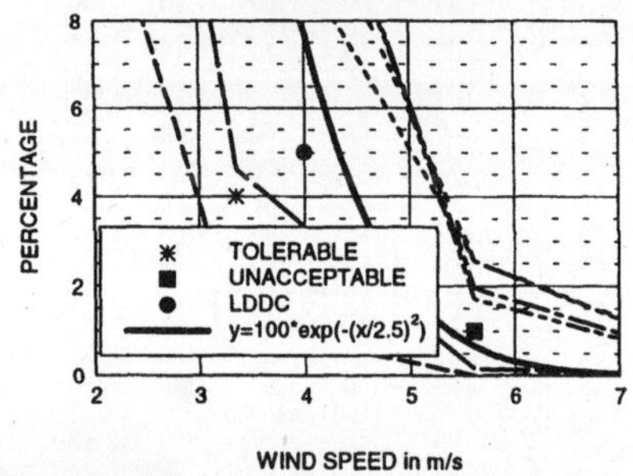

FIG 4.07 (e) ENTRANCES

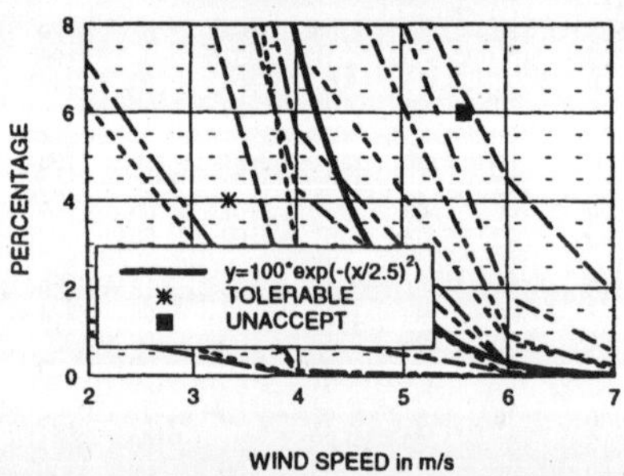

"Distress Criterion". It is going to be more difficult to define this criterion because comfort levels for most people fall between reasonable limits, but distress levels will vary widely depending upon the age and infirmity of the person. It is therefor considered that the "Distress Criterion" should be "notifiable". This flags the area, and allows the designer to limit the use of the area to certain groups of people, or the performance of certain jobs, within the general classification above.

A wind of Beaufort Force 6 can upset a frail old lady (this is not a sexist remark, a lady is specified because she normally presents a greater area of clothing to the wind). The effect of wind on the disabled is difficult to assess as it is much more variable. It is the Bristol custom to define Beaufort Force 6 wind speeds as the limit of safety, and to identify locations in which this wind speed has a 0.01% probability of being exceeded in any specified month (or the whole Year). This is a frequency of less that Once a Year. The locations where these wind speeds, either gust or mean hourly, have been exceeded are listed by the months when the exceedence occurred. An example of the presentation is shown in Figure 4.08.

MONTH	LOCATIONS				
JANUARY	4	9	24		
FEBRUARY	4	9	16	24	
MARCH	24				
APRIL					
MAY					
JUNE					
JULY	24				
AUGUST					
SEPTEMBER	24				
OCTOBER	4	5	9	12	20
NOVEMBER	4				
DECEMBER	24				
YEAR	24				

FIGURE 4.08

DISTRESS CRITERIA

BUILDING AERODYNAMICS

The accuracy of values from the tails of parent probability distributions is always dubious. In the present case the distributions are those for the "Meteorological Standard Wind Speed", which are outside the investigator's control. Additional confidence can be achieved if Extreme Value Analysis has been applied to the parent distributions, and the results compared with the "Once in 50 Years" values used for wind loading calculations.

Gust speeds ought to be converted to values of "Equivalent Hourly-Average Wind Speed" as explained in Section 4.3.1.1. This means that the same table of probabilities can be applied to both gust and hourly-average data for the derivation of "Comfort" and "Distress" criteria.

Thought must be given the implementation of the notification process. The wind speed value was based upon the walking ability of an old lady, which was deemed the most critical, with a probability of less than one occurrence a year: the accuracy of this calculation has been discussed in the last paragraph. Probability has further aspects in this context, for example, the probability whether a member of a critical group would be at that location at the instant of the strongest gust in the windiest hour of wind on one of the windiest day of the year: this is a joint probability of unrelated matters. Coupled to this consideration is the question "Is the location on a major route through the complex, and are there suitable alternate routes which are not "distressful"?

In preparing the document for the LDDC, it was agreed with Nick Isumov of the Boundary Layer Tunnel Laboratory at the University of Western Ontario that the probability for the distress criterion should be "Once a Year". Consequently the LDDC document requires notification of exceedences of greater than 0.025% for the Year and 0.04% for each month in the parent distributions. In the LDDC document the wind speed limit for the "General Public" was an hourly average wind speed of 15 m/s, and in areas where any frail person or a cyclist would not be expected, the wind speed was 20 m/s.

4.3.1.3. Comparisons with Empty Spaces.

A question often posed by clients is whether their building makes conditions in its environment more windy or less: this is a reasonable question, but the answer is not as simple as it would appear.

A tall building, which is defined as one which protrudes above the surrounding buildings, will always make some part of its surroundings windier. For one wind direction some areas will be windy and others will be sheltered, whilst for a different wind direction, the windy and sheltered areas could reverse. Because the wind speed increases with height, the taller the building, the faster the wind impinging upon its surface, and the faster will be the winds brought down to ground level. Different shapes of building behave differently as discussed in Section 2.2.1 .

If there is a small space within a densely packed neighbourhood of buildings of all the same height, then conditions within that area will be pleasant if the area is less than 5 times the square of the average heights of the surrounding buildings. If that open space is filled with a building of the same height as its surroundings, then there will be little change. If the proposed building is taller than its neighbours, then it will act as a scoop and bring wind down into its immediate surroundings. This wind, once down at ground level, has to go somewhere, and will flow through the surrounding streets until it is slowed by friction with the buildings, which will cause air to disperse over and around the neighbouring buildings. Not only will the immediate surroundings of the new building be windier, but so also will be the surroundings of the neighbouring buildings.

If the "open" area is greater than 5 times the square of the average height of the surrounding buildings, then significant wind will enter the area. The addition of a new building of the same height as its surroundings will improve matters. The addition of a new tall building will make matters worse in places and better in others, depending upon the wind direction.

Some experimenters take the model of the proposed building out from the model of its surroundings and measure, for all wind directions, local wind speeds at the same locations they studied with the proposed building in place. This gives a real comparison and is the best way to proceed; a comparison between two sets of tables of the form of Figure 4.04. This procedure does however, doubles the cost of the investigation.

If the open area is large compared with the heights of the surrounding buildings, then the empty site can be studied in "meteorological" terms rather than in "building environmental" terms. This means that the computer programme, which has been used to determine the approaching wind speeds and profiles, can be used with an assumed ground roughness of 0.03m for the site to obtain the ratio of the wind speed at 1.7m (head height) to the "Meteorological Standard Wind Speed". At Bristol we take a single value at the centre of the open site, determine the velocity ratio as above and assume that it applies for all wind directions. We then produce a table as Figure 4.06 for the open site and comparisons can be made with the values presented in Figures 4.04 for every location with the proposed building in place. It is then obvious at which locations overall shelter is provided, and at which locations wind speeds are increased. In this form of presentation, even though the results show that there is shelter at a given location, it does not mean that, for some wind directions, the proposed building has not made matters worse. It does present the data in the same form as that on which the acceptability of the area is judged, and, at Bristol, we maintain that this is the appropriate presentation.

4.4. Response to Vibration.

The response of the human body to vibrations is not often considered in the building context, although much work has been done on it in relation to transport. Different parts of the body respond to different frequencies. This is obvious when the human body is considered to consist of a number of masses joined by springs and dampers; in fact Figure 3.08 applies. The smallest parts, say the eyes, respond to the highest frequencies, with the larger masses, say the stomach, being excited by lower frequencies. It is generally accepted that the body responds more critically to accelerations for frequencies below 5 Hz, and to velocities for frequencies above 15 Hz.

The results of early work were contained in a Draft for Development number DD32:1974, which was subsequently republished as BS 6841:1987. These data are essentially for transport situations where movement is of the essence, and vibrations are to be expected. Three attitudes of the body are considered, standing, sitting and lying, but if the axes are body axes, that is to say are located in the body (x facing forward, y sideways and z from head to toe, with the origin at the heart) then it is found that response depends upon the axis and not the attitude. The data are presented in terms of the variation of the root-mean-square of the acceleration in m/s^2 with frequency for exposure times between 1 minute to 24 hours. Separate graphs are presented for three different acceptability levels. The most tolerant is called "Exposure Limit" and relates to safety and health requirements; the second is entitled "Fatigue Decreased Proficiency Boundary", and the third is named "Reduced Comfort Boundary".

When vibrations occur at, either more than one frequency, or in more than one direction, the draft for development gives no firm guidance as to the procedures to be adopted; sometimes it is suggested that the criterion of the most restrictive of the motions be used, and other times a summation be used. In this latter case it is suggested that a rms. summation of the weighted components in each 1/3 octave band be undertaken.

Data on the reaction of people are also contained as a section in a report on the response of buildings entitled "Structural Vibration and Damage" by R.J.Steffens, a BRE Report dated 1974. Here the classification is in terms of "K" values, following DIN 4025 and 4150, but the descriptions of the reactions are more vague, for example, one description is "Strongly noticeable. Still tolerable, but very unpleasant if lasting over an hour: work is affected, but still possible".

The only structures where large amplitudes or accelerations are found in practice are bridges; this is reasonable because transportation is concerned. In buildings comfort, or even perception, is more likely to be the criterion. The slightest perceptible movement causes a feeling of foreboding or even disaster. The Steffens report is a better reference in these cases.

Just to illustrate the difference between transportation and buildings, consider two examples. Firstly a bridge, with a lateral movement of 300mm at a period of 2 seconds, would be safe for about 40 seconds exposure, ability to work would be impaired after about 1 to 4 minutes, and comfort would be destroyed immediately. On the other hand, for a tall building with a natural frequency of 2 Hz, an amplitude of 50μ (0.05 mm) would be the "Threshold of Perception" and would be the limit for vibrations occurring repeatedly at night for all but business, industrial and port users.

5. Rain and Snow

In the absence of wind, rain and snow fall vertically downwards. The effect of wind is to give the rain drops and snow flakes a horizontal component of velocity. Unfortunately, to date, little data on the simultaneous records of wind and rain are available, and consequently data on the correlation of these two events is vague.

There are three consequences of this horizontal movement. The first is on the building where the rain can now impinge on non-horizontal surfaces and so cause staining, or allow mosses and lichens to grow, or can cause damp to penetrate the walls to the detriment of its inhabitants. The second effect is on the comfort of people because the rain can penetrate beneath canopies and other protective devices. The third is a combination of building and people: in the past the materials of which buildings were made could absorb water, and during a storm, the surface of a large building would absorb tons of water, water which would be evaporated by the wind once the rain had stopped. Modern buildings are often clad in impervious materials, which keep the water on the surface whence it can be blown off by the wind or can flow down the surface. If an arcade occurs under the face of a building, then the rain descending the face can drip at the edge of the arcade in large drops which are annoying to the people passing under: gutters must be placed in this situation.

Canopies are placed over entrance doors to provide local shelter from the rain to people entering or leaving: bus and train stations have roofs with open sides for the protection of the travelling public. It would therefor be very useful to be able to estimate the penetration of the rain under a canopy or roof, and this can only be done by an understanding of the movement of the raindrop in the wind.

Snow, because it is lighter, will move more horizontally, but is a much less common occurrence. This will be dealt with separately.

5.1. Rain.

5.1.1. Terminal Velocity.

A rain storm is made up of rain drops of a range of sizes and our consideration is with the movement of all these drops.

The drag force on the rain drop moving through still air is the same as the drag of a stationary drop in an airstream, and will be given by

$$D = C_D \times 1/2\, \rho_a\, V^2 A,$$

where C_D is the Drag Coefficient, ρ_a is the density of the air, A is the cross sectional area of the drop, and V is the "slip" velocity. The slip velocity is the relative velocity of the drop and the wind.

FIG 5.01 TERMINAL VELOCITY OF RAIN DROPS

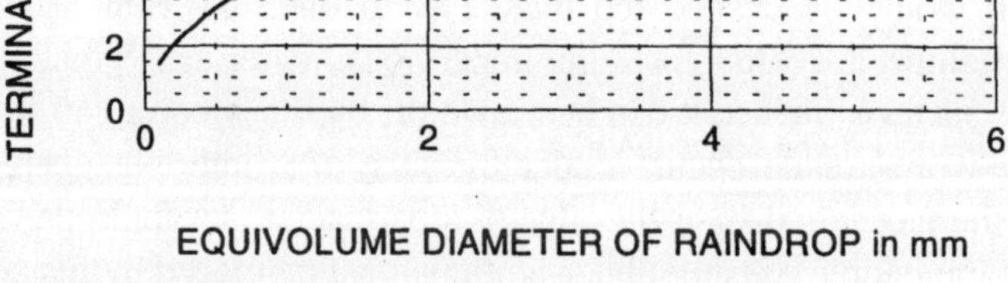

It is found that, if a drop is allowed to fall freely in still air, it accelerates initially, but very quickly settles down to a constant velocity, called its "Terminal Velocity" when the Drag of the drop equals its weight. The terminal velocity is easy to measure, and it is found to be a function of the drop size. Various investigators have measured the relationship and produced several empirical expressions, the one preferred by the author is due to Daws, who states that

$$V_{term} = 4.5\ D^{0.5}\ ,$$

where D is the equivolume diameter of the drop in mm, and V_{term} is the terminal velocity in m/s. To give a feel for the velocities, these are shown in Figure 5.01. Some other investigators present expressions which allow for the change of shape of the raindrop with size and wind speed.

5.1.2. Size of Rain Drops.

A shower contains raindrops of a variety of sizes, the range and distribution of sizes depends upon the overall rainfall. The relationship is again expressed in a variety of expressions by different investigators, the one preferred by the author is

$$dR/dD = 49.25 \times D^{3.5}\ exp(\ -4.1 \times R^{-0.222} \times D)$$

where R is the total rainfall in mm/hr, D is the equivolume diameter of the raindrop in mm and dR/dD is the contribution to R from raindrops between the sizes of $(D\text{-}dD/2)$ and $(D+dD/2)$. This is presented in Figure 5.02 for rainfall rates of 1.25, 12.5 and 125 mm/hr. When plotted in this way, the shape of the curve for the small rainfall rate is difficult to see. In Figure 5.03 the same data are presented as the variation of the (contribution to the rainfall divided by the total rainfall) with the diameter of the raindrop.

It can be seen that, as the rainflow increases, larger sized raindrops are included in the storm and that the size of the most frequent raindrops increases.

5.1.3. Effect of Wind.

Just as the raindrop reaches a constant vertical velocity in still air, in wind the raindrop reaches the constant horizontal velocity equal to the wind speed. The only difference is that the wind speed is continually changing, so the horizontal velocity of the drop will also continually vary.

FIG 5.02. DISTRIBUTION OF RAIN DROPS

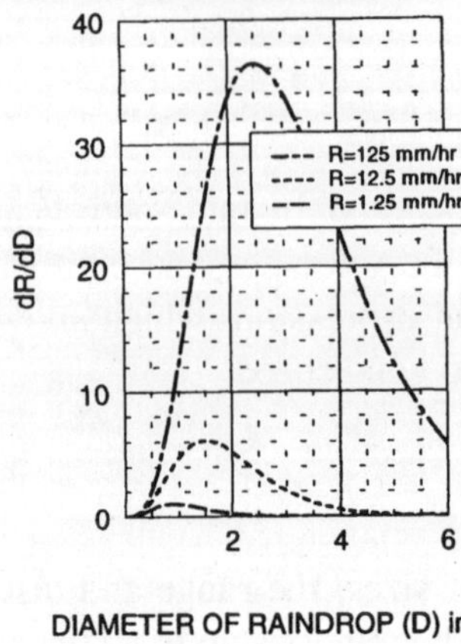

FIG 5.03. DISTRIBUTION OF SIZES OF RAINDROPS

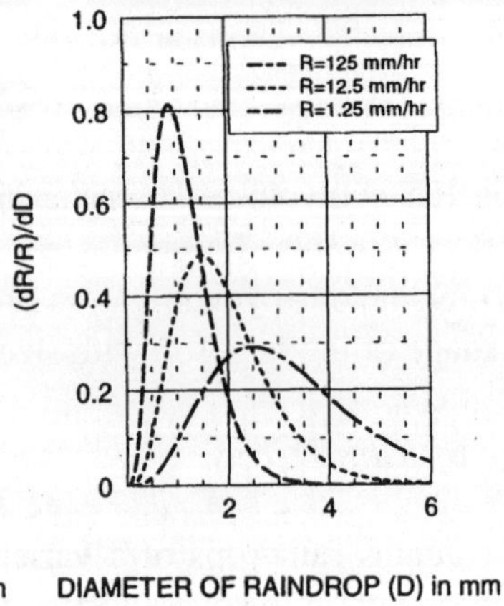

If the wind speed and the raindrop speed are not identical, a drag force is exerted on the raindrop as the first equation in section 5.1.1 predicts with the slip velocity rapidly tending to zero. In practice it is usual to assume that this correction occurs instantaneously.

The path of the raindrop in a constant wind speed follows the triangle of velocities, this is shown in Figure 5.04. If the wind speed varies in space and not in time, the raindrop would follow a curved path.

FIG.5.04 TRADJECTRY OF RAINDROP

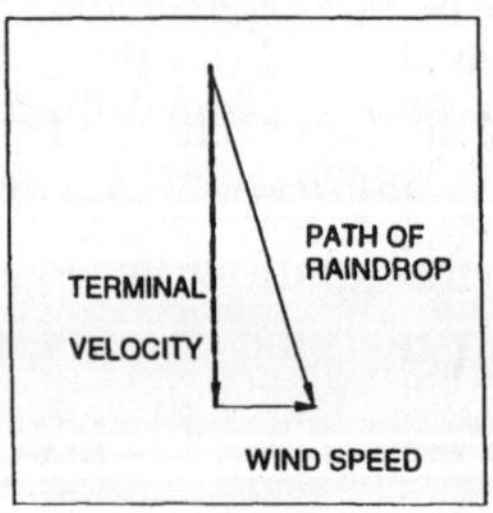

However, if the wind followed a curved path, a raindrop in the wind would not follow that path exactly, but would be "centrifuged" out to follow a path of greater radius. This can be explained as follows: Consider a particular spherical drop of air within the air mass flowing towards a wall. Pressures are established around that particular drop of air which will cause it to move it its curved path, that is why it moves in that path. Now consider that particular spherical drop of air being replaced by a drop of water of identical size. The pressure around it will be the same as around the original drop of air, but the mass of that drop of water is greater than the original drop of air. When Newton's second Law of Motion (Force = Mass × Acceleration) is applied to the water drop, as the same forces are applied by the surrounding air, the acceleration will be less because the mass is greater. The water drop will follow a curve of a greater radius. This is shown in Figure 5.05 with the raindrop centrifuging out from the horizontal curved path of the wind. The picture in reality is further complicated by the vertical movement of the raindrop which is falling at its terminal velocity.

FIG 5.05 HORIZONTAL CURVED TRAJECTRY OF RAINDROP

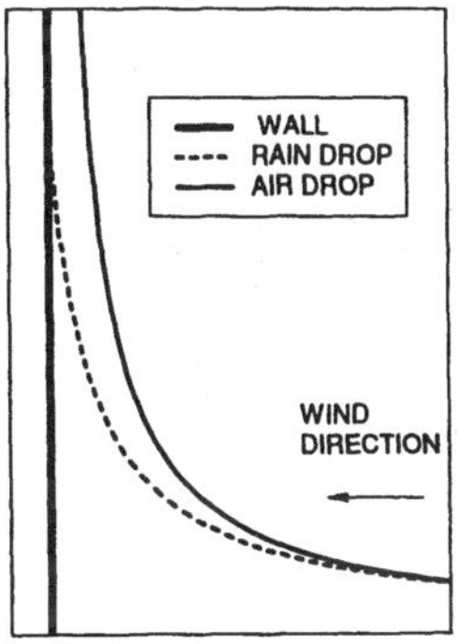

5.1.4. Impingement of Rain on a Vertical Wall.

Work has continued over the years aimed at predicting the volume of water which will impinge on a vertical wall. The original work in 1962 produced a "Driving Rain Index", which was the product of the mean annual wind speed and the mean annual rainfall. This was updated in 1976 (Driving-rain Index by R.E.Lacy: Building Research Establishment Report 1976) with the introduction of larger scale maps and better working instructions. With the advent of the analysis of longer samples of data from the Meteorological Office, direction variations were established, leading ultimately to BS 8104: 1992 (Code of Practice for Assessing exposure of walls to wind-driven rain).

5.1.4.1. Prediction of the Probability of the Occurrence of Rain.

Early workers discovered that the greater the wind speed in general, the more likely it was to rain, although data on simultaneous records of rainfall and wind speed are scarce. However, even in the UK, the differences geographically were very noticeable. In Figures 5.06 and 5.07 the variation of the percentage of the time when there was rain in the wind with the wind speed are presented; in Figure 5.06 for the Western parts of the UK and in Figure 5.07 for the Eastern parts. There is scatter in the data, and the limiting values are presented in those Figures.

FIG. 5.06 LIMITING % OF TIME RAINING WESTERN UK

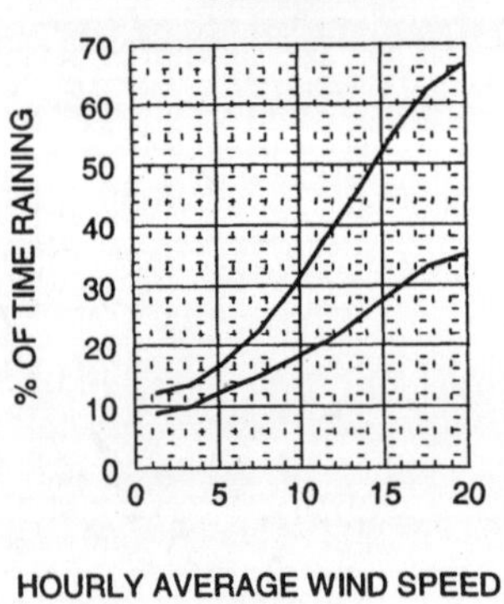

FIG 5.07 LIMITING % OF TIME RAINING EASTERN UK

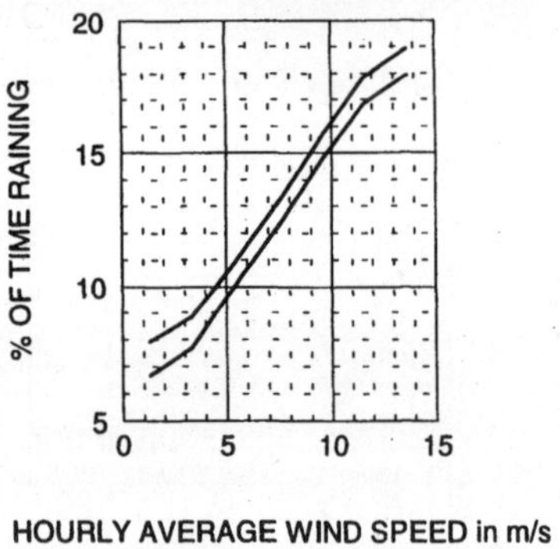

The probability tables for the variation of wind speed and direction have been discussed in the Chapter on the Wind Environment, and one for Kingsway in January is presented in Figure 5.08. From these data the percentage of time, assuming that it is the same as probability of occurrence, when it is raining can be estimated, within limits, but these data do not tell how much rain is falling. As the rain can only impinge on a vertical wall when the wind is from a limited arc of direction, it is possible to predict within limits, the percentage of time when some rain will reach the wall by an integration of percentages from Figure 5.06 (or Figure 5.07) and Figure 5.08. To simplify this procedure, the mean values for each range of the Beaufort Scale have been extracted from Figures 5.06 and 5.07 and are presented in Figure 5.09.

WD	BEAUFORT RANGE							
	1	2	3	4	5	6	7	8
0	.0	.4	1.2	1.8	1.2	.3	.0	.0
30	.1	.3	1.1	1.5	.9	.2	.0	.0
60	.1	.6	1.9	2.7	1.6	.3	.0	.0
90	.0	.3	1.0	1.8	1.2	.2	.0	.0
120	.1	.3	.8	.9	.4	.1	.0	.0
150	.1	.4	.8	.8	.3	.1	.0	.0
180	.3	.7	1.1	.9	.5	.2	.0	.0
210	.1	.6	2.1	4.1	3.7	1.6	.2	.0
240	.1	.8	3.4	6.9	7.7	4.7	1.3	.0
270	.1	.9	2.9	5.1	5.1	3.2	1.1	.1
300	.2	.8	2.3	3.1	2.3	.9	.1	.0
330	.1	.5	1.1	1.2	.7	.3	.1	.0

FIG.5.08 PERCENTAGE OF TIME WIND SPEED IS IN EACH RANGE OF THE BEAUFORT SCALE FOR JAN

BEAUFORT FORCE	1	2	3	4	5	6	7	8
MEAN WIND SPEED	1.03	2.45	4.48	6.93	9.60	12.53	15.65	19.00
EASTERN UK	7.25	7.80	9.45	12.10	15.25	17.75		
WESTERN UK LOWER	8.8	9.5	11.5	14.1	17.5	22.5	28.7	34.2
WESTERN UK UPPER	11.9	12.6	15.25	21.0	29.5	41.5	54.5	64.5

FIG. 5.09 LIMITING VALUES OF PERCENTAGES OF TIME WHEN IT IS RAINING

The values of "Mean Wind Speed" are in m/s and the other values in the Figure are percentages. As the upper and lower limits for Eastern UK were close an average value is given the Figure above. For example, in the Eastern UK when the wind is Beaufort Force 5, then it will be raining for about 15.25 % of the time. If the wall faces the SouthWest (240°), then from Figure 5.08 this will be happening in January at Kingsway for 7.7% of the time. The contribution from Beaufort Force 5 winds for this wind direction will then be about 1.2% of the total time. To this must be added the time when the wind is from directions 180° , 210° , 270° and 300°. The calculation needs to be repeated for the other ranges of the Beaufort Scale and the percentages aggregated. This has only told us the percentage of the time when it is raining and might impact on a vertical wall.

5.1.4.2. Prediction of the Probability of the Quantity of Rain.

The quantity of rain impinging on a vertical wall depends, in the first instance, on the angle of the rain to the vertical. The sideways movement of the wind is governed by the local wind speed and the terminal velocity (see Figure 5.04); the terminal velocity depends upon the size of drop (Figure 5.01), and the range of drop sizes in a storm depends upon the total intensity of the storm (Figures 5.02 and 5.03). So information on the intensity of the storm is crucial to a meaningful calculation.

Holland ("Rain Intensity Frequency Relationships in Britain" Meteorological Office Hydrology Memo No 33 1964 with Appendix 1968) presented a relationship between Rainfall in mm/hr, Duration of storm, and Return Period: a single set of curves applying to the whole UK.

More recently data for the UK has been produced and is presented in BS 8104: 1992 ("Code of Practice for Assessing exposure of Walls to Wind-driven Rain"). The UK is presented on 19 maps, each of which is divided into about 10 regions, and within these regions small corrections to the values are shown on the map. For each location values of "Spell Map Value" and "Annual Map Value" are presented, and can be converted into values of "Airfield Spell Index" and "Airfield Annual Index" by Tables 1 and 2. These are values of litres /m^2 , which is the same as mm of rain. The spell values are "Once in 3 Year" values; corrections for "Once a Year" and "Once in 10 Year" values are presented. The impingement of rain on vertical walls depends thereafter on 4 factors called "Terrain Roughness Factor (R)", "Topography Factor (T)", "Obstruction Factor (O)" and "Wall Factor (W)". The first two allow for the effect the surroundings have on the approaching wind, the Obstruction Factor allows for the shelter presented by surrounding buildings, and the most interesting of all, the Wall factor allows for the centrifuging of the rain from the wind, which was depicted in Figure 5.05. Values are presented for different parts of walls on several types of buildings.

The annual value speaks for itself, and is appropriate when considering the moisture content of exposed building material or when assessing the likely growth of mosses and lichens.

The spell index was designed for assessing the resistance of the wall to water penetration. The idea of a "spell" was devised by Caton, who considered that a spell should last as long as the input of rain to a wall exceeded the output by evaporation. This required a period of 96 hours without rain to follow a "spell". Later his evaporation model was considered inappropriate, but the concept of the spell as he defined it was kept. The "Spell" is officially defined as "A period, or sequence of periods, of wind-driven rain on a vertical surface of given orientation. A spell is of variable length and can include several periods of wind-driven rain interspersed with periods of up to 96 hours without appreciable wind-driven rain (see Appendix D)". It is impossible to derive a maximum value of rainfall in mm over a stated period from these data.

For the assessment of the maximum value of rain in a stated period, data from Holland can be replotted to present, on a "Once in 3 Years" (the same as used in BS 8104) basis a correspondence between the rainfall in mm/hr and the duration of the shower. These data are presented in Figure 5.10. Added to that Figure are values of the total rainfall during the shower. Both the above rainfall values should be multiplied by 0.69 to obtain "Once a Year" values and by 1.44 to obtain "Once in 10 Years" values. These data are omni-directional. An approximate correction for wind direction could be achieved using BS 8104 as follows: for the location under consideration find the highest value of the Airfield Spell Index for all wind directions in BS 8104, then find the value of the Airfield Spell Index for the appropriate wind direction and correct the value from Figure 5.10 by the ratio of the two values. This is not exact, but it will give an order of magnitude value for the rainfall in a storm or shower whereby to assess the comfort of pedestrians in the open.

FIG 5.10. VARIATION OF EXTREME RAINFALL WITH DURATION

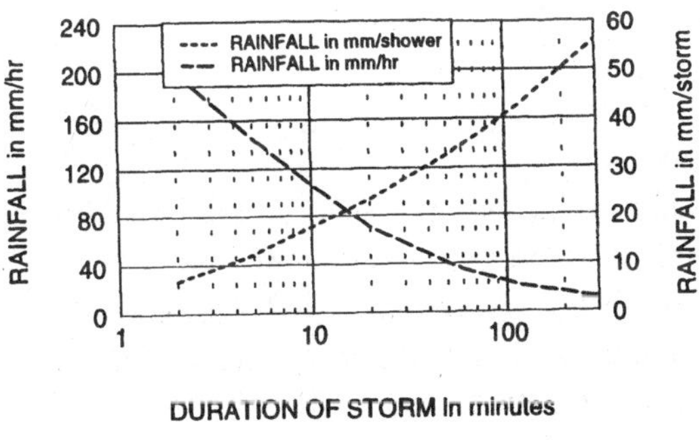

In spite of their failings, these data are the best available for the UK at present.

5.1.5. Protection from the Rain.

5.1.5.1. On the Face of a Building with a Solid Wall.

The vertical movement of the raindrop is also affected by the effect of the building on the wind speeds, this is the "Wall Factor" mentioned in the last Section. If the building creates a down draught, then the downward velocity of the raindrop will be its terminal velocity plus the downward component of the wind speed. On the other hand, if the component of wind from the building is upwards, and of equal value to the terminal velocity of the raindrop, then the raindrop will travel horizontally. It other situations, if the air path is curved in horizontal and vertical planes, then the raindrop will centrifuge out in both planes.

An overhang or canopy is often placed on a building to shelter parts from the rain. In an experiment where overhangs were placed both at the top of the wall, and half way up the wall, it was found that the overhang at the top of the wall, not only did not provide shelter, but sometimes increased the volume of water reaching the wall. On the other hand, the canopy placed half way down the wall always provided some shelter lower down.

A canopy is often placed over a door to provide protection to those entering or leaving. If the door is on the centreline of the building, then the down flow will make the rain fall in a path more aligned to the vertical, which means that the canopy will give a larger depth of protection. Unfortunately the down flow only occurs very close to the surface of the building, of the order of a meter, so this assistance is minimal. If the open door beneath the canopy allows air to flow into the building, then this will tend to give the rain under the canopy a component of velocity towards the door, and the effectiveness of the canopy will be reduced: this is another reason to reduce the inflow through doors to a minimum.

Very little data in published form are available on wind speeds in these areas. If the protection from the rain is important, then measurements of wind speed in this area should be commissioned from a wind tunnel investigation or other source. If this is very important, then a special form of wind tunnel experiment can be conducted.

5.1.5.2. A Roof Over an Area with Open Sides.

An interesting situation exists when an open area is to be protected from the rain by a roof and partially open sides such as the bus or train station. Data for the "Wall Factor" are generally unavailable, and recourse must be made to wind tunnel measurements of the wind environment of the building, with special emphasis on local wind speeds around the open area. Further protection can be provided by a barrier at ground level, but this is not essential. This arrangement is shown in Figure 5.11. Because there is a through-flow of air, the rain penetrates under the roof. The passage of the rain in Figure 5.11 is oversimple, in that the centrifuging of the rain from curved air paths is ignored, and the flow under the roof and behind the barrier, which is complex with the rain driven in all directions is not allowed for because the analysis ends once the rain has entered the vertical gap. However it is possible to make an estimate of the volume of rain entering.

FIG.5.11. ELEVATION OF 45° BARRIER

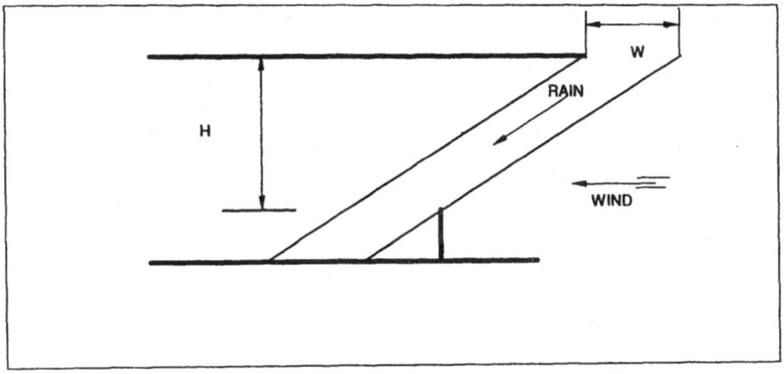

In the following discussion it will be assumed that the line joining the edge of the roof and the top of the barrier is at 45° to the vertical, although any angle is possible. Rain will enter when its path is at a greater angle than 45° to the vertical. The catchment area of this rain will be W per meter width on Figure 5.11, in that all the rain which would have fallen on the area W in the open will ènter beneath the roof. As this angle increases, it is obvious that the catchment, zero at 45° , will increase to a value greater than the height of the opening H. Thus the higher wind speeds, which create the higher angles of the rain, will increase the concentration of rain at entry, although, if the path of the rain within were unaffected by the presence of other obstacles, the deposition on the floor would be of the same concentration as in the open.

FIG 5.12. PENETRATION OF 45° BARRIER

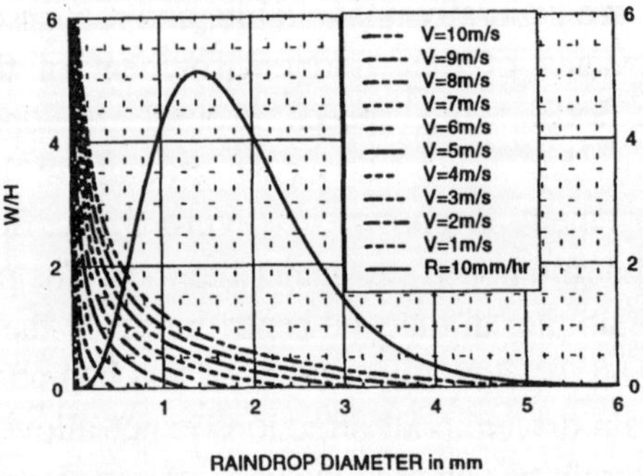

Because the rainflow contains an assortment of raindrops of different sizes, each of which has a different terminal velocity, and therefor trajectory, the distribution of raindrop sizes at a given location inside will be different from that of the parent rain storm. In Figure 5.12 the variations of both the contribution to the volume of water from the range of drop sizes, and the catchment areas for the different wind speeds with raindrop size are presented. These quantities can be combined to show the contribution to the volume flow from each size of raindrop as a function of wind speed. The total water content of the rain can be obtained by integration of these curves for a given wind speed, and it is interesting to note that, for the higher wind speeds and the lower rates of rainfall, the volume of flow entering per unit of vertical

FIG 5.13 DISTRIBUTION OF RAIN PENETRATING R=1mm/hr

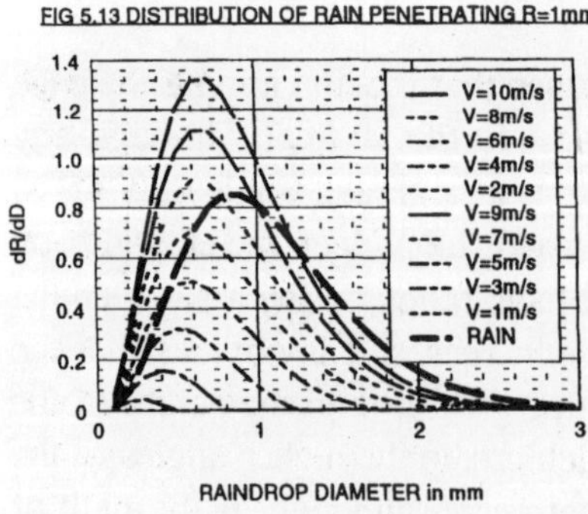

FIG 5.14 DISTRIBUTION OF RAIN PENETRATION R=30mm/hr

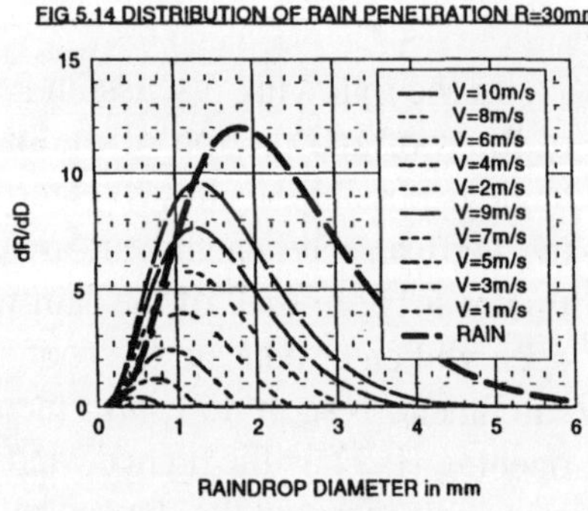

area can be greater that the volume of flow reaching unit area of ground in the open. This is clear from Figures 5.13 and 5.14, the first is for a basic rainfall rate of 1mm/hr, and the second for 30 mm/hr.

FIG 5.15. PROBABILITY OF RAIN PENETRATION JANUARY WD 0°

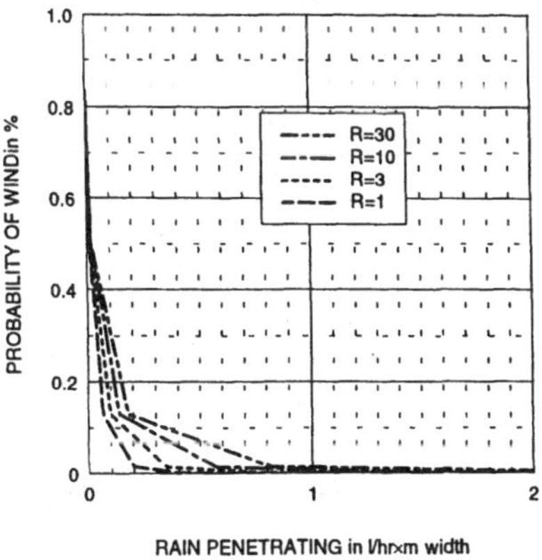

FIG 5.16 PROBABILITY OF RAIN PENETRATION FEBRUARY WD 240°

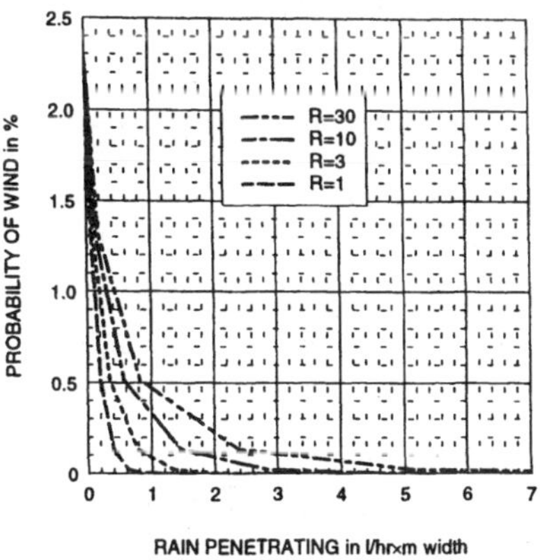

FIG 5.17 PROBABILITY OF RAIN PENETRATION AUGUST WD 90°

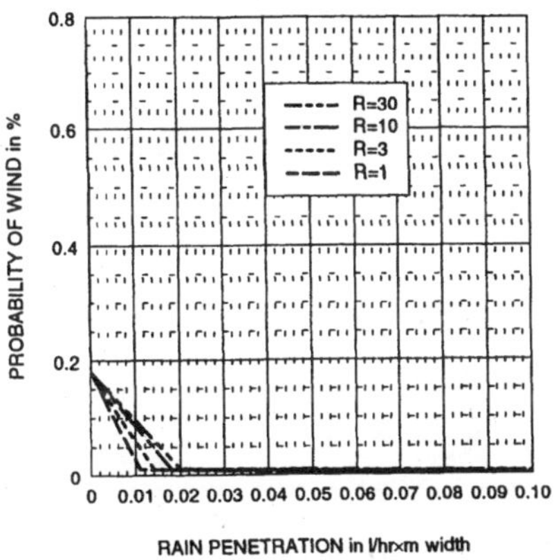

FIG 5.18 PROBABILITY OF RAIN PENETRATION YEAR WD 240°

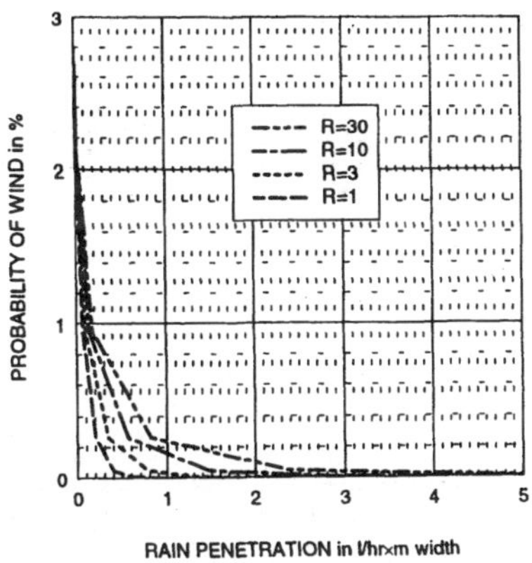

It would be very useful to turn these data into curves of the variation of probability of occurrence with rainflow rates entering. The probability statistics for the wind speed are available, and these have been introduced in Figure 5.15 for January winds from the North in London, Figure 5.16 February wind direction from the SouthWest, Figure 5.17 (August from the

East) and Figure 5.18 (Year from the SouthWest). Comparing these figures it is clear that the differences in probability vary much more with the time of year and the wind direction than with the rainfall rate.

FIG 5.19 PROBABILITY OF RAIN PENETRATION ANGLE 60° JANUARY WD 0°

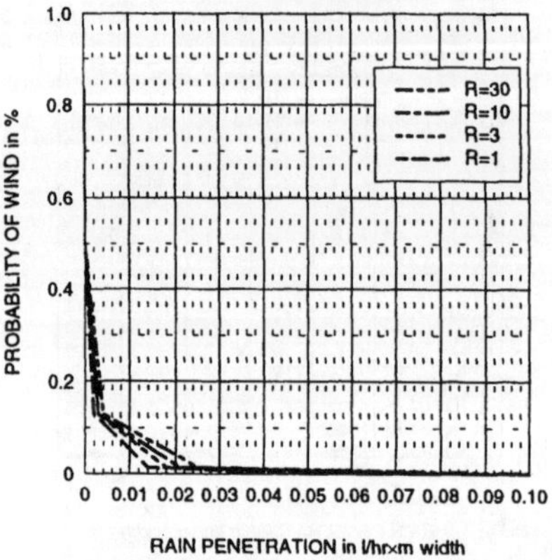

FIG 5.20 PROBABILITY OF RAIN PENETRATION ANGLE 60° FEBRUARY WD 240°

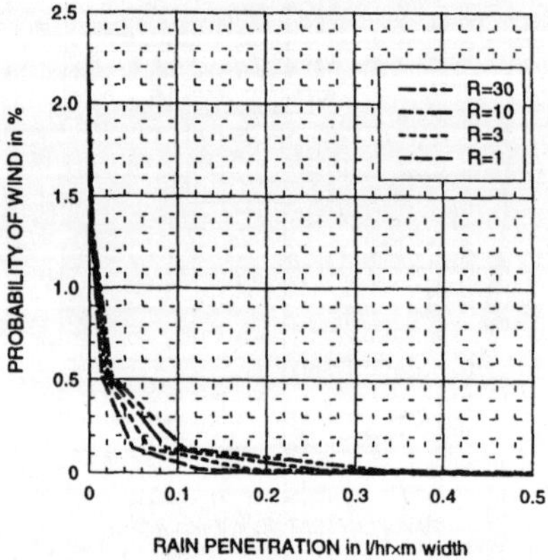

FIG 5.21 PROBABILITY OF RAIN PENETRATION ANGLE 60° AUGUST WD 90°

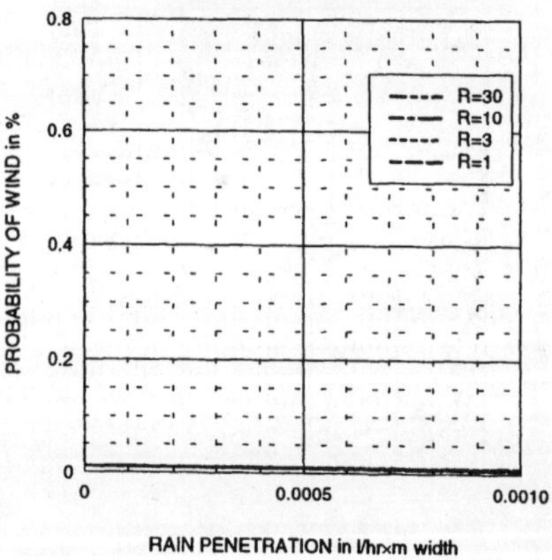

FIG 5.22 PROBABILITY OF RAIN PENETRATION ANGLE 60° YEAR WD 240°

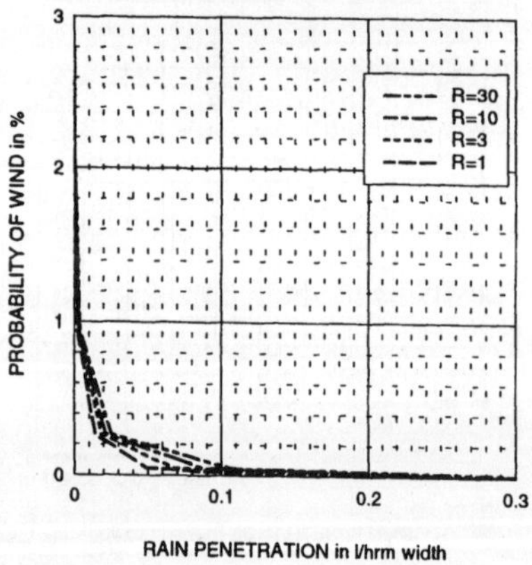

The data on those figures have not taken into account the probability that there will be rain of that rate when the wind is blowing at that speed from that direction. The data are for an average velocity through the gap equal to 40% of the Meteorological Standard Wind Speed and are expressed in Rain Penetration of litres per (hour × m^2 of vertical open area). The data of Figure

5.09 could be used to allow for this, but those data are omni-directional data, and recent attempts to obtain, not only directional data, but also data refereed to geographical locations, have not yet come to fruition. In the UK the winds from the SouthWest tend to bring in much rain, but there are no statistics to quantify this.

This is as far as the study goes at present, the actual values of probability will be smaller than the values presented in Figures 5.15 to 5.18, but the factor is unknown, and the author's guess is that it will be about an order in magnitude. This approach can be used to compare two or more different systems with some confidence. To this end the calculations have been repeated for an overhang of 60° and the results are presented in Figures 5.19 to 5.22.

5.1.6. Louvres.

Louvres at the entrances to ventilator systems usually consist of flat slats so inclined that the rain impinging on their outside surfaces, assumed to have a downward component of velocity, runs down externally. The curved path of the air entering the louvre centrifuges more rain out of the wind, but the centrifuged rain, if it impinges on the louvre, must be intercepted and removed.

A more complicated shape for the louvre "blade" could remove more rain by decreasing the radius of curvature of the air path (incurring a pressure loss penalty), but it is essential in this case for the rain impinging on the louvre blades to be removed, and not be allowed to be blown back into a lower louvre.

Where dry air is essential it is possible to place a second set of louvres internally so designed and positioned to remove the rain entering through the first set of louvres. In this case, rain removal from each blade of the inner louvre must be achieved.

5.1.7. Calculations Which Can Be Made.

In the UK the following calculations can be made.

5.1.7.1. Possibility of the Occurrence of Rain.

Values for this can be obtained, with wide scatter, from a combination of Figure 5.09 and an appropriate Figure 5.08 for the location in question.

5.1.7.2. Estimates of the Maximum Deposition on a Wall in a Spell.

Use BS 8104.

5.1.7.3. Estimates of the Maximum Deposition on a wall in a Short Period.

A value for the shower duration is assumed. For the shower duration, the rainfall in mm/hr is read from Figure 5.10, and corrected for the required Return Period. The rainfall rate is then corrected for the site location in the UK and for wind direction using BS 8104. To do this, it is assumed that the data for Figure 5.10 have been corrected for a "Spell Rose Value" of 26, or an "Airfield Spell Index" of 127 mm/hr (Table 1). For sake of the example, assume that the "Spell Rose Value" for location and wind direction is 23 from Appendix B of BS 8104, which corresponds to an "Airfield Spell Index" of 89.8 mm/hr: the value of Rainfall Rate from Figure 5.10 should be multiplied by 89.8/127. For other wind directions the ratio will be different.

The procedure of BS 8104 is then followed.

5.1.7.4. Estimation of the Probability of Rain Penetration of Overhang Barrier.

For a barrier system use the procedure outlined in Section 5.1.5.2. The data for the percentage of time when the wind is blowing and there is rain present (from Figure 5.09) have been added to the Yearly data presented in Figures 5.18 and 5.22.

To make a direct comparison between blockages forming a 45° angle with the vertical, and those forming a 60° angle, the penetration curves for wind from the SouthWest for the whole year are presented in Figures 5.23 and 5.24.

It will be clear, after all the caveats about the accuracy of obtaining the probability of Extreme Values of Rain Penetration, that the chance of obtaining meaningful values for the probability of penetration of lower value of rain is small.

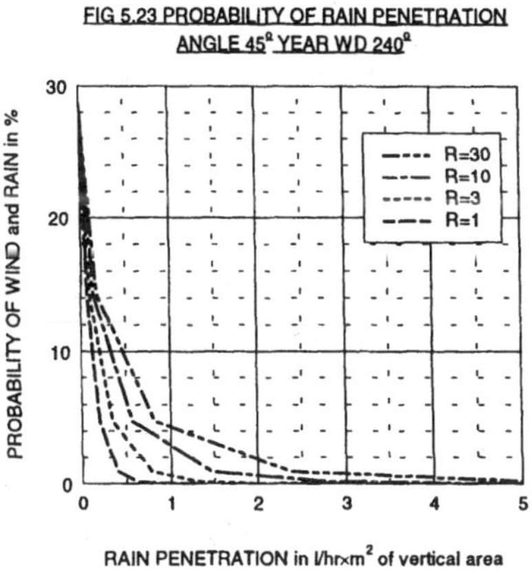

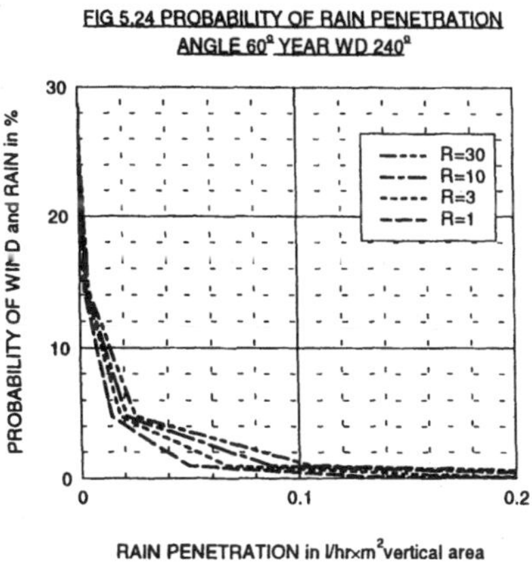

It is to be hoped that data of greater accuracy for these quantities will become available soon as the fruits of research work at present in hand.

5.2 Snow.

Even less data are available about snow in the wind as rain in the wind. Its main effect is on Snow Loading, and the latest data are contained in the appropriate National Snow Codes.

A word of warning might be appropriate here. In the UK the usual procedure is that there is a snow storm, which lies for a short time during which time the wind might blow and cause drifts, and it might freeze during this time, then the snow melts, and the problem departs. In other countries, many in Europe, the procedure is different. There is a snow fall, and the wind causes drifting, or not, and it freezes. Then there is another snow storm on top of the first frozen drifted snow. The build-up of the snow is different in this case that that for the UK. The National Codes for the country must be studied and followed. They all contain advice for the inclusion of the wind content in the final loading picture.

In case anyone wants to study the movement of snow flakes by themselves, the following data might be useful.

5.2.1. Data on Snowflakes.

As with rain there are several expressions for the variation of Terminal Velocity with size, the simplest of which is

$$V_{term} = D^{\,0.31},$$

where D related to the diameter of a raindrop which has the same mass as the snowflake.

An expression for the variation of snowflake sizes within a snowstorm, comparable to that for the raindrop, is as follows

$$R^{1.94} = 0.938 \int_o^{D_{max}} D^{3.5} \exp\left(-2.29 \times D \times R^{-0.45}\right) dD.$$

However, the author has not been able to use this expression with much success, it is presented here as an expression which occurs in the literature.

6. Ventilation

Ventilation, and its allied subject Fire, has become a greater part of Wind Engineering in the last decade. This has partly come about because the heating and ventilation engineers in the profession are realising how much wind engineering has to offer.

A ventilation study usually follows a wind tunnel investigation of the pressures on a building in which the surface pressures are integrated into loads and moments for the structural engineer. In the structural study the pressure tappings have been distributed to cover the surface required, with the greatest concentration on areas where the pressure is changing most rapidly. Pressure tappings have been placed at doors and other openings so that values of internal pressure can be calculated to obtain pressure differentials across the cladding. For the ventilation study these tappings at doors and other openings are used, and a few additional tappings have to be placed at all possible inlet and outlet points of the ventilation system. It is better to include all possible positions and select those most suitable, than omit some which could have been efficient.

Forced systems can be studied as well as natural ones, although the data required is different. In this case the fan has been "sized" to pass sufficient air, but it must be established that the fan is capable of so doing against the back pressure created by the position of its inlet and outlet. The calculation to ensure a satisfactory result is detailed in Section 6.3.

In the study of a natural system two different presentations of data are required. The first is the number of Air Changes per Hour (ACH) through the whole volume of the building. Too much inflow of cold air can upset the heating balance. If the air flow through the system is satisfactory, then the velocities through doors and openings can be considered.

This chapter will start with the assumptions made, and will then discuss the alternative systems, natural and forced. The ventilation of Car Parks will be treated separately in Section 6.4.

6.1. Assumptions Made.

The building will be assumed to be sealed, except for prescribed openings such as doors, windows, make-up air apertures and ventilation openings. It is well known that all buildings leak to some extent, some would say like a sieve, and this can be taken into account as will be explained in Section 6.2.3.2 , although this is seldom done.

The internal pressure within the building will be assumed uniform. To justify this a "reducio ad absurdum" argument is used. If there were a pressure gradient within the building, it would produce a velocity irrespective of the internal size. This velocity over the large cross sectional area would move a large volume of air. Where would it come from and where would it go? That is not to say that there could be local draughts caused by obstacles. The areas adjoining entrance doors require attention from this point of view.

The pressures used in the calculations will be those averaged over a long time period, several minutes. The internal pressure for the building used for the calculation of structural loads on the cladding is calculated with an expression depending upon the internal volume of the building. This is explained in Paragraph 3.1.7. The averaging time used is given by

$$T = 45 \times (\text{Volume of building or storey})^{1/3} / V$$

where V is the hourly-average wind speed at the height of the most significant opening, usually the top of the building. This is to allow for the fact that the short period pulses do not pump enough air into the building during the gust to increase its internal pressure appropriately. In a ventilation study the same value should be used, but, as there is little change in the value of pressure averaged over long periods, and as the results are related in Air Changes per **Hour**, it is usual in ventilation work to consider an averaging time of about

15 minutes as applicable for any building. This eliminates the necessity to make a choice of whether to use gusts or lulls.

It is also assumed that the pressure difference across an opening creates both a velocity through the opening and a loss of energy in the form of separations and turbulence. The loss of energy is allowed for in Bernoulli's Equation by the introduction of a "Pressure loss coefficient", which can differ from opening to opening. Once the air has entered the volume, it is assumed that all its kinetic energy is dissipated in heat; this is explained in paragraph 6.2.1.

To summarise, the building is assumed leak-proof, except for stated openings, which can be assumed to be open or shut and sealed: the internal volume will be treated as a single volume with a value of internal pressure (except in the cases when the building is treated as two separate volumes joined by an opening, which can be open or shut): values of external pressure averaged over about 15 minute will be used in the calculations: that the openings themselves create a loss of pressure: and that the whole of the kinetic energy generated in the opening is dissipated in heat within the volume.

6.2. Natural Systems.

6.2.1. Losses through Openings.

The pressure difference across an opening will create a velocity through the opening, by converting the pressure energy to kinetic energy, thus

$$p_e - p_i = dp = 1/2\rho V^2,$$

where p_e is the value of external pressure, and p_i is the value of internal pressure, both averaged over about 15 minutes. But there will be losses dissipated by turbulence at the edges of the opening and in any louvres across the opening. Manufacturers of ventilators present pressure loss data for their products. Thus, in practice

$$V = \{(dp / C_D) / (1/2\rho)\}^{1/2}$$

where C_D is the total pressure loss coefficient for the opening (see Section 6.2.3). The data presented in a wind tunnel investigation, or retrieved from published data, are in the form of pressure coefficients. Thus

$$dp = 1/2\rho V_{ref}^{\ 2} (C_{pe} - C_{pi}),$$

and so

$$V / V_{ref} = \{(C_{pe} - C_{pi}) / C_D\}^{1/2},$$

The volume flow through the opening is therefor

$$Q = V \times A.$$

It is important that a separate value of loss coefficient be associated with each opening, because they may be of different types within a single building.

6.2.2. Effect of Partitions.

Many buildings have internal partitions or are sub-divided internally.

If a partition is directly associated with an individual opening, such as a window in a room for example, which is separated from the main internal volume by a door, then this can be allowed for by applying an additional loss to the window opening to allow for the loss through the door as well as through the window. When the door is shut, it is usual to assume zero open area for the window, or a very small area to allow for leakage.

If a building is divided into two separate volumes by a single partition, then a simple calculation can be performed on the whole building ; this is described in Section 6.2.5.

If however, the building consists of a central volume with several satellites, each with several openings to the outside, then a much longer analysis is required; this is described in Section 6.2.6

6.2.3. Values for Losses.

6.2.3.1. Doors and Louvres.

The conventional louvre has a pressure loss coefficient of about 0.67. The total loss factor (C_D), taking into account the subsequent loss of kinetic energy, will be 1.67.

It is our practice to assume a total loss factor of 1.30 for an open door with sharp edges.

If heaters or coolers are attached to openings, the loss of these devices must be added to that of the opening. This results in the total loss factor being increased by about 2.0.

6.2.3.2. General Leakiness in the Building.

If a full wind loading study has been performed, and values of pressure are available on the roof and walls of the building, then very small open areas can be associated with each (proportional to the area they represent), and the same calculation undertaken.

6.2.4. The Value of the Internal Pressure and the Calculation Precedure.

Values of internal pressure cannot be measured in a wind tunnel investigation. The reason is that the model can have received rough treatment, either in handling or by sustaining higher than ambient temperatures for an extended time during testing. As a result all the joints are not, or might not be, 100% air tight. Measured values of internal pressure would thus depend on the size and location of leaks in the model, an uncontrollable factor. Further, if measured in an air-tight model, the value would correspond to one set of openings (doors, windows and other openings), and a complete reinvestigation would have to be carried out for every scenario to be studied.

When a conventional wind tunnel investigation is carried out, values of pressure coefficient are measured at every location which includes all doors and other possible openings in the fabric. Those locations chosen for a purely structural purpose are ignored in this study. An area and a loss coefficient are attributed to each location, and the volume flow through the whole volume is assumed to be zero for natural ventilation. Thus

$$Q = 0 = \sum_{I=1}^{N} (V_i / V_{ref}) \times A_i$$

where V_i is the velocity through the opening at location i, and A_i is its open area.. The only unknown in this equation is the value of the internal pressure coefficient. In the computation a value is assumed, and the value for Q calculated. A step-by-step calculation is undertaken, wherein corrections to the assumed value for the internal pressure are made progressively until the continuity of mass requirement is achieved with sufficient accuracy. The value of internal pressure coefficient is recorded and the calculation proceeds for the next wind direction.

Once the value of internal pressure coefficient is known for a given wind direction, the volume flow through each opening can be calculated, and the sum of either inflow and or outflow can be made (these should be the same). This sum is then the volume flow through the volume. But it, and the flow rates through individual openings are dependent upon the value of the reference wind speed used in the calculation.

It is our custom at Bristol to present the "Volume Flow" data for a unit value of reference wind speed in the first case. An example of this presentation is shown in Figure 6.01. Occasionally, but of greater significance, in a fire situation (see Chapter 7), the flow through one or more opening is excessive, or of the wrong sign, for several wind directions, and it would be convenient to close it / them for those wind directions alone, and yet retain it/them for the other wind directions. This procedure has the additional complication that it is requires a wind vane to be mounted on the roof of the building, and a control box to organise that the louvres at predetermined locations are opened and closed depending upon the wind direction. This procedure has been allowed for in the example illustrated in Figure 6.01. Down the left hand side of the Figure are three sets of Areas (1,2 and 3), and across the top, under the value of wind direction, is the number of the set of areas which apply for that wind direction. The values in the body of the table are values of volume flow in m^3/s which flow through each opening per m/s of reference wind speed. The row along the bottom entitled "Internal Pressure Percent" is the value of the internal pressure (in percentages), which gives zero through- flow of air. The two rows below that are values of inflow and outflow respectively which flow through the whole volume in cubic meters per second per unit of reference wind speed.

LOC	AREA 1	LOSS	AREA 2	AREA 3	WIND DIRECTION 0	30	60	90	120	150	180	210	240	270	300	330
					2	2	2	1	1	1	1	3	3	1	1	1
5	.00	.00	.00	.00	.00	.00	.00	.00	.00	.00	.00	.00	.00	.00	.00	.00
6	.00	.00	.00	.00	.00	.00	.00	.00	.00	.00	.00	.00	.00	.00	.00	.00
7	.00	.00	.00	.00	.00	.00	.00	.00	.00	.00	.00	.00	.00	.00	.00	.00
8	.00	.00	.00	.00	.00	.00	.00	.00	.00	.00	.00	.00	.00	.00	.00	.00
9	.00	.00	.00	.00	.00	.00	.00	.00	.00	.00	.00	.00	.00	.00	.00	.00
10	.00	.00	.00	.00	.00	.00	.00	.00	.00	.00	.00	.00	.00	.00	.00	.00
11	.00	.00	.00	.00	.00	.00	.00	.00	.00	.00	.00	.00	.00	.00	.00	.00
12	.00	.00	.00	.00	.00	.00	.00	.00	.00	.00	.00	.00	.00	.00	.00	.00
13	2.00	.67	2.00	2.00	-.79	-1.25	-1.26	-.85	-.65	-.40	-.09	.37	.16	-.71	-.61	-.56
14	2.00	.67	2.00	2.00	-1.06	-1.29	-.86	-.48	-.47	-.16	.30	.26	-.27	-.78	-.73	-1.04
15	2.00	.67	2.00	2.00	-.84	-.95	-.52	-.40	-.54	-.40	-.33	-.71	-.90	-.93	-.71	-.94
16	2.00	.67	2.00	2.00	-.36	-.08	-.18	.07	-.50	-.44	-.56	-1.03	-1.34	-1.07	-.88	-.96
17	2.00	.67	.00	2.00	.00	.00	.00	.07	-.54	-.57	-.80	-1.15	-1.38	-1.08	-.78	-.50
18	2.00	.67	.00	2.00	.00	.00	.00	-.44	-.72	-.85	-.88	-1.11	-1.28	-.95	-.61	.22
19	2.00	.67	.00	2.00	.00	.00	.00	-.75	-.92	-1.00	-.80	-.84	-.74	-.84	-.49	.39
20	2.00	.67	2.00	2.00	-.45	-.93	-1.26	-1.06	-.79	-.65	-.42	-.18	-.38	-.66	-.49	-.23
21	1.00	.67	1.00	.00	-.20	.22	.22	.03	-.37	-.31	-.19	.00	.00	-.35	-.47	-.39
22	1.00	.67	1.00	.00	-.09	.24	.20	-.15	-.37	-.27	-.14	.00	.00	-.33	-.44	-.41
23	1.00	.67	1.00	.00	-.13	.18	.16	-.18	-.34	-.25	-.16	.00	.00	-.35	-.50	-.57
24	1.00	.67	1.00	.00	-.18	.15	.09	-.18	-.32	-.20	-.19	.00	.00	-.18	-.55	-.60
25	1.00	.67	1.00	.00	-.34	.08	.09	-.22	-.32	-.27	-.26	.00	.00	-.18	-.53	-.64
26	1.00	.67	1.00	.00	-.35	.08	.09	-.24	-.25	-.22	-.21	.00	.00	-.21	-.42	-.58
27	1.00	.67	1.00	.00	-.30	.18	.16	-.22	-.25	-.24	-.25	.00	.00	-.21	-.38	-.51
28	1.00	.67	1.00	.00	-.26	.08	.13	-.18	-.17	-.30	-.25	.00	.00	-.30	-.48	-.54
29	1.00	.67	1.00	.00	-.22	.18	.13	-.18	-.17	-.27	-.14	.00	.00	-.18	-.52	-.54
30	1.00	.67	1.00	.00	-.34	.20	.20	-.12	.06	-.27	-.14	.00	.00	.20	-.52	-.54
31	1.00	.67	1.00	.00	-.36	.15	.16	-.09	-.12	-.24	-.19	.00	.00	.22	-.50	-.54
32	1.00	.67	1.00	.00	-.36	.22	.22	-.09	-.12	-.25	-.16	.00	.00	.26	-.47	-.53
34	3.00	.30	3.00	3.00	2.11	1.27	-.93	-1.16	-1.06	.15	.68	.44	.41	1.03	1.02	1.63
36	.00	.30	.00	.00	.00	.00	.00	.00	.00	.00	.00	.00	.00	.00	.00	.00
38	3.00	.30	3.00	3.00	1.55	.97	-.31	-.75	-.67	.34	.27	.88	1.23	2.03	2.50	2.71
47	.00	.30	.00	.00	.00	.00	.00	.00	.00	.00	.00	.00	.00	.00	.00	.00
50	3.00	.30	3.00	3.00	2.08	.97	.54	.33	.48	-1.02	-1.36	-.69	1.27	2.10	2.65	2.49
53	3.00	.30	3.00	3.00	1.49	.81	.62	.33	.19	-1.02	-1.53	-1.55	1.06	2.03	2.44	1.92
55	3.00	.30	3.00	3.00	.44	.60	.82	1.49	1.56	1.53	1.83	1.08	-.15	-.88	-.55	.49
58	.00	.30	.00	.00	.00	.00	.00	.00	.00	.00	.00	.00	.00	.00	.00	.00
60	3.00	.30	3.00	3.00	.06	-.56	.31	1.17	1.68	1.53	1.75	1.55	1.11	.82	.87	.66
61	.00	.30	.00	.00	.00	.00	.00	.00	.00	.00	.00	.00	.00	.00	.00	.00
62	3.00	.30	3.00	3.00	.06	-.34	.44	1.28	2.20	2.53	1.31	.93	.68	.53	.68	.38
63	.00	.30	.00	.00	.00	.00	.00	.00	.00	.00	.00	.00	.00	.00	.00	.00
64	.00	.30	.00	.00	.00	.00	.00	.00	.00	.00	.00	.00	.00	.00	.00	.00
68	3.00	.30	3.00	3.00	-.53	-.46	-.02	1.25	1.74	1.82	1.48	.98	.86	.43	.61	-.49
71	.00	.30	.00	.00	.00	.00	.00	.00	.00	.00	.00	.00	.00	.00	.00	.00
73	.00	.30	.00	.00	.00	.00	.00	.00	.00	.00	.00	.00	.00	.00	.00	.00
75	3.00	.30	3.00	3.00	-.62	-.71	.76	1.73	1.74	1.71	1.41	.76	-.35	.53	.87	.22
77	.00	.30	.00	.00	.00	.00	.00	.00	.00	.00	.00	.00	.00	.00	.00	.00
INTERNAL PRESSURE					-46.0	-28.7	-29.1	-44.6	-46.5	-63.1	-44.0	-36.8	-42.5	-51.9	-65.5	-55.8
PERCENT VOLUME					7.8	6.6	5.3	7.7	9.7	9.6	9.0	7.3	6.8	10.2	11.6	11.1
FLOW m**3/s/m/s					-7.8	-6.6	-5.3	-7.7	-9.7	-9.6	-9.0	-7.3	-6.8	-10.2	-11.6	-11.1

FIG 6.01 VOLUME FLOWS ENTERING

SCENARIO 47

Any number of scenario (combinations of area openings) can be studied. This procedure is therefor used as a design tool to select the optimum combination.

As explained in Section 1.5.2, the reference wind speed is related to the surrounding buildings, and to the geographical location. Thus it can be directly related to the "Meteorological Standard Wind Speed" (the hourly-average value of wind speed measured 10m above flat level ground geographically close to the site). These data for sites around the world are available in the form of "Table of Wind Speed and Direction". These are probability tables, so the data on ventilation has to be presented on a probability basis (see Section 1.5.2).

	VOL per SEC										
MONTH	.00	20.00	40.00	60.00	80.00	100.00	120.00	140.00	160.00	180.00	200.00
JAN	100.00	67.02	35.59	16.95	7.55	3.21	1.31	.52	.20	.07	.02
FEB	100.00	64.22	31.83	14.13	5.95	2.44	.98	.38	.15	.06	.02
MAR	100.00	64.17	29.09	11.40	4.22	1.53	.55	.20	.07	.03	.01
APR	100.00	63.56	28.38	11.26	4.41	1.73	.66	.25	.09	.03	.01
MAY	100.00	67.23	29.53	10.70	3.69	1.24	.39	.12	.04	.01	.01
JUNE	100.00	61.07	22.68	7.00	2.06	.57	.14	.03	.01	.01	.01
JULY	100.00	61.54	24.08	7.94	2.48	.74	.21	.06	.02	.01	.01
AUG	100.00	56.71	22.27	7.76	2.55	.80	.24	.07	.02	.01	.01
SEPT	100.00	65.10	29.93	11.97	4.47	1.59	.53	.17	.05	.02	.01
OCT	100.00	71.85	34.99	13.85	4.87	1.56	.45	.12	.03	.01	.01
NOV	100.00	66.25	33.30	15.17	6.70	2.90	1.23	.51	.20	.08	.03
DEC	100.00	72.28	41.61	21.14	10.15	4.86	2.37	1.18	.59	.30	.15
YEAR	100.00	65.87	32.39	14.02	5.73	2.27	.88	.33	.12	.05	.02

FIG 6.02
CUMULATIVE PROBABILITY FOR Vol Per Sec
BUILDING AERODYNAMICS
SCENARIO 47

Once the statistics of the reference wind speed have been introduced, the volume of data increases. In Figures 6.02 and 6.03 are presented value of probability that the Volume flow (Figure 6.02) or the velocity (Figure 6.03) are exceeded for the whole volume (Figure 6.02) and the opening at location 34 (Figure 6.03): in the case of the locations, inflow and outflow data are presented separately.

If the volume flow per second through the whole volume is multiplied by 3600 and is divided by the volume of the building in m^3 , then the units for the value obtained are Air Changes per Hour (ACH). If the volume of the building is known during the preparation of the data, the steps in the Figure can be adjusted so that each represents a multiple or fraction of ACH.

MONTH	VEL in m/s .00	1.00	2.00	3.00	4.00	5.00	6.00	7.00	8.00	9.00	10.00
JAN	92.23	37.01	14.19	5.46	2.07	.79	.31	.12	.04	.02	.01
FEB	86.61	35.45	14.04	5.70	2.31	.93	.37	.14	.06	.02	.01
MAR	63.88	24.15	9.06	3.30	1.11	.35	.11	.03	.01	.00	.00
APR	75.83	31.56	12.48	4.69	1.61	.53	.17	.06	.02	.00	.00
MAY	56.08	25.23	10.41	3.95	1.42	.52	.20	.08	.03	.02	.00
JUNE	57.81	21.88	7.09	2.15	.71	.27	.11	.04	.02	.00	.00
JULY	75.88	28.59	8.82	2.15	.48	.12	.03	.00	.00	.00	.00
AUG	72.33	24.97	7.49	2.18	.63	.19	.06	.02	.00	.00	.00
SEPT	79.41	30.81	10.59	3.21	.87	.24	.07	.03	.00	.00	.00
OCT	89.97	32.33	10.68	3.61	1.27	.47	.17	.06	.02	.00	.00
NOV	88.14	30.58	10.76	3.81	1.26	.40	.12	.04	.02	.00	.00
DEC	88.74	35.53	12.21	4.77	1.86	.73	.29	.13	.06	.03	.02
YEAR	77.46	30.63	11.33	4.32	1.68	.69	.30	.13	.06	.03	.01

FIG 6.03
CUMULATIVE PROBABILITY FOR VEL in m/s.
BUILDING AERODYNAMICS
SCENARIO 47
FOR LOC 34 INFLOW

MONTH	VEL in m/s .00	1.00	2.00	3.00	4.00	5.00	6.00	7.00	8.00	9.00	10.00
JAN	7.77	5.76	3.16	1.38	.49	.14	.03	.00	.00	.00	.00
FEB	13.39	9.13	4.36	1.58	.46	.12	.03	.00	.00	.00	.00
MAR	36.12	20.87	6.92	1.57	.26	.04	.01	.00	.00	.00	.00
APR	24.17	11.77	2.93	.53	.08	.02	.00	.00	.00	.00	.00
MAY	43.93	25.47	7.24	1.21	.14	.02	.00	.00	.00	.00	.00
JUNE	42.19	21.09	4.34	.46	.03	.01	.00	.00	.00	.00	.00
JULY	24.12	11.49	2.23	.22	.02	.01	.00	.00	.00	.00	.00
AUG	27.67	12.24	2.71	.39	.04	.01	.00	.00	.00	.00	.00
SEPT	20.59	11.10	3.02	.52	.07	.01	.00	.00	.00	.00	.00
OCT	10.03	6.51	2.11	.42	.07	.01	.00	.00	.00	.00	.00
NOV	11.86	7.61	3.85	1.73	.72	.28	.11	.04	.02	.00	.00
DEC	11.25	9.18	5.91	3.10	1.37	.54	.20	.08	.03	.01	.00
YEAR	22.54	12.80	4.84	1.42	.35	.08	.02	.01	.00	.00	.00

FIG 6.03
CUMULATIVE PROBABILITY FOR VEL in m/s.
BUILDING AERODYNAMICS
SCENARIO 47
FOR LOC 34 OUTFLOW

If location 34 were a door, then it would be preferable for the maximum wind speed to be below 3 m/s, although values up to 6 m/s can be tolerated for very low values of probability. The probability for zero velocity expresses the dividing probability between inflow and outflow. These data are of interest to the Heating Engineer who has to supply sufficient heating capacity for all air entering the building.

6.2.5. *Two Separate Volumes Joined by an Opening.*

There are situations in which the building is in two parts, or there are two separate buildings, but they are joined by a passage or opening. The same analysis applies, the internal pressure in the first building is assumed, and the net inflows through all the openings in that building are summed. The internal pressure in the second building can be calculated such that the pressure difference across the opening between them would produce the velocity required to pass the excess air from the first building to the second. This determines the internal pressure in the second building. The net inflow into the second building (including that through the opening between the buildings) can be calculated. This value must be zero. The original guess for the value of

NO	AREA	LOSS	WIND DIRECTION 0	30	60	90	120	150	180	210	240	270	300	330
1	.0	.0	.00	.00	.00	.00	.00	.00	.00	.00	.00	.00	.00	.00
2	.0	.0	.00	.00	.00	.00	.00	.00	.00	.00	.00	.00	.00	.00
3	3.0	.7	.73	.66	.13	.48	.43	.44	.44	.65	.82	.64	.50	.85
4	3.0	.7	.66	.69	.35	.74	.54	.29	.20	-.40	-.27	-.74	.72	.31
5	3.0	.7	.08	.57	-.19	.42	.59	.44	.30	.69	1.29	1.39	.45	-.10
7	2.0	.7	.05	.38	.39	-.25	.11	-.18	.25	.21	-.18	.29	.13	.34
12	.0	.0	.00	.00	.00	.00	.00	.00	.00	.00	.00	.00	.00	.00
19	.0	.0	.00	.00	.00	.00	.00	.00	.00	.00	.00	.00	.00	.00
20	.0	.0	.00	.00	.00	.00	.00	.00	.00	.00	.00	.00	.00	.00
23	.0	.0	.00	.00	.00	.00	.00	.00	.00	.00	.00	.00	.00	.00
24	.0	.0	.00	.00	.00	.00	.00	.00	.00	.00	.00	.00	.00	.00
25	.0	.0	.00	.00	.00	.00	.00	.00	.00	.00	.00	.00	.00	.00
26	.0	.0	.00	.00	.00	.00	.00	.00	.00	.00	.00	.00	.00	.00
27	.0	.0	.00	.00	.00	.00	.00	.00	.00	.00	.00	.00	.00	.00
28	.0	.0	.00	.00	.00	.00	.00	.00	.00	.00	.00	.00	.00	.00
29	.0	.0	.00	.00	.00	.00	.00	.00	.00	.00	.00	.00	.00	.00
30	.0	.0	.00	.00	.00	.00	.00	.00	.00	.00	.00	.00	.00	.00
31	15.0	.3	1.39	2.94	3.13	1.53	3.83	4.69	3.52	-.57	.19	2.35	-4.34	1.84
32	.0	.0	.00	.00	.00	.00	.00	.00	.00	.00	.00	.00	.00	.00
33	.0	.0	.00	.00	.00	.00	.00	.00	.00	.00	.00	.00	.00	.00
34	15.0	.3	-2.91	-4.16	-3.80	-2.84	-5.35	-5.47	-4.71	-.57	-1.85	-3.17	2.67	-3.24
35	5.0	.3	1.52	1.22	.68	1.30	1.50	.76	1.19	1.15	1.66	.81	1.65	1.40
INTERNAL			-28.1	-28.1	-28.3	-28.4	-28.5	-28.6	-24.7	-29.9	-27.6	-27.6	-27.7	-34.8
PRESSURE			-40.1	-36.0	-30.7	-37.3	-40.5	-31.7	-32.2	-36.8	-42.0	-31.2	-42.1	-45.0
PERCENT VOLUME FLOW			-2.91	4.17	3.80	2.84	5.35	5.47	4.71	1.15	1.85	3.17	4.34	3.24
m**3/s/m/s			-2.91	-4.16	-3.80	-2.84	-5.35	-5.47	-4.71	-1.15	-1.85	-3.17	-4.34	-3.24

FIG 6.04 VOLUME FLOWS ENTERING

BUILDING AERODYNAMICS

the internal pressure in the first building is changed, and a step-by-step calculation proceeds until the error is acceptably small. An example of the flow data for unit reference wind speed is presented in Figure 6.04. In this illustration the same openings applied to all wind directions, although this is not a limitation to the method. In Figure 6.04 there are two rows of data under the heading "Internal Pressure Percent", the upper row is for the first building and the lower for the second. The last row presents values of the overall flow through both buildings per unit reference wind speed. The opening between

VEL in m/s

MONTH	.00	.50	1.00	1.50	2.00	2.50	3.00	3.50	4.00	4.50	5.00
JAN	100.00	92.63	72.34	49.81	31.13	18.19	10.08	5.14	2.32	.90	.29
FEB	100.00	90.42	67.54	43.78	25.81	14.40	7.73	3.97	1.92	.86	.35
MAR	100.00	85.63	57.52	34.83	19.90	10.97	5.93	3.10	1.54	.71	.30
APR	100.00	86.58	61.54	38.90	22.38	12.16	6.33	3.10	1.38	.55	.19
MAY	100.00	84.06	53.24	29.00	13.91	5.91	2.25	.76	.22	.06	.01
JUNE	100.00	85.06	55.23	30.36	15.37	7.55	3.49	1.44	.52	.16	.04
JULY	100.00	87.16	58.90	32.79	16.36	7.55	3.09	1.07	.30	.07	.01
AUG	100.00	83.99	55.49	31.50	16.22	7.74	3.39	1.35	.48	.15	.04
SEPT	100.00	86.06	58.35	34.34	18.62	9.62	4.71	2.13	.87	.31	.10
OCT	100.00	81.77	51.93	29.14	15.23	7.52	3.44	1.41	.51	.16	.04
NOV	100.00	87.22	62.46	39.73	23.27	12.75	6.58	3.17	1.40	.56	.20
DEC	100.00	87.20	62.32	39.60	23.00	12.56	6.49	3.12	1.37	.54	.19
YEAR	100.00	86.20	59.97	36.89	20.98	11.35	5.86	2.85	1.29	.53	.20

FIG 6.05
CUMULATIVE PROBABILITY FOR VEL in m/s.
BUILDING AERODYNAMICS
FOR LOC 35 INFLOW

VEL in m/s

MONTH	.00	.50	1.00	1.50	2.00	2.50	3.00	3.50	4.00	4.50	5.00
JAN	.00	.00	.00	.00	.00	.00	.00	.00	.00	.00	.00
FEB	.00	.00	.00	.00	.00	.00	.00	.00	.00	.00	.00
MAR	.00	.00	.00	.00	.00	.00	.00	.00	.00	.00	.00
APR	.00	.00	.00	.00	.00	.00	.00	.00	.00	.00	.00
MAY	.00	.00	.00	.00	.00	.00	.00	.00	.00	.00	.00
JUNE	.00	.00	.00	.00	.00	.00	.00	.00	.00	.00	.00
JULY	.00	.00	.00	.00	.00	.00	.00	.00	.00	.00	.00
AUG	.00	.00	.00	.00	.00	.00	.00	.00	.00	.00	.00
SEPT	.00	.00	.00	.00	.00	.00	.00	.00	.00	.00	.00
OCT	.00	.00	.00	.00	.00	.00	.00	.00	.00	.00	.00
NOV	.00	.00	.00	.00	.00	.00	.00	.00	.00	.00	.00
DEC	.00	.00	.00	.00	.00	.00	.00	.00	.00	.00	.00
YEAR	.00	.00	.00	.00	.00	.00	.00	.00	.00	.00	.00

FIG 6.05
CUMULATIVE PROBABILITY FOR VEL in m/s.
BUILDING AERODYNAMICS
FOR LOC 35 OUTFLOW

the buildings is designated as location 35 and the statistics for the flow rate through the opening is presented in Figure 6.05.

6.2.6. A Central Building with Multiple Satellites.

If there is one building connected to a second one, as described in Section 6.2.5 the calculation is simple as there is only one value of internal pressure whose value has to be guessed, and corrected by step-by-step calculations. If there is more than one satellite, then the problem is more involved.

The calculation procedure is as follows:

Divide the building into a main volume plus a number of satellites. Assume a value for the internal pressure in the main volume, and consider this the value of external pressure at the junction locations with the satellites. Consider each satellite in turn by assuming a value for its internal pressure, evaluate the nett flow through all its openings, including the one with the main volume. This value must be zero, so, by a step-by-step procedure adjust the assumed value for the internal pressure in the satellite until the mass flow through all openings in the satellite equals zero within sufficient accuracy. Repeat the process for all the satellites. Then treat the values of internal pressure in each satellite as the value of external pressure at their junctions with the main volume, and evaluate the mass flow through the main volume. This value must be zero.

Adjust the assumed value for the internal pressure in the main volume and repeat the whole procedure until the volume flow through all the openings in the main volume is acceptably close to zero.

Values of internal pressure in the main volume and in all the satellites are then known, so the flow through all the openings to atmosphere, and the flow between the main volume and the satellites can be calculated.

This is a much longer procedure than for a single satellite, but, with the use of computers, it can be accomplished .

6.3. Forced Systems.

6.3.1. Wind Tunnel Calculations.

At first glance these systems are easier to analyse because the fans are

FIG 6.06 EXAMPLE OF FAN CHARACTERISTIC

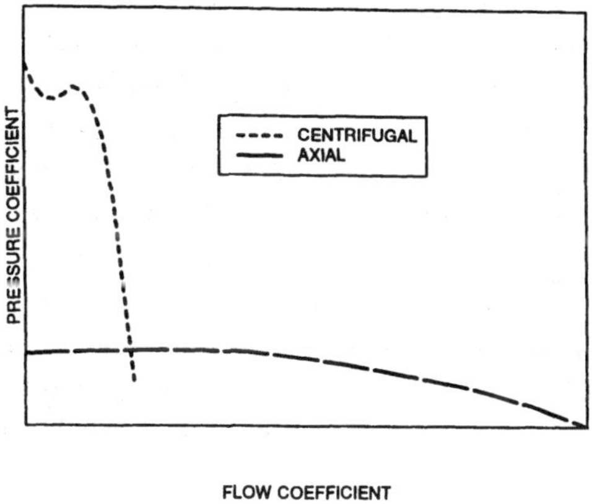

LOC	AREA 1	LOSS	AREA 2	AREA 3	W I N D				D I R E C T I O N							
					0	30	60	90	120	150	180	210	240	270	300	330
					1	1	1	1	1	1	1	1	1	1	1	1
1	.00	.00	.00	.00	.00	.00	.00	.00	.00	.00	.00	.00	.00	.00	.00	.00
8	.00	.00	.00	.00	.00	.00	.00	.00	.00	.00	.00	.00	.00	.00	.00	.00
9	.00	.00	.00	.00	.00	.00	.00	.00	.00	.00	.00	.00	.00	.00	.00	.00
12	.00	.00	.00	.00	.00	.00	.00	.00	.00	.00	.00	.00	.00	.00	.00	.00
13	.00	.00	.00	.00	.00	.00	.00	.00	.00	.00	.00	.00	.00	.00	.00	.00
14	.00	.00	.00	.00	.00	.00	.00	.00	.00	.00	.00	.00	.00	.00	.00	.00
15	.00	.00	.00	.00	.00	.00	.00	.00	.00	.00	.00	.00	.00	.00	.00	.00
16	.00	.00	.00	.00	.00	.00	.00	.00	.00	.00	.00	.00	.00	.00	.00	.00
17	.00	.00	.00	.00	.00	.00	.00	.00	.00	.00	.00	.00	.00	.00	.00	.00
18	.00	.00	.00	.00	.00	.00	.00	.00	.00	.00	.00	.00	.00	.00	.00	.00
19	.00	.00	.00	.00	.00	.00	.00	.00	.00	.00	.00	.00	.00	.00	.00	.00
55	9.70	.30	.00	.00	-12.02	-11.69	-12.31	-12.92	-13.71	-13.16	-13.12	-13.12	-13.16	-13.66	-13.54	-13.04
56	10.00	.30	.00	.00	-13.93	-14.62	-13.51	-13.24	-13.08	-13.41	-13.52	-14.23	-15.19	-13.08	-11.15	-12.16
57	3.00	.30	.00	.00	-3.84	-4.00	-4.05	-4.00	-4.09	-4.06	-3.91	-3.67	-3.38	-3.45	-3.66	-3.78
58	15.60	.30	.00	.00	-20.07	-19.98	-20.76	-21.23	-21.73	-21.33	-20.61	-19.51	-18.36	-18.34	-19.55	-19.89
59	6.00	.30	.00	.00	-7.73	-7.70	-8.05	-8.22	-8.18	-8.32	-7.94	-7.25	-7.64	-7.72	-7.91	-7.89
60	8.20	.30	.00	.00	-10.73	-10.75	-10.82	-10.48	-9.47	-8.68	-8.66	-9.72	-10.76	-11.49	-11.26	-11.02
61	6.50	.30	.00	.00	-8.54	-8.45	-7.99	-7.64	-6.84	-7.77	-8.72	-9.01	-8.75	-8.86	-8.96	-8.74
67	7.80	.30	.00	.00	-10.55	-10.27	-10.13	-10.04	-10.07	-10.13	-10.41	-10.33	-10.38	-10.63	-10.71	-10.71
76	9.00	.30	.00	.00	-12.59	-12.54	-12.39	-12.22	-12.83	-13.13	-13.11	-13.16	-12.39	-12.78	-13.26	-12.78
	INTERNAL PRESSURE				199.6	200.7	206.1	203.7	192.6	206.3	215.5	220.7	226.0	230.6	218.6	204.4
	PERCENT VOLUME				.0	.0	.0	.0	.0	.0	.0	.0	.0	.0	.0	.0
	FLOW m**3/s/m/s				-100.0	-100.0	-100.0	-100.0	-100.0	-100.0	-100.0	-100.0	-100.0	100.0	100.0	-100.0

FIG 6.07 VOLUME FLOWS ENTERING

BUILDING AERODYNAMICS

REFERENCE WIND SPEED 1 m/s

assumed to provide all the air required irrespective of wind strength and direction but in practice the computation is more complex as will be explained below. A fan has a "characteristic", which describes its performance. The characteristic (see Figure 6.06 for example) is the variation of the flow rate through the fan with the pressure difference against which the air has to be delivered: the greater the adverse pressure difference the smaller the flow rate. Conversely, the greater the advantageous pressure difference, the greater the flow rate. Because the internal pressure, the external pressure at the openings to the atmosphere, and the external pressure at the location of the fan all depend upon wind, the performance of the fan depends upon the wind.

If the fan, or fans, are designed to supply the required volume of air in the most disadvantageous case, the volume flow in all other situations will be excessive. It might be thought that excessive air is a good thing, but, in cold weather it has to be heated, which puts up the requirement for the heating plant. There might also be excessive flow through doors making them

					W I N D			D I R E C T I O N								
LOC	AREA 1	LOSS	AREA 2	AREA 3	0 1	30 1	60 1	90 1	120 1	150 1	180 1	210 1	240 1	270 1	300 1	330 1
1	.00	.00	.00	.00	.00	.00	.00	.00	.00	.00	.00	.00	.00	.00	.00	.00
8	.00	.00	.00	.00	.00	.00	.00	.00	.00	.00	.00	.00	.00	.00	.00	.00
9	.00	.00	.00	.00	.00	.00	.00	.00	.00	.00	.00	.00	.00	.00	.00	.00
12	.00	.00	.00	.00	.00	.00	.00	.00	.00	.00	.00	.00	.00	.00	.00	.00
13	.00	.00	.00	.00	.00	.00	.00	.00	.00	.00	.00	.00	.00	.00	.00	.00
14	.00	.00	.00	.00	.00	.00	.00	.00	.00	.00	.00	.00	.00	.00	.00	.00
15	.00	.00	.00	.00	.00	.00	.00	.00	.00	.00	.00	.00	.00	.00	.00	.00
16	.00	.00	.00	.00	.00	.00	.00	.00	.00	.00	.00	.00	.00	.00	.00	.00
17	.00	.00	.00	.00	.00	.00	.00	.00	.00	.00	.00	.00	.00	.00	.00	.00
18	.00	.00	.00	.00	.00	.00	.00	.00	.00	.00	.00	.00	.00	.00	.00	.00
19	.00	.00	.00	.00	.00	.00	.00	.00	.00	.00	.00	.00	.00	.00	.00	.00
55	9.70	.30	.00	.00	3.54	4.47	2.88	-2.58	-5.20	-3.32	-2.95	-4.12	-3.81	-5.22	-5.03	-3.49
56	10.00	.30	.00	.00	-5.22	-6.88	-3.59	-2.23	-.35	-2.74	-3.04	-6.13	-7.89	-1.31	6.62	4.47
57	3.00	.30	.00	.00	.50	-.99	-1.05	-.84	-1.15	-1.00	.60	1.18	1.93	1.82	1.32	.89
58	15.60	.30	.00	.00	1.85	2.37	-4.21	-6.00	-7.51	-5.94	-1.45	4.56	8.54	8.71	5.16	3.58
59	6.00	.30	.00	.00	.50	.76	-1.91	-2.52	-2.31	-2.69	-.75	2.62	1.50	1.18	-1.45	-1.37
60	8.20	.30	.00	.00	-1.68	-1.90	-1.74	2.15	5.03	6.37	6.46	4.07	-1.55	-4.25	-3.72	-2.95
61	6.50	.30	.00	.00	-1.54	-1.05	2.80	3.68	5.04	3.53	-1.65	-3.38	-2.31	-2.63	-3.05	-2.34
67	7.80	.30	.00	.00	-3.13	-2.03	.82	1.71	1.57	1.50	-1.63	-2.51	-2.27	-3.16	-3.54	-3.54
76	9.00	.30	.00	.00	-4.82	-4.74	-4.01	-3.38	-5.11	-5.72	-5.59	-6.29	-4.13	-5.13	-6.31	-5.24
	INTERNAL PRESSURE				-39.0	-37.3	-36.6	-39.9	-51.8	-40.3	-32.8	-15.2	-14.9	-11.5	-21.6	-35.5
	PERCENT VOLUME FLOW				6.4	7.6	6.5	7.5	11.6	11.4	7.1	12.4	12.0	11.7	13.1	8.9
	m**3/s/m/s				-16.4	-17.6	-16.5	-17.5	-21.6	-21.4	-17.1	-22.4	-22.0	-21.7	-23.1	-18.9

FIG 6.08 VOLUME FLOWS ENTERING

BUILDING AERODYNAMICS

REFERENCE WIND SPEED 10 m/s

MONTH	FAN PRESSURE DIFFERENCE									
	3.0	6.0	9.0	12.0	15.0	18.0	21.0	24.0	27.0	30.0
JAN	8.23	5.00	3.25	2.24	1.57	1.12	.80	.58	.43	.33
FEB	10.92	5.43	2.86	1.62	.95	.57	.35	.23	.15	.10
MAR	11.61	5.66	2.79	1.46	.78	.42	.23	.13	.08	.04
APR	10.60	4.59	2.07	1.01	.50	.25	.13	.07	.04	.02
MAY	9.68	4.45	2.16	1.14	.62	.35	.21	.13	.08	.05
JUNE	4.75	1.37	.41	.13	.04	.02	.01	.00	.00	.00
JULY	2.32	.63	.18	.06	.02	.01	.00	.00	.00	.00
AUG	3.90	1.43	.56	.24	.10	.05	.02	.01	.01	.00
SEPT	4.13	1.44	.53	.21	.09	.04	.01	.01	.00	.00
OCT	9.15	4.21	1.99	.98	.49	.25	.12	.06	.03	.02
NOV	6.42	3.11	1.59	.86	.47	.26	.15	.08	.05	.03
DEC	7.81	3.90	2.04	1.12	.63	.35	.20	.11	.07	.04
YEAR	7.93	3.88	2.00	1.10	.61	.35	.20	.11	.07	.04

MONTH	FAN PRESSURE DIFFERENCE									
	-3.0	-6.0	-9.0	-12.0	-15.0	-18.0	-21.0	-24.0	-27.0	-30.0
JAN	20.96	5.79	1.96	.82	.24	.05	.01	.01	.00	.00
FEB	14.01	3.68	1.21	.68	.18	.05	.02	.01	.00	.00
MAR	16.04	4.00	1.16	.50	.06	.01	.00	.00	.00	.00
APR	11.82	2.62	.59	.18	.03	.00	.00	.00	.00	.00
MAY	9.21	1.81	.31	.07	.01	.00	.00	.00	.00	.00
JUNE	10.43	1.52	.27	.04	.01	.00	.00	.00	.00	.00
JULY	12.62	1.67	.20	.04	.01	.00	.00	.00	.00	.00
AUG	10.90	1.87	.29	.08	.00	.00	.00	.00	.00	.00
SEPT	15.26	3.39	.88	.32	.07	.01	.00	.00	.00	.00
OCT	12.68	2.24	.53	.17	.03	.01	.00	.00	.00	.00
NOV	21.30	5.44	1.58	.78	.21	.05	.02	.01	.00	.00
DEC	21.12	5.68	1.68	.75	.21	.03	.01	.00	.00	.00
YEAR	16.12	3.90	1.07	.40	.07	.01	.00	.00	.00	.00

FIG 6.09 PROBABILITY OF VALUES OF FAN PRESSURE DIFFERENCES

FOR FAN AT LOCATION 19

unpleasant to use.

A forced system is not a doddle.

A wind tunnel investigation can supply useful information in this case too. Areas and Loss Coefficients are allocated to all the locations, zero area being allocated to those areas where there are fans. The volume flow rate through all the other openings (with zero open area at the fan location) must be equal and opposite to the flow through the fans. The value of the Internal Pressure adjusts itself automatically for this to occur. The difficulty is immediately obvious, the fan passes a given volume rate in absolute terms against a given pressure difference in absolute terms: the integrated flow rate through all the other openings is a function of the reference wind speed. The basic presentation for the natural system (Figure 6.01) does not apply because the value of the Internal Pressure varies with the reference wind speed, and, as the value of the Internal Pressure varies, so will the flow rate through every one of the openings, some increasing and some decreasing. This is shown in Figures 6.07 and 6.08: Figure 6.07 is for a reference wind speed of 1 m/s, and Figure 6.08 for a reference wind speed of 10 m/s, both having a fan which is supplying 100 m^3/s of air. Notice that the total volume flows in and out in the last two rows of the Figures are in units of m^3 / sec per unit of reference wind speed, so that the difference between in and out on Figure 6.08 is only 10 m^3/s per m/s. For some values of Reference Wind Speed the wind could enter at a location, whilst it would leave at the same location for a different value of Reference Wind Speed, for example at location 55 for a wind from the North (0°) in Figures 6.07 and 6.08.

The required output from the wind tunnel investigation is a series of values of probability for the pressure difference across the fan (and fans in different locations will have different probabilities). The Meteorological data present probabilities for the Reference Wind Speed. Thus, for a given wind direction, the probabilities of various values of reference wind speed are known. For a whole range of values of reference wind speed, values of Internal Pressure are calculated for each wind direction. and for each of these values of Internal Pressure values of Pressure Difference across a fan can be calculated. Thereafter, working backwards, for chosen values of Pressure Difference, the value of Reference Wind Speed is calculated, and the Probability of its Occurrence (different for each month) is computed. The calculation is performed for each wind direction and the values summed to get the Probability in the chosen month or the Year as a whole. A typical presentation at Bristol is shown in Figure 6.09. These data should be compared with the characteristic of the fan (Figure 6.06) to ensure that its performance is satisfactory.

Once this is accomplished, the probabilities of volume flows through doors and other openings should be examined and the data presented as in Figure 6.10. The value of the velocity through the door when there is no wind is stated in the rubric (-1.32 m/s in the example of Figure 6.10). This makes the tables look rather odd. If January is considered, the probabilities for velocities through the door of -4, -3, -2 -1 and 0 m/s are 17.07, 35.01, 63.02, 13.23 and 10.15 respectively. There is a step in the probabilities between -2

MONTH	VELOCITY THROUGH OPENING										
	-10.00	-9.00	-8.00	-7.00	-6.00	-5.00	-4.00	-3.00	-2.00	-1.00	.00
JAN	.00	.14	.43	1.18	3.14	7.59	17.07	35.01	63.02	13.23	10.15
FEB	.00	.02	.09	.34	1.35	4.30	11.76	27.15	54.50	19.59	15.37
MAR	.00	.00	.06	.31	1.24	4.26	12.89	30.94	55.86	24.40	20.77
APR	.00	.01	.07	.30	1.02	3.28	9.89	25.73	49.49	30.01	25.59
MAY	.00	.00	.02	.11	.48	2.07	8.26	25.44	52.69	23.52	19.78
JUNE	.00	.00	.01	.09	.46	1.98	8.01	27.79	57.94	18.70	14.51
JULY	.00	.00	.03	.12	.51	2.18	9.41	30.78	61.83	13.22	9.35
AUG	.00	.00	.01	.08	.39	1.86	0.71	28.59	57.56	15.03	9.65
SEPT	.00	.03	.11	.38	1.33	4.42	13.30	31.74	58.07	14.19	10.03
OCT	.00	.01	.06	.23	.89	3.18	10.09	26.00	54.22	16.65	12.51
NOV	.00	.03	.15	.56	2.09	6.52	17.51	38.32	65.30	14.16	11.93
DEC	.00	.12	.36	.96	2.58	6.83	17.16	37.18	62.93	17.57	14.17
YEAR	.00	.04	.14	.48	1.53	4.68	13.33	31.60	58.22	18.23	14.47

MONTH	VELOCITY THROUGH OPENING										
	.00	1.00	2.00	3.00	4.00	5.00	6.00	7.00	8.00	9.00	10.00
JAN	10.15	8.09	4.90	2.24	.94	.30	.15	.05	.00	.00	.00
FEB	15.37	12.13	6.78	2.52	.80	.26	.08	.03	.00	.00	.00
MAR	20.77	17.54	11.14	4.63	1.33	.27	.04	.00	.00	.00	.00
APR	25.59	21.41	12.90	4.64	1.07	.16	.02	.00	.00	.00	.00
MAY	19.78	16.41	9.82	3.63	.92	.17	.02	.00	.00	.00	.00
JUNE	14.51	10.92	4.99	1.07	.11	.00	.00	.00	.00	.00	.00
JULY	9.35	6.61	2.72	.53	.06	.00	.00	.00	.00	.00	.00
AUG	9.65	6.36	2.36	.45	.06	.00	.00	.00	.00	.00	.00
SEPT	10.03	7.29	3.44	.98	.21	.03	.00	.00	.00	.00	.00
OCT	12.51	9.72	5.55	2.37	.93	.34	.11	.03	.00	.00	.00
NOV	11.93	10.02	6.45	2.97	1.15	.39	.11	.03	.00	.00	.00
DEC	14.17	11.57	7.04	2.97	1.00	.28	.07	.01	.00	.00	.00
YEAR	14.47	11.56	6.62	2.50	.73	.18	.04	.00	.00	.00	.00

FIG 6.10 PROBABILITY OF VALUES OF
VELOCITY ENTERING THROUGH OPENING

FOR LOCATION 55

FLOW FOR ZERO WIND SPEED= -1.32

BUILDING AERODYNAMICS

and -1 m/s. The inconsistency arises because, for wind speeds more negative than -1.32 m/s (the velocity through the door when there is no wind), the wind is assisting the fan, but for more positive values than -1.32 m/s, the wind is opposing the fan. For a continuous curve of probability with velocity through the door, the probability % on one side of the divide should be presented as (100 - probability %). In the case of the natural system, whose results are presented in Figure 6.03, this has been taken into account because the change-over occurred for zero flow through the door at the known wind speed of zero. Similar probability data for the whole volume can be produced, as in Figure

6.11. In this the minimum volume flow is in the absence of wind, the presence of wind always increases the volume flow through the whole volume.

The increase in volume flow caused by the wind is interesting. In the example shown in Figure 6.11, the fan was installed to introduce 100 m^3/s, (the example is from a food store), and in January there is about a 1% probability that the flow rate will be 300 m^3/s. In January the air is cold, and

MONTH	TOTAL VOLUME FLOW								
	105.00	130.00	155.00	180.00	205.00	230.00	255.00	280.00	305.00
JAN	82.12	57.15	38.04	24.38	14.98	8.57	4.60	2.38	1.19
FEB	81.14	50.25	29.92	17.46	9.74	5.05	2.46	1.17	.56
MAR	85.13	54.53	34.16	20.48	11.37	5.63	2.47	.98	.36
APR	82.82	46.98	26.91	14.87	7.74	3.66	1.52	.56	.19
MAY	81.72	47.27	26.31	13.71	6.29	2.47	.81	.22	.06
JUNE	80.93	47.44	26.72	14.40	6.74	2.60	.81	.21	.05
JULY	79.69	49.04	29.53	16.69	8.19	3.35	1.11	.31	.07
AUG	76.45	46.28	27.86	15.62	7.48	2.92	.91	.23	.05
SEPT	78.06	48.39	30.75	19.26	11.23	5.92	2.79	1.21	.47
OCT	79.22	47.49	27.76	15.64	8.25	3.94	1.71	.69	.26
NOV	85.66	59.38	39.91	25.64	15.22	8.17	4.00	1.87	.84
DEC	84.76	58.68	39.65	25.42	15.05	8.03	3.87	1.76	.77
YEAR	81.55	52.18	33.01	20.15	11.46	5.92	2.75	1.18	.46

FIG 6.11 PROBABILITY OF VALUES OF TOTAL VOLUME FLOW

a complex arrangement of operating the fans and openings to reduce this excessive flow can be installed, but this would require a wind vane and anemometer on the roof of the building.

6.3.2. Choice of Fans.

This is a specialist subject and will only be mentioned briefly here.

In general "Axial" fans produce large flow rates against small pressure differences. "centrifugal" fans produce relatively small flow rates against large pressure differences. This is a generalised statement. Special design features have been added to both to increase their ranges.

It is advised that the ESDU Data Item "A Guide to Fan Selection and Performance" Item number 79037 Amendment A 1980 is studied, otherwise specialist advice should be obtained.

6.4 Car Parks.

These require special attention. Once again ventilation can either be natural or forced

6.4.1. Natural Ventilation.

It is possible to enclose the edges of multi-storey Car Parks in a wind tunnel model, and insert pressure tappings in a variety of positions around the perimeter. Then carry out an investigation as described in Section 6.2, and present probabilities for a range of volume flows through the whole Car Park. This would give an overall value of Air Changes per Hour for the whole Car Park: this is not good enough. Within a Car Park, or a part of a Car Park, it is possible to get pockets of stagnation where fumes can collect and are not ventilated. Some time ago we investigated a Car Park where the overall assessment suggested an ACH value of 10. On detailed study, most of the air entered on one side and left on the adjoining side, the remaining two sides being almost completely unventilated.

The way to study these stagnation regions is in a wind tunnel investigation. A special wind tunnel model is made of perspex with all the openings correctly represented. Consider the simplest case of a single deck of underground car parking underneath the building, the roof of the building would be perspex, and the roof of the car park would also be perspex. The floor of the car park would be painted matt black and be supplied with a tube for the admission of smoke. A camcorder would be mounted in the wind tunnel looking down through the building to the floor of the car park. Smoke is injected into the car park and the timer on the camcorder is started running. At a noted time, the supply of smoke to the car park is cut off, and the recorder shows the subsequent movement of the smoke. A series of stills from a video of an investigation are presented in Figure 6.12

Time Scales for the investigation must be established. If the linear, velocity and time scales for the study are L , V and T, given by

$$L = \mathrm{L}_{\mathrm{model}} / \mathrm{L}_{\mathrm{full\ scale}}$$
$$V = \mathrm{V}_{\mathrm{model}} / \mathrm{V}_{\mathrm{full\ scale}}$$
$$T = \mathrm{T}_{\mathrm{model}} / \mathrm{T}_{\mathrm{full\ scale}},$$

Time = 10 seconds

Time = 70 seconds

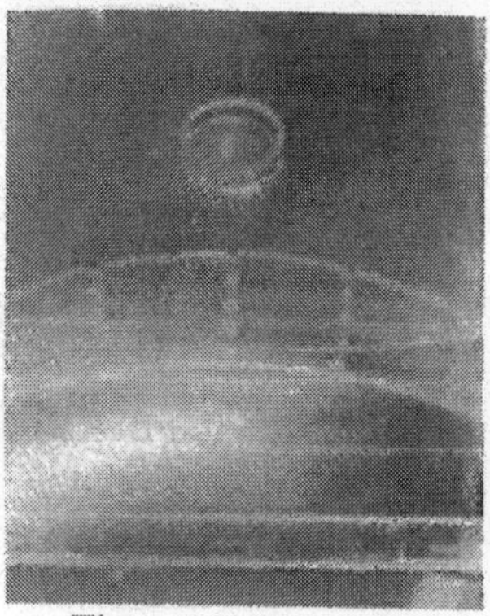

Time = 130 seconds

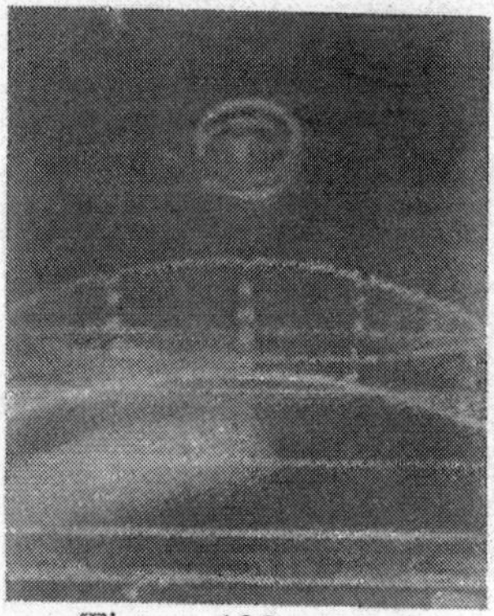

Time = 190 seconds

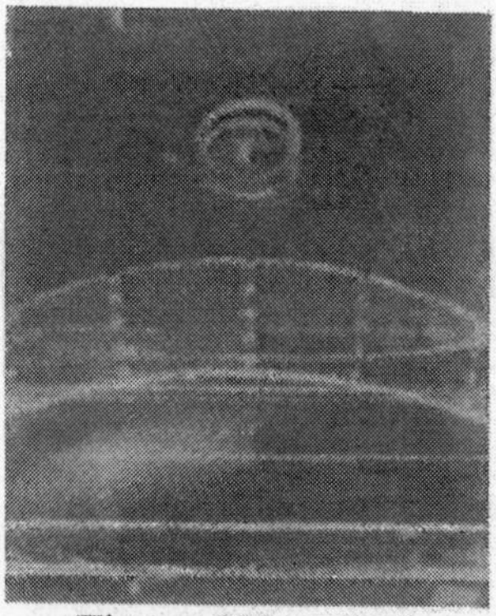

Time = 238 seconds

FIG 6.12 SMOKE PHOTOGRAPHS

then

$$T = L / V.$$

The time from the switch off of smoke on the video is marked on the recording, so the time in full scale to reach the same clearance is given by

$$(Time\ in\ fs) = (Time\ in\ wt) \times (V_{wt} / L) / V_{fs}.$$

where (V_{wt} / L) is a known constant for the investigation and V_{fs} is the full scale Meteorological Standard Wind Speed.

For sake of illustration, assume that the constant (V_{wt}/L) for the investigation presented in Figure 6.12 was 100, that the photographs were taken at times from the cessation of smoke introduction of 10s, 70s, 130s, 190s and 238s respectively, and that the wind direction was 240°.

The Probabilities that the Meteorological Standard Wind Speed are greater than the stated value are presented in Figure 6.13. Using full scale wind speed as the common factor, it is now possible to produce a table showing the probability that conditions would be better than those shown in each photograph. These data are presented in Figure 6.14.

SPEED m/s	WIND DIRECTION 345	15	45	75	105	135	165	195	225	255	285	315	345	ALL
0	5.01	4.04	7.19	4.57	2.63	2.52	3.83	12.41	25.22	18.73	9.82	4.04		100.00
1	4.97	3.99	7.12	4.55	2.57	2.42	3.53	12.35	25.13	18.59	9.67	3.90		98.79
2	4.76	3.79	6.78	4.41	2.37	2.17	3.03	12.04	24.66	18.07	9.16	3.55		94.79
3	4.34	3.41	6.12	4.09	2.05	1.80	2.46	11.37	23.63	17.08	8.30	3.08		87.73
4	3.74	2.87	5.16	3.56	1.64	1.39	1.92	10.30	21.95	15.62	7.16	2.55		77.87
5	3.00	2.25	4.02	2.87	1.21	1.00	1.45	8.87	19.64	13.79	5.87	2.02		65.99
6	2.23	1.62	2.88	2.10	.82	.67	1.06	7.20	16.84	11.72	4.56	1.53		53.23
7	1.52	1.07	1.87	1.38	.51	.42	.75	5.48	13.75	9.55	3.36	1.11		40.78
8	.95	.64	1.09	.81	.29	.25	.51	3.88	10.65	7.46	2.33	.78		29.63
9	.53	.35	.57	.41	.15	.13	.35	2.54	7.78	5.56	1.53	.52		20.42
10	.27	.17	.27	.18	.07	.07	.23	1.52	5.34	3.96	.95	.33		13.35
11	.12	.08	.11	.07	.03	.03	.14	.83	3.43	2.68	.55	.21		8.28
12	.05	.03	.04	.02	.01	.01	.09	.42	2.05	1.73	.30	.12		4.87
13	.02	.01	.01	.01	.00	.01	.05	.19	1.14	1.06	.16	.07		2.71
14	.01	.00	.00	.00	.00	.00	.03	.08	.58	.61	.07	.04		1.43
15	.00	.00	.00	.00	.00	.00	.02	.03	.27	.34	.03	.02		.72
16	.00	.00	.00	.00	.00	.00	.01	.01	.12	.17	.01	.01		.34
17	.00	.00	.00	.00	.00	.00	.01	.00	.05	.08	.01	.01		.15
18	.00	.00	.00	.00	.00	.00	.00	.00	.02	.04	.00	.00		.07
19	.00	.00	.00	.00	.00	.00	.00	.00	.01	.02	.00	.00		.03
20	.00	.00	.00	.00	.00	.00	.00	.00	.00	.01	.00	.00		.01

FIG 6.13 PROBABILITY IN PERCENTAGE
THAT WINDSPEED IS GREATER THAN STATED VALUE
IN JANUARY

WIND SPEED		5 m/s	7 m/s	9 m/s	11 m/s	13 m/s	15 m/s
PROB in %		19.6	13.8	7.8	3.4	1.1	0.3
	TIME ON FIG6.12						
TIME	70secs	23.3	16.7	13.0	10.6	9.0	7.8
in	130secs	43.3	31.0	24.1	19.7	16.7	14.4
minutes	190secs	63.3	45.2	35.2	28.8	24.4	21.1
	238secs	79.3	56.6	44.1	36.1	30.5	26.4

FIG 6.14 PROBABILITY OF TIME FOR PHOTOGRAPHS

Figure 6.14 can be interpreted in words as saying that conditions have a 3.4% probability of being better than those shown in the 70 secs photograph after 10.6 minutes from the cessation of the smoke. Any areas which have just cleared in that time have the equivalent of 6 ACH. These data are further presented in graphical form in Figure 6.15.

FIG 6.15 PROBABILITY v TIME FOR PHOTOGRAPHS

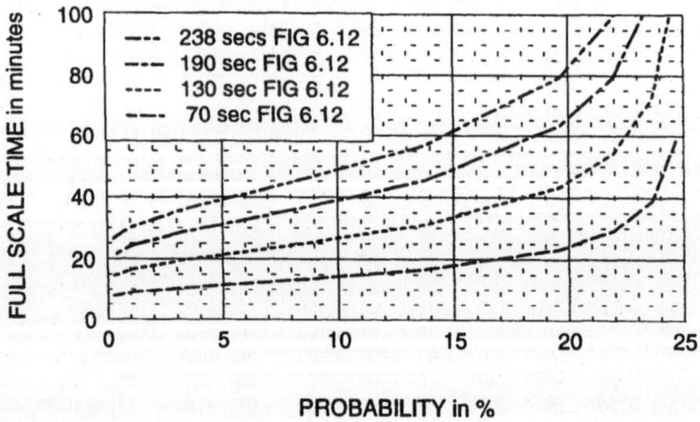

Let us assume that the area in question just clears on the 130 seconds photograph, then the probability that the area in full scale will clear can be read from Figure 6.15 as any co-ordinates of the 130 seconds line. For example there is a probability of 18.2% of clearing in 40 minutes; 13.2%

probability of clearing in 30 minutes and 4.2% probability of clearing in 20 minutes. These probabilities are for the one wind direction only. To get values for the overall probability of clearing in a given, or a range , of times, the above study must be performed for the complete range of wind directions, and the probabilities for a given clearance time summed for all.

6.4.2. Mechanical Ventilation.

Problems do not evaporate if Mechanical Ventilation is used. If there are two locations from which air is drawn from the Car Park, then there is likely to be a region between them where the drawing power from each is equal and opposite. This is likely to be a stagnation region. Air must enter somewhere to be drawn out: if there are a limited number of locations where this can occur, there are also possible stagnation regions between them. The cure is to have the source points as well distributed as possible.

If the system supplies fresh air, then the same problems are possible.

6.4.3. Hybrid System.

Natural Ventilation is simpler and avoids all the complications of ducting; it is also cheaper to run and does not lend itself to man-created problems.

If a natural system works for the majority of the Car Park, it is possible to augment it with fans in the Car Park itself. The purpose of the fans is to move the pollution from the stagnation regions to others which are well ventilated naturally. This would involve a fan mounted to the ceiling in the stagnation region which would be switched on automatically as soon as a pre-arranged level of pollution had been reached. The system would be slightly improved if the fan were made to gyrate through a limited angle at the same time; this would ensure that no new area became a stagnation one.

This system requires no ducting, but would require that all electric cables met the fire regulations.

7. Fire

This chapter is not seen as a manual for design as far as fire is concerned. It only highlights those aspects which directly relate to wind matters, where the wind engineer can have a useful input.

The basic approach for the containment of fire in a building, as far as the wind engineer is concerned, is that there shall be an internal volume at roof level, called a smoke reservoir, where the smoke from a fire can collect prior to being removed from the building. There are also considerations for false ceilings and escape routes.

The areas of openings in a fire situation should be sufficient to vent the smoke when there is no wind. This specifies the area of the openings which must work under buoyancy forces alone. The purpose of the wind engineer is to ensure that, under no circumstances, shall the wind inhibit this state of affairs.

Studies of fire situations are very similar to those for Ventilation with the exception that external flow is never allowed **into** smoke reservoirs. It is no good claiming that, on average, more air leaves a reservoir than enters it, because the air entering is cold, and when it mixes with the smoke, it will reduce the temperature of the smoke and cause it to lose its buoyancy, causing secondary flows which might bring the smoke into contact with people.

In a large complex, it is almost impossible to treat the whole complex as an entity as escape paths are too long. The building can be split into a series of smoke zones, and, when a fire is sensed in one zone curtains are dropped to create an individual smoke reservoir in that zone, then the smoke from that

LOC	AREA 1	LOSS	AREA 2	AREA 3	WIND DIRECTION											
					0	30	60	90	120	150	180	210	240	270	300	330
					2	2	2	1	1	1	1	3	3	1	1	1
5	.00	.00	.00	.00	.00	.00	.00	.00	.00	.00	.00	.00	.00	.00	.00	.00
6	.00	.00	.00	.00	.00	.00	.00	.00	.00	.00	.00	.00	.00	.00	.00	.00
7	.00	.00	.00	.00	.00	.00	.00	.00	.00	.00	.00	.00	.00	.00	.00	.00
8	.00	.00	.00	.00	.00	.00	.00	.00	.00	.00	.00	.00	.00	.00	.00	.00
9	.00	.00	.00	.00	.00	.00	.00	.00	.00	.00	.00	.00	.00	.00	.00	.00
10	.00	.00	.00	.00	.00	.00	.00	.00	.00	.00	.00	.00	.00	.00	.00	.00
11	.00	.00	.00	.00	.00	.00	.00	.00	.00	.00	.00	.00	.00	.00	.00	.00
12	.00	.00	.00	.00	.00	.00	.00	.00	.00	.00	.00	.00	.00	.00	.00	.00
13	2.00	.67	2.00	2.00	-.79	-1.25	-1.26	-.85	-.65	-.40	-.09	.37	.16	-.71	-.61	-.56
14	2.00	.67	2.00	2.00	-1.06	-1.29	-.86	-.48	-.47	-.16	.30	.26	-.27	-.78	-.73	-1.04
15	2.00	.67	2.00	2.00	-.84	-.95	-.52	-.40	-.54	-.40	-.33	-.71	-.90	-.93	-.71	-.94
16	2.00	.67	2.00	2.00	-.36	-.08	-.18	.07	-.50	-.44	-.56	-1.03	-1.34	-1.07	-.88	-.96
17	2.00	.67	.00	2.00	.00	.00	.00	.07	-.54	-.57	-.80	-1.15	-1.38	-1.08	-.78	-.50
18	2.00	.67	.00	2.00	.00	.00	.00	-.44	-.72	-.85	-.88	-1.11	-1.28	-.95	-.61	.22
19	2.00	.67	.00	2.00	.00	.00	.00	-.75	-.92	-1.00	-.80	-.84	-.74	-.84	-.49	.39
20	2.00	.67	2.00	2.00	-.45	-.93	-1.26	-1.06	-.79	-.65	-.42	-.18	-.38	-.66	-.49	-.23
21	1.00	.67	1.00	.00	-.20	.22	.22	.03	-.37	-.31	-.19	.00	.00	-.35	-.47	-.39
22	1.00	.67	1.00	.00	-.09	.24	.20	-.15	-.37	-.27	-.14	.00	.00	-.33	-.44	-.41
23	1.00	.67	1.00	.00	-.13	.18	.16	-.18	-.34	-.25	-.16	.00	.00	-.35	-.50	-.57
24	1.00	.67	1.00	.00	-.18	.15	.09	-.18	-.32	-.20	-.19	.00	.00	-.18	-.55	-.60
25	1.00	.67	1.00	.00	-.34	.08	.09	-.22	-.32	-.27	-.26	.00	.00	-.18	-.53	-.64
26	1.00	.67	1.00	.00	-.35	.08	.09	-.24	-.25	-.22	-.21	.00	.00	-.21	-.42	-.58
27	1.00	.67	1.00	.00	-.30	.18	.16	-.22	-.25	-.24	-.25	.00	.00	-.21	-.38	-.51
28	1.00	.67	1.00	.00	-.26	.08	.13	-.18	-.17	-.30	-.25	.00	.00	-.30	-.48	-.54
29	1.00	.67	1.00	.00	-.22	.18	.13	-.18	-.17	-.27	-.14	.00	.00	-.18	-.52	-.54
30	1.00	.67	1.00	.00	-.34	.20	.20	-.12	.06	-.27	-.14	.00	.00	.20	-.52	-.54
31	1.00	.67	1.00	.00	-.36	.15	.16	-.09	-.12	-.24	-.19	.00	.00	.22	-.50	-.54
32	1.00	.67	1.00	.00	-.36	.22	.22	-.09	-.12	-.25	-.16	.00	.00	.26	-.47	-.53
34	3.00	.30	3.00	3.00	2.11	1.27	-.93	-1.16	-1.06	.15	.68	.44	.41	1.03	1.02	1.63
36	.00	.30	.00	.00	.00	.00	.00	.00	.00	.00	.00	.00	.00	.00	.00	.00
38	3.00	.30	3.00	3.00	1.55	.97	-.31	-.75	-.67	.34	.27	.88	1.23	2.03	2.50	2.71
47	.00	.30	.00	.00	.00	.00	.00	.00	.00	.00	.00	.00	.00	.00	.00	.00
50	3.00	.30	3.00	3.00	2.08	.97	.54	.33	.48	-1.02	-1.36	-.69	1.27	2.10	2.65	2.49
53	3.00	.30	3.00	3.00	1.49	.81	.62	.33	.19	-1.02	-1.53	-1.55	1.06	2.03	2.44	1.92
55	3.00	.30	3.00	3.00	.44	.60	.82	1.49	1.56	1.53	1.83	1.08	-.15	-.88	-.55	.49
58	.00	.30	.00	.00	.00	.00	.00	.00	.00	.00	.00	.00	.00	.00	.00	.00
60	3.00	.30	3.00	3.00	.06	-.56	.31	1.17	1.68	1.53	1.75	1.55	1.11	.82	.87	.66
61	.00	.30	.00	.00	.00	.00	.00	.00	.00	.00	.00	.00	.00	.00	.00	.00
62	3.00	.30	3.00	3.00	.06	-.34	.44	1.28	2.20	2.53	1.31	.93	.68	.53	.68	.38
63	.00	.30	.00	.00	.00	.00	.00	.00	.00	.00	.00	.00	.00	.00	.00	.00
64	.00	.30	.00	.00	.00	.00	.00	.00	.00	.00	.00	.00	.00	.00	.00	.00
68	3.00	.30	3.00	3.00	-.53	-.46	-.02	1.25	1.74	1.82	1.48	.98	.86	.43	.61	-.49
71	.00	.30	.00	.00	.00	.00	.00	.00	.00	.00	.00	.00	.00	.00	.00	.00
73	.00	.30	.00	.00	.00	.00	.00	.00	.00	.00	.00	.00	.00	.00	.00	.00
75	3.00	.30	3.00	3.00	-.62	-.71	.76	1.73	1.74	1.71	1.41	.76	-.35	.53	.87	.22
77	.00	.30	.00	.00	.00	.00	.00	.00	.00	.00	.00	.00	.00	.00	.00	.00
	INTERNAL PRESSURE				-46.0	-28.7	-29.1	-44.6	-46.5	-63.1	-44.0	-36.8	-42.5	-51.9	-65.5	-55.8
	PERCENT VOLUME FLOW				7.8	6.6	5.3	7.7	9.7	9.6	9.0	7.3	6.8	10.2	11.6	11.1
	m**3/s/m/s				-7.8	-6.6	-5.3	-7.7	-9.7	-9.6	-9.0	-7.3	-6.8	-10.2	-11.6	-11.1

FIG 7.01 VOLUME FLOWS ENTERING

BUILDING AERODYNAMICS

SCENARIO 47

reservoir must be removed successfully. It is even satisfactory not to evacuate all the other zones while the fire is dealt with in its own zone.

7.1 Natural Systems.

In natural systems, the only required presentation of data is for values of the volume flow entering at all the locations for all wind directions. A copy of the presentation of these data is shown on Figure 7.01. These data are for a reference wind speed of 1 m/s, and, because all flows in a natural system are factored by the value of the reference wind speed, any value of the reference wind speed will do for this discussion. The important word is entering, and all positive values in that Figure show flow entering. It is only necessary to study Figure 7.01 for all locations in smoke reservoirs to ensure that the values in the body of the Figure are negative for all wind directions.

In the illustration, scenario 47, shown in Figure 7.01 locations 13 to 32 (total loss coefficients 1.67) are possible locations for outlets, although in this case they are not all in smoke reservoirs, and locations 34 to 77 (total loss coefficients 1.30) are doors or other possible openings. These data are for 1 m/s of reference wind speed, and, because it is a natural system, this presentation is satisfactory (for a reference wind speed of 10 m/s, all the values in the body of the Figure would be multiplied by 10). A very quick look at the Figure shows that the situation presented therein is unsatisfactory because there are many positive values of flow rates for locations 13 to 32, assuming that they are all in smoke reservoirs. The reason for the Scenario number is that different combinations of areas have to be tried, even allowing different openings for different wind directions as shown in the fourth row from the top in the Figure and explained in Section 6.2.4. The giving of Scenario numbers shows the development of the thought process used. The results from all the scenario can be summarised on a single table in the report.

Success is a scenario with no positive values at locations in smoke reservoirs.

7.2. Forced Systems.

The same process does not work in the case of a Forced system. The reason has been explained in Section 6.3.

MONTH	VELOCITY THROUGH OPENING										
	-10.00	-9.00	-8.00	-7.00	-6.00	-5.00	-4.00	-3.00	-2.00	-1.00	.00
JAN	.00	.00	.03	.31	1.70	6.90	20.20	49.79	.14	.03	.02
FEB	.00	.00	.00	.13	.93	4.27	14.25	39.03	.18	.03	.02
MAR	.00	.00	.00	.06	.76	4.56	16.76	45.60	.03	.00	.00
APR	.00	.00	.00	.05	.53	3.18	13.00	39.06	.00	.00	.00
MAY	.00	.00	.00	.01	.21	2.10	10.84	37.59	.02	.00	.00
JUNE	.00	.00	.00	.00	.19	1.92	11.94	40.37	.00	.00	.00
JULY	.00	.00	.00	.01	.19	2.12	14.15	45.24	.00	.00	.00
AUG	.00	.00	.00	.00	.17	2.11	12.72	40.40	.00	.00	.00
SEPT	.00	.00	.00	.08	.71	4.20	16.72	42.44	.00	.00	.00
OCT	.00	.00	.00	.04	.42	2.91	12.75	38.76	.02	.00	.00
NOV	.00	.00	.00	.16	1.29	6.71	23.55	55.62	.02	.00	.00
DEC	.00	.00	.05	.28	1.61	6.57	20.97	52.18	.00	.00	.00
YEAR	.00	.00	.01	.11	.86	4.64	16.94	44.65	.04	.00	.00

MONTH	VELOCITY THROUGH OPENING										
	.00	1.00	2.00	3.00	4.00	5.00	6.00	7.00	8.00	9.00	10.00
JAN	.00	.00	.00	.00	.00	.00	.00	.00	.00	.00	.00
FEB	.00	.00	.00	.00	.00	.00	.00	.00	.00	.00	.00
MAR	.00	.00	.00	.00	.00	.00	.00	.00	.00	.00	.00
APR	.00	.00	.00	.00	.00	.00	.00	.00	.00	.00	.00
MAY	.00	.00	.00	.00	.00	.00	.00	.00	.00	.00	.00
JUNE	.00	.00	.00	.00	.00	.00	.00	.00	.00	.00	.00
JULY	.00	.00	.00	.00	.00	.00	.00	.00	.00	.00	.00
AUG	.00	.00	.00	.00	.00	.00	.00	.00	.00	.00	.00
SEPT	.00	.00	.00	.00	.00	.00	.00	.00	.00	.00	.00
OCT	.00	.00	.00	.00	.00	.00	.00	.00	.00	.00	.00
NOV	.00	.00	.00	.00	.00	.00	.00	.00	.00	.00	.00
DEC	.00	.00	.00	.00	.00	.00	.00	.00	.00	.00	.00
YEAR	.00	.00	.00	.00	.00	.00	.00	.00	.00	.00	.00

FIG 7.02 PROBABILITY OF VALUES OF
VELOCITY ENTERING THROUGH OPENING

FOR LOCATION 12 FLOW RATE 150 cub meters / sec

FLOW FOR ZERO WIND SPEED= -2.26

BUILDING AERODYNAMICS

In a Forced system every single opening into a smoke reservoir has to be examined separately, and the probabilities for velocities entering every outlet in the smoke reservoir have to be presented. An example of this was shown in Figure 6.10 which is for the case of flow being supplied into the building. The location shown there, location 55, would not be acceptable if it was in a smoke reservoir, as there is a probability of inflow. A further illustration of this solution is shown in Figures 7.02 and 7.03. Data in Figure 7.02 represents a fan supplying 150 m^3 /s into the building, and, if location 12 is in a smoke zone, shows zero probability for flow entering through that location.

MONTH	VELOCITY THROUGH OPENING										
	-10.00	-9.00	-8.00	-7.00	-6.00	-5.00	-4.00	-3.00	-2.00	-1.00	.00
JAN	.00	.00	.00	.09	.58	2.52	9.96	29.60	59.49	.63	.38
FEB	.00	.00	.00	.02	.22	1.36	6.42	22.10	50.76	.81	.47
MAR	.00	.00	.00	.00	.13	1.18	7.03	26.99	61.27	.28	.12
APR	.00	.00	.00	.01	.14	.88	5.08	22.57	59.85	.08	.03
MAY	.00	.00	.00	.00	.05	.38	3.72	20.43	56.20	.18	.08
JUNE	.00	.00	.00	.00	.03	.36	3.55	22.08	58.44	.04	.01
JULY	.00	.00	.00	.00	.05	.40	3.96	25.73	62.39	.00	.00
AUG	.00	.00	.00	.00	.03	.33	3.90	22.99	55.40	.11	.04
SEPT	.00	.00	.00	.03	.20	1.16	6.45	25.95	56.48	.06	.02
OCT	.00	.00	.00	.01	.11	.73	4.75	21.37	51.94	.35	.13
NOV	.00	.00	.00	.03	.33	2.01	10.15	35.67	70.46	.20	.09
DEC	.00	.00	.00	.12	.58	2.38	9.63	31.66	64.18	.06	.02
YEAR	.00	.00	.00	.03	.25	1.35	7.07	26.75	59.17	.29	.15

MONTH	VELOCITY THROUGH OPENING										
	.00	1.00	2.00	3.00	4.00	5.00	6.00	7.00	8.00	9.00	10.00
JAN	.38	.25	.07	.01	.00	.00	.00	.00	.00	.00	.00
FEB	.47	.30	.08	.01	.00	.00	.00	.00	.00	.00	.00
MAR	.12	.06	.00	.00	.00	.00	.00	.00	.00	.00	.00
APR	.03	.01	.00	.00	.00	.00	.00	.00	.00	.00	.00
MAY	.08	.04	.00	.00	.00	.00	.00	.00	.00	.00	.00
JUNE	.01	.00	.00	.00	.00	.00	.00	.00	.00	.00	.00
JULY	.00	.00	.00	.00	.00	.00	.00	.00	.00	.00	.00
AUG	.04	.02	.00	.00	.00	.00	.00	.00	.00	.00	.00
SEPT	.02	.00	.00	.00	.00	.00	.00	.00	.00	.00	.00
OCT	.13	.06	.00	.00	.00	.00	.00	.00	.00	.00	.00
NOV	.09	.05	.00	.00	.00	.00	.00	.00	.00	.00	.00
DEC	.02	.00	.00	.00	.00	.00	.00	.00	.00	.00	.00
YEAR	.15	.09	.02	.00	.00	.00	.00	.00	.00	.00	.00

FIG 7.03 PROBABILITY OF VALUES OF
VELOCITY ENTERING THROUGH OPENING

FOR LOCATION 12 FLOW RATE 100 cub meters / sec

FLOW FOR ZERO WIND SPEED= -1.50

BUILDING AERODYNAMICS

On he other hand, the data of Figure 7.03, for the same situation but with the fan supplying 100 m^3 /s, shows that there is a probability of air entering, and that this latter situation is unacceptable.

Although in the above examples, air was supplied into the volume by the fans outside the smoke reservoirs, a better system might appear to be to place the fans in the smoke reservoirs sucking the smoke out. This is not always a better solution because the action of the fan then is to reduce the internal pressure. This reduction of pressure could cause air to enter other outlets in the smoke reservoir, an unacceptable situation. For this system to work, fans often have to be placed at every outlet location. The only requirement on the Wind Engineer in this case is to ensure that the fans are capable of moving the required volume of smoke against the pressure difference.

In some special cases, for example in a Food Hall of a Department store, the ventilation requirements might require the removal of odours directly by fans in the roof. For the rest of the store, the fire situation might require that the store is pressurised as the cheapest solution for the removal of smoke. In this case it is possible to supply bi-directional fans for the roof extracts in the Food Hall, so that, in the normal operating condition, they extract odours directly, but in the fire situation they are reversed to assist the pressurisation of the store for the removal of smoke from the other openings in the smoke reservoirs. The efficiency of bi-directional fans is lower than that of uni-directional ones, but the difference nowadays is not all that great.

7.3. Smoke Zones.

When a building is large and is to be split into several smoke zones, it is possible that adjoining zones can be connected by malls and other large openings to the one where the fire is assumed to occur. Smoke curtains are dropped from the roof to create the smoke reservoirs in the one zone where there is a fire, no obstructions are made at ground level. Air can then pass in and out of the zone at ground level. The analysis of the situation, discussed in the last two sections takes into account all the openings in the skin of the whole building because this affects the internal pressure. The general approach will be to close the roof openings in the other zones without a fire, and open all those designated roof openings in the fire zone. All doors must be assumed to be open to allow people to leave. The reason for closing adjoining roof openings is that the external pressure on the roof of buildings tends to be negative, and the closing of all those not used for the extraction of the smoke will cause the internal pressure to rise, increasing the pressure difference across the openings in the fire zone forcing the smoke to leave. This applies to both natural and forced systems.

7.4. Make-up Air.

It seems unreasonable to set out on purpose to provide air into the smoke zone, but, to ensure the egress of smoke from the reservoir this is necessary. The provision of make-up air gives the engineer some latitude because the locations of the openings for make-up air are open to choice. The purpose is to ensure as positive a value of internal pressure as possible, so the location / locations of the openings for make-up air can be chosen in regions of positive (or least negative) pressure. They should be positioned, if possible, to ensure that the velocity of the entering air does not annoy people, although in the fire situation this is less important, unless the velocities are excessive and hinder the movement of the people. If the system has different openings in the smoke reservoirs for different wind directions, then there can be different openings for make-up air, controlled by the same computer programme. An occasion for more scenarios!

7.5. False Ceilings.

If a fire is in a passage, or in an adjoining room which discharges into a passage, which has a false ceiling, it must be impossible for the smoke to travel in the space above the ceiling, and to be returned to the passage at a position away from the fire, such that a person, emerging into the passage near the returned smoke, seeing the smoke, would turn away from the smoke and walk into the fire zone.

The same phenomena, although not exactly a false ceiling, must be avoided regardless of the means whereby the smoke is transferred from the location of the fire, or smoke outlet, to another location directly connected to the location of the fire or smoke outlet at some distance from it along which no smoke is travelling.

7.6. Escape Routes.

In most instances smoke reservoirs are at roof level, and any escape routes over the roof must not be through areas where the smoke will be discharged.

However, some smoke discharges from underground premises with forced systems can be at ground level, or a short distance above the ground.

Although it is obvious that the discharge should not be directly over an escape route, the passage of the smoke from the outlet until it has dispersed into the atmosphere should be examined (in the wind tunnel investigation) to ensure that it does not subsequently cross an escape route. It is also necessary to ensure that if the smoke is emitted into a complex of paths and escapes along one path, it is not possible for a person to encounter the smoke and flee along a different path which is free of smoke, but which leads directly back to the fire or smoke outlet.

8. Emissions from Buildings

The subject of "Air Pollution", which results from "Emissions from Buildings" in the first place, is a subject in its own right, and many books are devoted solely to its study. At one time the government in the UK had a laboratory (Warren Spring) entirely devoted to its study. The subject can only be touched on lightly in a book on Building Aerodynamics; the reader who wants an in-depth study should start with such works as "Atmospheric Diffusion" by Frank Pasquill or one of the many books by Dick Scorer. But, for the reader basically interested in buildings and their environment, this chapter will explain the study of emissions which can be integrated with the other aerodynamic studies carried out on buildings.

A distinction can be drawn between the emissions from ventilating systems and emissions of combustion products, kitchen outlets and gases from laboratories, hospitals and other specialist sources. The purpose of a ventilating system is to replace the oxygen supply and to remove minor smells and odours that are produced in the normal way of life. The other emissions can be divided into three categories, toxic, annoying and unnoticeable.

The effect of the wind on the plume is the first concern. When there is no wind at all, the plume will rise vertically until it loses all its vertical momentum and buoyancy, and then the heavier-than-air content of the plume will start to fall and will arrive at the ground at the site of the chimney. If there is very little wind, this phenomena will occur modified by a slight diffusion of the effluent by the wind causing a reduction of the value of maximum ground level concentration, which will occur a short distance downwind of the chimney. Gradually, as the wind speed increases, the value of maximum ground level concentration will reach a minimum value at some distance from the chimney. As the wind speed increases further, the maximum ground level concentration will rise due to the lower height at which the plume levels out. Thereafter the maximum value of ground level concentration will increase with further increase in wind speed due to the progressive lowering of

FIG 8.01 VARIATION OF glc WITH WIND SPEED

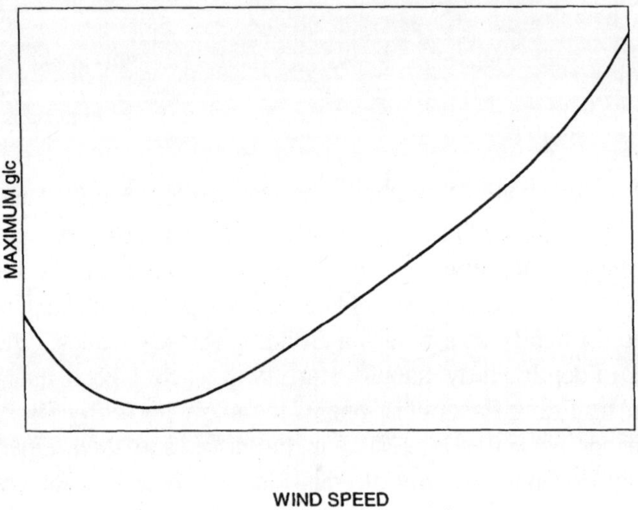

the horizontal plume. This is shown in Figure 8.01

The study divides into two areas, The Far Field and the Near Field. In this book only the Near Field will receive any consideration in depth: this book is not for readers interested in the Far Field.

How then to define the Near Field? There are two aspects that will be covered. The first is to ensure that the effluent leaves the point of emission cleanly, and the second is to ensure that the emitted gases do not interact with the building from which they are emitted, or any surrounding building. "Interact" with the building is a interesting phrase: obviously the effluent, in a reasonable concentration, should not impinge on the surface of the building where there are inlets to a ventilation system otherwise reinjestion will occur. If the building is naturally ventilated using windows, then reinjestion through windows, which can be opened at the whim of the occupants, is not a desirable feature. Doors, dining rooms and managing directors suites are other important areas.

Once clear of the emitting orifice, the effluent will be diluted by mixing with the air, the prime activator of the mixing process is atmospheric turbulence. Turbulence in the duct leading to the orifice is of too small a scale to contribute significantly to diffusion. Near Field covers the emitting building and the surrounding ones as well. But how far? This will become clearer in the following sections.

Conditions for the top of a Tall Chimney are somewhat simpler, so will be considered first.

8.1. The General Flow Pattern.

The flow of the effluents will be considered in two parts, firstly the breaking cleanly from the top of the chimney, and secondly their subsequent passage downwind.

The general assumption will be that the effluent breaks cleanly at the top of the chimney and thereafter continues to rise whilst, at the same time, being turned into the wind direction by the wind. Once the plume has lost its initial vertical velocity it travels downwind, diffusing all the time. In calculations it is often common practice to assume a fictitious point source for the plume at a height above the chimney from which the same downwind plume would have formed in the absence of vertical velocity.

If a jet emerges from a pipe into still air, it diffuses as a cone, the cone angle depending upon the turbulence in the pipe; a value of 7° for the semi-cone angle is an average value. The diffusion of the plume from the chimney does not diffuse in such an orderly fashion because it is diffused by the turbulence in the atmosphere. The large eddies throw whole of bits of the plume, called "Puffs" about in the air without really diffusing them, and the plume is described as "looping". Simultaneously the smaller eddies of the atmosphere are eating into the "puffs", and gradually diffusing them. This is shown in Figure 8.02.

Diffusion is therefor not a nice clean simple situation of the concentration gradually reducing inversely with the square of the distance from the source. At a given point in space, the concentration could be zero for a considerable time, then of a high value as a puff passes, and then back to zero again. The

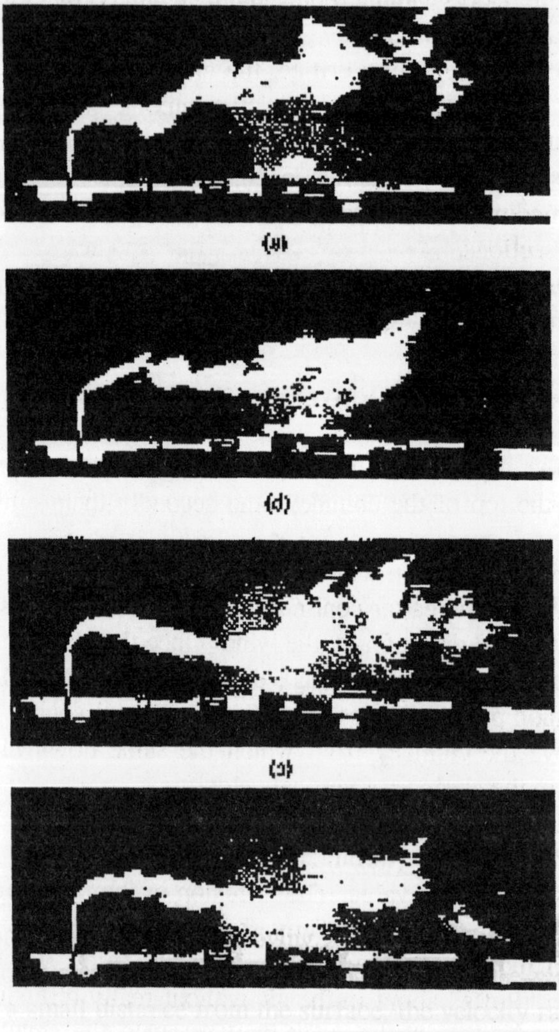

FIG 8.02. CHIMNEY SHOWING LOOPING

mean value of concentration will decrease with distance downwind, but not in a simple inverse square fashion. It is also possible for puffs of high concentration to reach the ground. For a tall chimney it is usually the

"Ground Level Concentration" which is of importance, and this will vary dramatically whether the location is in a puff or not.

8.2. Breaking Cleanly at the Top of a Chimney.

The first essential is that the emission shall break cleanly from the top of the chimney. All readers have seen examples when this does not happen. One is shown in Figure 8.03.

If the plume does not break cleanly from the top of the chimney, the effective height of the chimney is much less than its actual height, and it is even possible for the effluent to reach ground level at the base of the chimney

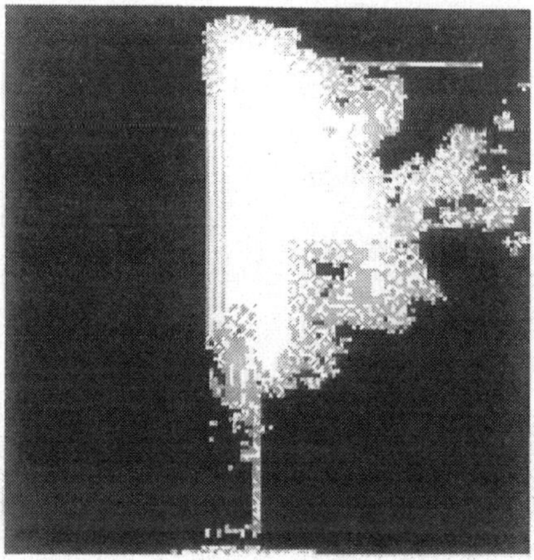

FIG 8.03. NOT BREAKING CLEANLY

8.2.1. Dynamic Similarity for Tall Chimneys.

In section 2.1.1 the requirements for the dynamic similarity of the flow of air over a body are stated in terms of non-dimensional groups of the dependant variables. The same type of study can be undertaken for the effluent emerging from the top of a chimney.

In the chimney the gas has velocity, pressure, density and viscosity. Outside the air has density, velocity, ambient pressure, viscosity and turbulence. Viscosity can be eliminated in a discussion of separation from the lip of the chimney.

The velocity of the gasses in the chimney will be determined by the pressure at entrance to the chimney and the pressure at the top, and it is normal to assume that the internal and external pressures at the top of the chimney are equal..

The chimney can be considered as a member in an airstream, the air generating a pressure around the external surface of the member. But the flow pattern around the top and sides (within about 4 diameters of the top) of a tall chimney is very complex as the surface patterns of Figure 8.04 shows. Figure 8.04(a) is for Reynolds Number of 0.14×10^6 with no efflux, (b) Re = 2.7×10^6 with no efflux, (c) Re = 5.4×10^6 with no efflux, and (d) Re = 5.4×10^6 with efflux = 0.3V. The variation of pressure around the rim of the chimney is almost impossible to quantify in simple terms.

The study of section 2.1.1 showed that all the "Numbers" were, in fact, ratios of the inertia force on the element of air to another force on the same

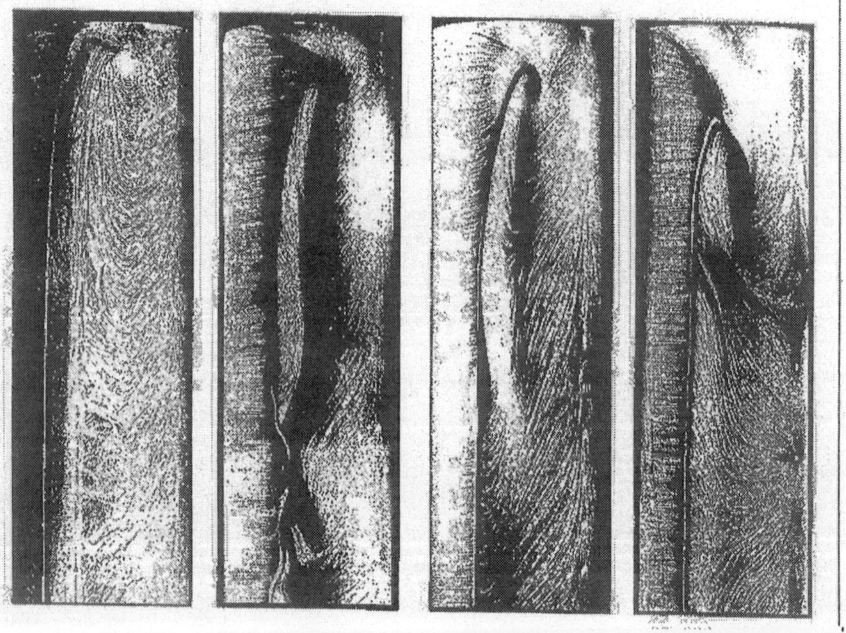

(a) (b) (c) (d)

FIG 8.04. FLOW PATTERNS AT TOP OF CHIMNEY

element, depending on the property considered. If the same approach is applied in this case, then the dynamic similarity should depend upon the ratio of the inertia force of the internal gasses to the inertia force of the surrounding air. Thus it would appear that the requirement for similarity of two flows is that the ratio of inertia forces external and internal should be the same. Thus

$$\rho_g V_g^{\,2} = \rho_a V_a^{\,2},$$

where ρ_g and V_g are the density and velocity of the gasses in the chimney and ρ_a and V_a are the density and the velocity of the wind outside.

The temperature difference between the gasses and the air on emission is often small, so, in the majority of cases, the requirement for similarity reduces to the velocity ratio

$$V_g \,/\, V_a .$$

There are times when the temperature of the gasses is important, and in that case, the requirement for similarity is for the ratio of inertias to be the same.

8.2.2. The Value of the Velocity Ratio.

The value of the Velocity Ratio is defined as the ratio of the mean Efflux Velocity to the 15-minute average wind speed at the height of the top of the chimney.

It is our experience that the flow will break cleanly from the top of a tall chimney when the velocity ratio is between 1 and 1.5. In Figure 8.05 are shown two photographs for velocity ratios of 0.8 and 1.3.

Before the use of cine cameras, and later video cameras or camcorders, became common practice, still photographs were taken. In that case a great number of stills had to be taken for each situation in an attempt to capture the extreme patterns, but even then no information was available on the frequency of each type of pattern. The stills chosen for this book have the same drawback, but they are chosen to illustrate the situation; any serious decision would be taken using the video.

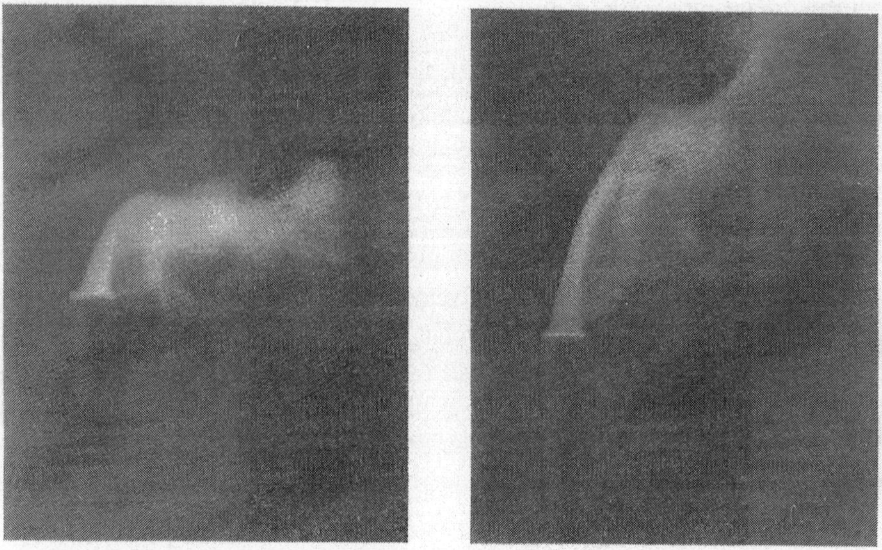

Velocity Ratio = 0.8 Velocity Ratio 1.3

FIG 8.05. FLOW AT CHIMNEY TOPS

8.2.3. Influence of Adjoining Buildings or Members.

Adjoining buildings or members can have a considerable effect on the performance of a chimney.

To illustrate an extreme example of interference, consider the case when an existing boiler house becomes too small, and a larger boiler house and associated chimney are constructed adjoining the original building. At one phase of the development the two chimneys are present simultaneously: the smaller chimney being still in use. This situation is depicted in Figures 8.06 and 8.07, the wind in both cases blows from left to right. In Figure 8.06 the wind direction is from the small chimney to the large one. The lower smaller chimney discharges into the oncoming flow of the large chimney and it is expected that there will be downflow in the front of the large chimney just as there is a downflow in the front of all buildings. However the interesting situation is when the wind direction is from the large to the small chimney (Figure 8.07). The small chimney is in the wake of the large chimney, and, under certain circumstances, the effluent flows upwind in the wake of the

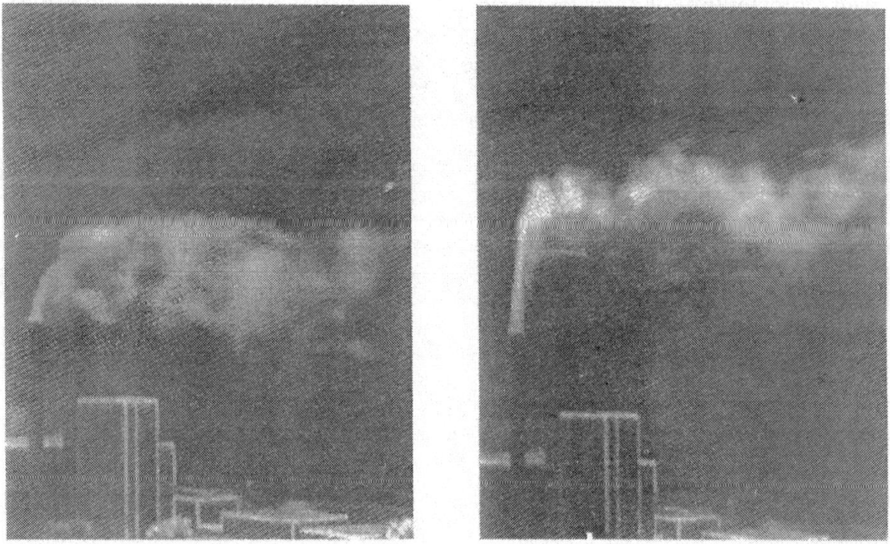

FIG 8.06. FLOW FROM SMALL CHIMNEY TO LARGE

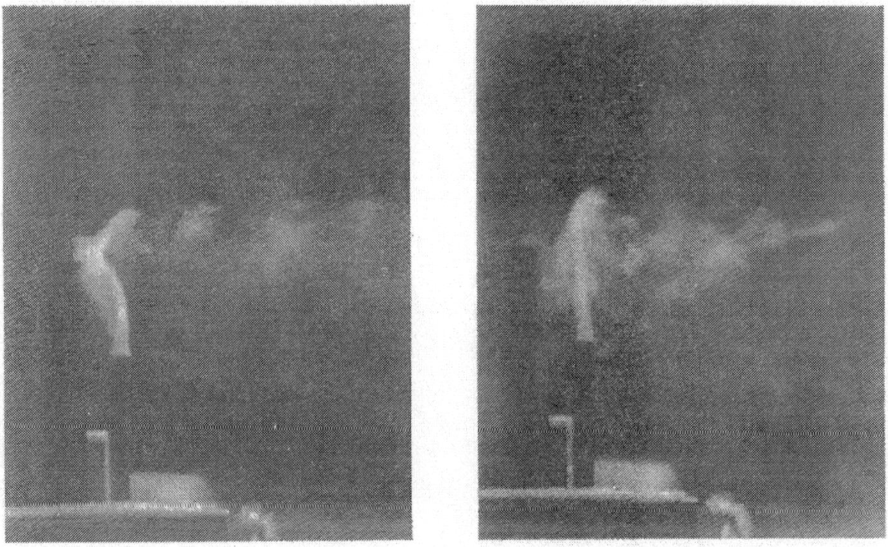

FIG 8.07. FLOW FROM LARGE CHIMNEY TO SMALL

large chimney until it reaches its surface, whereafter it flows in all directions, some down to ground level. The left hand photographs are for a velocity ratio of 1.2, and the right hand photographs for a velocity ratio of 2.5.

8.2.4. Importance of Parameters.

There are two parameters in this study; the Height of the chimney and the Velocity Ratio.

The height of a chimney can be determined as that required to provide the necessary amount of natural draught for the boiler, or other equipment, to operate. In that case the height of the chimney is determined from non-aerodynamic considerations. For the calculation of the height of a chimney from these considerations see Section 8.5.

In the past, in those cases where the height of the chimney is not required to produce draught, a "One and a Quarter" Rule was used wherein the height of a chimney was required to be 1.25 times the height of the building on which the chimney was situated. No mention was made of Velocity Ratio.

It will be obvious from Figure 8.03 that, if the effluent did not break cleanly from the top of the chimney, then the height of the chimney became of academic interest only. When the effluent gets into the wake of the chimney, it flows downwards until it is "plucked off" the surface by the wind flowing around the chimney. Thus the effluent starts its journey in the atmosphere at a considerable distance below the top of the chimney. The "virtual point source" (it is now a virtual line source) is then well below the height of the chimney, and the resulting Ground Level Concentration is equivalent to that from a much shorter chimney. The advantage of height for the chimney has been lost. Even applying the 1.25 rule, it is possible for the effluent to travel down the chimney sides and rear, and enter the separated flow over the building itself, with the possibility of entering the air intakes on the building.

The simplest solution would be to state that the Velocity Ratio should be high enough for the effluent to break cleanly from the top of the chimney (remembering that the atmospheric wind speed increases with height), and that the height of the chimney be determined such that the Ground Level Concentration is everywhere acceptable.

8.2.5. Ground Level Concentration.

This is usually spoken of as a nice constant value. Measurement of plumes being emitted into a turbulence-free airstream show the effluent diffusing within a cone from the virtual point source, the concentration within the cone being constant at a given distance downwind from the source. In practice the flow is completely different. Figure 8.02 shows the plume breaking up into a series of puffs in which the concentration is high. The delivery of a puff to the ground means a high value of local concentration while the puff is in contact, followed by an extremely low level of concentration at other times. In practice all measurements of concentration are made by instruments which have a finite sampling time. If the sample averaging time is long, a constant value of glc (ground level concentration) will be obtained. If the sampling time is shorter, but only contains the arrival of a few puffs, the value will be higher and variable depending upon the number of puffs included, but if the sampling time is shorter that the stay time of a single puff, then the values will be extremely variable from about zero when no puff is present, to the order of a high percentage of the concentration on emission in the middle of a puff.

This topic is further discussed in Section 10.1.7.

8.2.6. Concentration on Emission.

If the emission is toxic, or has a safety exposure limit, they my advice is that the concentration on emission should never be greater than 10% of the Safety Limit for Short Exposure. Documents presenting exposure limits are available in the UK in such documents as "Occupation Exposure Limits 1988: Guidance Note from the Health and Safety Executive". Such a document states both Short and Long Term concentrations for nearly all chemicals used in industry.

A difficulty arises when a factory is built for prescribed chemical processes. During its life span, other work may be carried out therein: it is the duty of the commissioning team for the alterations to ensure that the concentrations at emission of new chemicals meet the requirements for the new chemicals.

Should the new product not meet the requirements, then dilution must be made in the chimney before emission. It is nearly always better to make this dilution in the chimney or just before. The reasons are that if air from within the building is used for dilution, this air has already been heated or cooled, and is expensive air. It is better to take air at atmospheric conditions, cheap air, for dilution purposes. The second reason is that the internal area of ducts within the building will have to be enlarged to pass the additional volume of air or there will be additional pressure loss in the ducting.

8.2.7. Vertical Velocities and Inversions etc.

In a neutral atmosphere, the vertical movement of the plume arises from the initial vertical velocity in the chimney. It is essential that, if the chimney is not of constant diameter, that its cross sectional area decreases towards the top. This is to ensure that the efflux velocity is maximum at the point of emission. Reduction in area, and consequent increase in velocity anywhere else in the system, will give rise to higher losses in the ducting and the chimney.

On leaving the chimney the vertical velocity reduces to almost zero by the entrainment of atmospheric air, so the initial momentum of the plume is dissipated quickly, and the concept of a virtual point source is realised.

The buoyancy force on elements within the plume due to the difference of temperature between the puff and the outside air persists for much longer, and a hot plume will continue to rise over a considerable distance, well into the Far Field.

Inversions are layers of the atmosphere which are very stable. This was explained in Section 1.4.2.1. When a chimney discharges under an inversion, the remaining vertical motion is destroyed at the inversion, and the plume spreads out under it. The air in the inversion layer has very little turbulence, so almost no mixing takes place at the upper boundary of the plume: all diffusion takes place on the underside, so that, by the time the ground is reached, values of glc can still be high. This is the one example where high temperature plumes are at a distinct advantage.

8.2.8. Dealing with Many Chimneys on a Building.

When the 1.25 rule is followed, the chimney becomes a feature of the building. When the building is a laboratory, then the roof can bristle with chimneys. Some architects find this unpleasant aesthetically, or not consistent with the lines of their building. To combat this they sometimes collect the outlets from a number of, fume cupboards say, and emit the effluent through a limited number of chimneys. This has a series of drawbacks associated with it. Firstly, it appears illogical that, when the purpose is to disperse the effluent from a number of sources, that they should be collected together at a single point, with all the internal ductwork which that requires, before being delivered to the atmosphere at a single point for dispersion. Logic would suggest that the emissions should be made from a number of sources spread over as great an area as possible, so that the overall dispersion is part spatial and part atmospheric. Secondly the efflux velocity has to be of at least a minimum value for the clean break at the chimney top, clearance of the building itself and its surroundings and for an acceptable value of glc when the effluent eventually reaches the ground. If the efflux comes from a number of sources, then all sources must be operating to obtain the required efflux velocity. If some sources are not operating, then the efflux velocity will be reduced, unless separate ducts are used for each source; this means multi-flue chimneys. Part load operation from a single source means reduced efflux velocity unless the area at outlet can be controlled.

The architect, faced with a collection of chimneys at one place obeying the 1.25 rule, thinks of containing them in some "feature" which is consistent with his concept of the building rather than a single chimney-like sheath. If he encloses them in a structure, leaving the tops of the chimneys just showing out of the top of the "shroud", then what he has produced can, in certain circumstances, behave as a building which is 1.25 times the height of the original building, with chimney stacks of zero height.

There are some design features which will allow this type of chimney cluster to work. A solid structure behaves just as a building with all the separations and vortices associated with a building. The sheath must be made, to the wind at least, to appear unlike a solid building. For example, if the sides of the sheath are made of louvres, at least for their upper third. This will allow flow through the sheath and will prevent there being a separated flow over the "roof" of the sheath, in fact, if the louvres are flat members inclined to prevent the rain entering, they will also be aligned to give the air flowing through them an upwards velocity component, thus helping the effluent to rise. This form has the additional advantage that it will hinder, if not kill, the formation of "leading edge vortices" from the upwind corner of the sheath. This orientation of the slats also makes the sheath less visible from the ground, but this "disadvantage", because it has been conceived as a "feature", can be overcome by careful choice of material and colour.

8.3. Emissions from the Roof of a Building.

In the last section it was described as illogical to collect the outlets from a number of sources into an internal duct and to connect these to a single chimney somewhere on the roof. The same process might be repeated several times so that there could be several large chimneys, with the problems mentioned in the last section. It would be logical to emit the effluent as close to its source as possible. This would entail a large number of "Chimneys" on the roof, a requirement which would be abhorrent to most architects.

The answer is to have low chimneys, 600 mm to 800 mm tall (the choice of 800 mm as a maximum is because this is the greatest height of light chimney which will not need staying). These do not comply with the 1.25 times rule. If placed away from the edge of the roof, they could be invisible to anyone standing fairly close to the building; only being visible from afar, and even then not appearing as a feature. But they must work.

To make these low chimneys work, the efflux velocity should be at least 2.0 to 2.5 times the value of the 15 minute average wind speed at the top of the building. These values are much higher than the values necessary to make the effluent break cleanly from a tall chimney. In practice this means an efflux velocity of about 25 m/s. The separated region on the top of a building is usually of the order of a meter in depth, so these low chimneys are within the separated region on the roof. To work they have to "punch" the effluent through the shear layer which divides the separated region on the roof from the active air above, and still retain sufficient vertical velocity to avoid being entrained in the wake of the building. The efflux velocity of 25 m/s achieves this in most applications.

To make the point more clearly, a series of still photographs from a video record of a study are included as Figure 8.08. It is impossible to understand the problem from a still from a video, because the still could be anywhere within the cycle of a puff reaching the ground and there being no puff near the ground; the frequency of the arrival of puffs at ground level is the important perameter, and this information is missing with stills. However, one still from each value of velocity ratio are presented in Figure 8.08. The values of velocity ratio of 1.0, 1.5, 2.0, 2.5 and 3.0 cover the useful range.

Occasionally a cap is placed over a chimney, which effectively produces zero vertical velocity component on emission; this is disastrous as shown on Figure 8.09 for the same conditions as Figure 8.08.

Velocity Ratio = 1.0

Velocity Ratio = 1.5

FIG 8.08 SMOKE PATTERNS Velocity Ratio = 2.0

Velocity Ratio = 2.5

FIG 8.08 SMOKE PATTERNS Velocity Ratio 3.0

FIG 8.09 SMOKE PATTERN Velocity Ratio ZERO

When the 1.25 rule has been implemented (although I cannot find a reference to the original document presenting the arguments arriving at this value),it is accepted by planning authorities and planning permission will usually follow, even when the efflux velocity is so low that the effluent would dribble down the sides of the chimney. On the other hand, because the use of low chimneys is a new and unestablished procedure, it is likely that the low chimney solution would require a demonstration that it works: this would involve a wind tunnel investigation.

Noise is another pollutant, and it is our experience that an emission of greater than 25 m/s creates noise, and would not be recommended.

This low chimney system works because, by using many chimneys, the effluents have been distributed spatially, and, for a given wind direction, no single area receives pollution from two chimneys at the same time, so the quantity of pollution at a given location is reduced. Because each chimney is associated with few sources (fume cupboards say) it is easy to maintain full efflux velocity in the event of some of the sources not operating.

8.4. Measurements of Concentrations.

The measurement of Concentrations in wind tunnel investigations is discussed in Section 10.1.7.

8.5. The Chimney Effect.

A chimney works in producing a natural draught for a boiler because the weight of the hot gasses in the chimney is less than the weight of a similar column of cold air outside the chimney. As the pressure for both columns at the top of the chimney are the same, the pressure at the base of the chimney must be below that of the external column. This is shown in Figure 8.10.
Assume that the mean internal temperature in the chimney is T° C above ambient, and that the pressures inside and outside are the same at the top of the chimney where the efflux mixes with the atmosphere. Then, by the equation of state (see Section 1.4.1);

$$p = \rho_i R T_i \quad = \rho_o R T_o$$

where p is the pressure, R the Gas Constant, ρ the density and T the temperature.

FIG 8.10 CHIMNEY

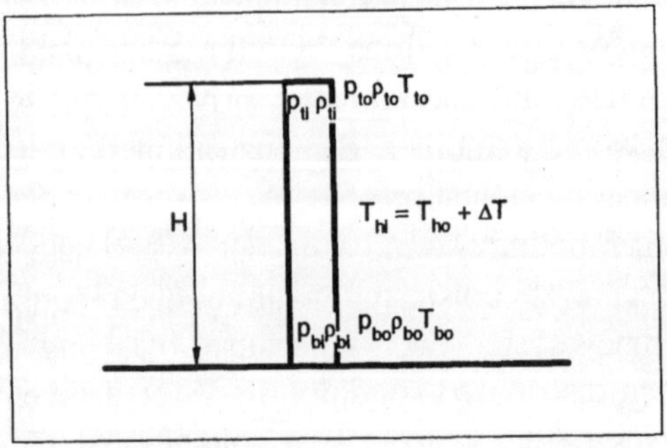

At the top of the chimney

$$\rho_i = \rho_o \times T_o / T_i$$

where suffices i and o refer to inside and outside.

The difference between the pressure at the base and top of the chimney is equal to the weight, per unit area, of the gases in the chimney

$$p_b - p_t = \rho \, g \, H,$$

where b and t refer to bottom and top respectively. Assuming that the difference in density inside and outside the chimney is the same at the bottom as at the top: this introduces an error in the final answer of about 0.2%, then the difference between the pressure at the base outside the chimney and the pressure at the base inside the chimney is given by

$$dp_b = p_{bo} - p_{bi} = (\rho_{bo} - \rho_{bi}) \, g \, H = \rho_o \, g \, H(T_i - T_o) / T_i \, .$$

Thus, for a 100 m high chimney with a mean temperature difference up the chimney of 50°C and an outside temperature of 15°C, the pressure difference created by the chimney would be 231 N/m^2, or 0.93 inches of water.

Occasionally the term "Inverse Chimney Effect" is used in reference to the flow up the face of a building in the sun. It means that the air in contact with the surface of the building is heated more than the general mass of air and so becomes lighter than the general mass, and will then flow up the face of the building.

9. Sailing

Sailing is mostly carried out in coastal areas where there are on-shore and off-shore winds to supplement the winds generated by normal mechanisms. These extra winds are usually of the gentle sort, in Beaufort ranges 2 to 4. During the development of London Docklands, many of whose waterways were to be used for water sports, discussions took place with sailing enthusiasts about conditions conducive to enjoyable sailing. As some of the clubs were to service beginners, their requirements, as well as those of experienced sailors, who want a challenge, had to be taken into consideration.

9.1 The Problem.

The major factor in the determination of suitability for sailing was wind speed. Three aspects of wind speed were considered. Firstly the mean value of wind speed, say an average over 10 minutes, was considered to be the most important. Secondly the turbulence, or the change of wind speed with time at a given location requires serious attention. Thirdly wind shear, the variation of wind speed with distance, can cause problems.

How were these three aspects to be written into "Criteria of Acceptability"? The first was relatively easy; discussions with sailors suggested limiting values of wind speed between which sailing would be possible. Sailors usually talk in terms of the Beaufort Scale, and the Beaufort Scale includes both mean wind speed and turbulence, the turbulence being specified by the environment. The same approach was made in determining the criteria of acceptability for built environments, and this was discussed in Chapter 4. In that chapter a shopping centre was used as the standard for the estimation of the relationship between mean wind speed and gustspeed. This would be inappropriate for sailing, so another standard must be chosen. Off-shore winds will have more turbulence than on-shore ones, so the intensity of turbulence for off-shore winds is a good starting point. But what fetch should be considered?

Should a long beach be the standard, or the edge of a quay with buildings along the front? Away from the coast, high winds create high waves which generate turbulence. At 2 m height above the sea the Turbulence Intensity is about 0.2 for strong winds, with higher values in rougher seas. If we accept the sailors estimate of the turbulence intensity implicit in the Beaufort Scale, and refer to the hourly-average numerical values in Figure 9.01, we should obtain comparison between observation of wind speeds and actual values. We will therefor take the hourly-average values for the ranges of the Beaufort Scale as the values defining both mean wind speed and turbulence.

Beaufort Force	Hourly-Average Windspeed m/s	Descriptionn of Wind	Noticable Effect of Wind
0	<0.45	Calm	Sea is mirror smooth
1	0.45 - 1.55	Light	Small wavelets like scales, but no foam crests
2	1.55 - 3.35	Light	Waves are short and more pronounced
3	3.35 - 5.60	Light	Crests begin to break: foam has glassy appearance, not yet white
4	5.60 - 8.25	Moderate	Waves are longer: many white horses
5	8.25 - 10.95	Fresh	Waves are more pronounced: white foam crests seen everywhere
6	10.95 - 14.10	Strong	Larger waves form: foam crests more extensive
7	14.10 - 17.20	Strong	Sea heaps up: foam begins to blow in streaks
8	17.20 - 20.80	Gale	Waves increase visibly: foam is blown in dense streaks
9	20.80 - 24.35	Gale	Waves increase further: continuous foam in streaks
10	24.35 - 28.40	Strong Gale	High waves with long overhanging crests: great foam patches
11	28.40 - 32.40	Storm	Waves so high that ships within sight are hidden in troughs; sea covered with streaky foam
12	> 32.40	Hurricane	Air filled with spray

FIGURE 9.01. THE BEAUFORT SCALE

The matter of shear has still to be considered, and this is more difficult. Ultimately it was decided to neglect shear in the calculations, but to consider it when discussing the results.

As a result of those discussions the following criteria were written to assess the suitability for sailing:

for beginners; wind speeds between 4 and 10 knots
for normal sailors; wind speeds between 4 and 14 knots
for expert sailors; wind speeds between 4 and 18 knots.

When the contours of "efficiency", defined in Section 9.3, were plotted, then regions of rapid change of efficiency would be examined with regard to the effect of shear.

9.2. The Theory.

It is assumed that the Probability Distribution of the "Meteorological Standard Wind Speed" close to the surface of the water follows a Weibull Distribution with reasonable accuracy.

Thus the Probability that the "Meteorological Standard Wind Speed" is between V_1 and V_2 is given by

$$P(V_1 < V < V_2, WD) = p\{exp[-(V_1/c)^k] - exp[-(V_2/c)^k]\},$$

where p is the probability that the wind is from wind direction WD, and c and k are the Weibull parameters for the Meteorological Standard Wind Speed. If the permissible limits of the local values of wind speed are v_1 and v_2 and the ratio of local to Meteorological Standard wind speed at the location is R; that is to say

$$R = v_1/V_1 = v_2/V_2,$$

the Cumulative Probability that the local wind speed shall be between the limits of v_1 and v_2 can be rewritten

$$P(v_1 < v < v_2, WD) = p\{exp[-(v_1/Rc)^k] - exp[-(v_2/Rc)^k]\},$$

and if the ratio of the limiting wind speeds is F, such that

$$F = v_2 / v_1 ,$$

the equation becomes

$$P(v_1 < v < v_2 , WD) = p\{exp[-(v_1 / Rc)^k] - exp[-(Fv_1 / Rc)^k]\}$$

$$= p\{exp[-(v_1 / Rc)^k] - (exp[-(v_1 / Rc)^k)^G \}$$

where $G = F^k$.

For simplification in writing, let

$exp[-(v_1 /Rc)^k = B$, then

$$P(v_1 < v < v_2 , WD) = P(dv,WD) = p\{ B - B^G)$$

and for a maximum value of the Cumulative Probability Function

$$dP(dv , WD) / dR = 0$$

or $$dP(dv,WD) / dB \times dB / d\{-(v_1 /Rc)^k \} \times d\{-(v_1 / Rc)^k \} / dR = 0.$$

$dP(dv,WD) / dB = 1 - G \times B^{(F-1)}$, and

$dB / d\{-(v_1 /Rc)^k\} = exp \{-(v_1 / Rc)^k \}$, which cannot = 0, and

$d\{-(v_1 /Rc)^k \} / dR = kc/v_1 \times (v_1 /Rc)^{(k+1)}$, which cannot = 0,

thus for $dP(dv,WD) / dR = 0$

$$-x^k = ln\ B = ln\ (1/F^k) / (F^k - 1)$$

$$x^k = (k \times ln(F)) / (F^k - 1)$$

where $x = v_1 / Rc$,

or $R = v_1 / cx$.

This is the value of R which gives the maximum Cumulative Probability for sailing; a value for which can be calculated by inserting this value into the equation defining B above, and substituting that value into the next equation.

9.3 Application.

A conventional wind environmental wind tunnel investigation is performed, in which the ratio of the local wind speed to the Meteorological Standard Wind Speed is measured at all locations. The only difference is that the locations chosen form a grid covering the whole of the water, see Figure 9.02. The 15 minute average values for the wind speed ratio (R) are used. An example of these data is presented in Figure 9.03.

The Cumulative Probability that the local wind speed shall be between the required limits is calculated from the equation

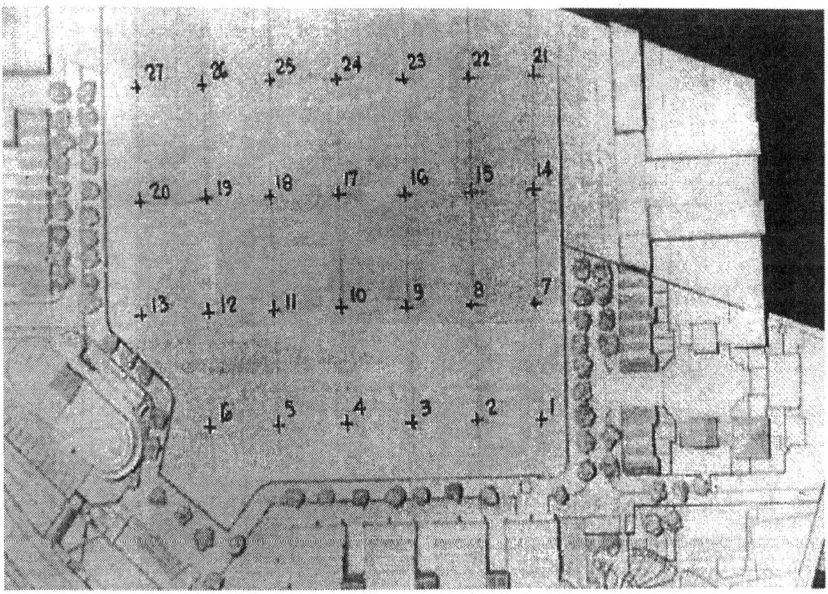

FIG 9.02 SHOWING LOCATION GRID

LOC	AVTM S/M	0	30	60	90	120	150	180	210	240	270	300	330
1	3	50	75	74	56	29	40	35	38	28	41	47	50
	15	22	44	40	22	7	20	11	16	8	13	17	17
2	3	64	74	67	58	52	40	43	50	49	62	44	61
	15	28	38	35	25	14	17	23	22	17	16	13	23
3	3	64	62	53	61	61	64	43	53	74	43	40	58
	15	25	31	25	26	25	23	16	23	32	14	11	20
4	3	50	61	47	62	80	61	53	68	47	62	46	49
	15	17	26	20	32	34	26	17	32	17	22	20	19
5	3	49	61	47	84	87	70	53	59	62	81	74	70
	15	16	25	34	43	32	29	17	25	20	53	41	32
6	3	50	53	89	73	87	56	44	47	73	74	68	73
	15	23	26	47	40	47	20	13	14	40	43	37	25
7	3	62	86	83	62	61	43	41	31	50	50	56	50
	15	29	46	47	26	25	14	14	7	14	11	17	16
8	3	71	87	89	83	71	58	34	53	61	67	46	56
	15	32	52	53	41	32	13	13	16	23	17	14	20
9	3	67	84	95	93	70	71	44	61	74	64	44	58
	15	31	47	56	50	22	20	17	25	31	25	16	22
10	3	68	89	92	78	70	75	52	68	83	74	64	62
	15	28	46	55	44	23	26	19	31	29	37	25	22
11	3	59	80	90	81	64	83	47	70	47	71	61	52
	15	20	41	55	43	29	28	19	34	11	37	20	16
12	3	64	74	87	75	81	58	53	75	70	77	40	58
	15	20	35	50	41	37	22	19	31	25	32	10	22
13	3	71	44	55	50	53	65	73	53	62	19	22	52
	15	25	20	25	22	23	22	29	17	28	5	8	20
14	3	73	89	96	95	29	43	31	37	56	71	61	62
	15	35	55	55	43	10	20	13	14	26	16	22	25
15	3	71	98	111	102	53	75	64	67	77	73	64	73
	15	34	59	70	56	17	43	19	26	34	22	23	34
16	3	67	92	120	104	86	75	64	67	81	61	61	75
	15	32	58	71	58	29	37	20	29	44	26	25	37
17	3	65	87	101	89	87	75	67	71	84	74	62	73
	15	26	49	58	47	38	34	29	34	37	32	22	34
18	3	61	93	92	102	105	70	75	80	73	62	64	65
	15	25	47	55	53	50	34	35	40	25	29	17	32
19	3	43	78	93	87	92	65	73	83	65	52	53	65
	15	16	41	56	50	47	28	34	40	20	14	19	28
20	3	38	80	83	89	77	68	58	71	70	31	50	49
	15	11	35	47	53	40	23	26	28	31	10	22	23
21	3	81	93	102	92	49	31	62	50	65	68	53	55
	15	43	56	68	47	14	8	37	16	31	26	22	23
22	3	80	98	107	93	81	43	78	55	71	86	71	64
	15	40	61	70	52	35	13	46	17	37	34	29	26
23	3	83	102	111	107	111	49	87	75	89	70	68	67
	15	40	62	70	55	56	13	47	29	44	32	26	28
24	3	68	105	114	87	105	49	89	74	95	77	65	67
	15	29	62	71	53	53	16	41	37	46	35	31	26
25	3	68	96	108	95	108	71	73	90	92	68	75	58
	15	25	53	68	53	62	23	31	44	35	31	31	20
26	3	67	84	101	102	89	80	81	78	71	61	62	50
	15	22	46	62	61	53	31	34	40	28	25	31	16
27	3	49	96	102	99	80	67	64	90	75	56	62	43
	15	17	50	53	59	41	26	29	43	35	22	31	14
28	3	74	80	98	86	84	32	55	92	90	78	68	64
	15	40	46	62	47	44	10	22	53	37	34	31	28

FIG 9.03 VELOCITIES AS PERCENTAGES OF THE REFERENCE VELOCITY

$$P(v_1 < v < v_2, WD) = p\{exp[-(v_1 / Rc)^k] - exp[-(v_2 / Rc)^k]\}$$

for all wind directions and for every location studied. These data are presented in Figures 9.04 to 9.07. For a location the first row of figures are values of the Cumulative Probability Percentage for sailing for each wind direction, and the total for all wind directions is presented in the column headed "ALL".

The second row of figures are the velocity percentages (R) from the wind tunnel study.

WIND DIRECTION

LOC	0	30	60	90	120	150	180	210	240	270	300	330	ALL	EFF
1	.9	4.1	4.2	.3	.0	.1	.0	.7	.0	.1	.0	.0	10.5	16.6
	22.0	44.0	40.0	22.0	7.0	20.0	11.0	16.0	8.0	13.0	17.0	17.0		
2	2.2	3.4	3.3	.7	.0	.0	.5	3.2	1.7	.7	.0	.1	15.9	25.1
	28.0	38.0	35.0	25.0	14.0	17.0	23.0	22.0	17.0	16.0	13.0	23.0		
3	1.6	2.3	1.3	.8	.2	.2	.0	3.6	10.9	.3	.0	.0	21.1	33.2
	25.0	31.0	25.0	26.0	25.0	23.0	16.0	23.0	32.0	14.0	11.0	20.0		
4	.1	1.3	.4	1.6	.7	.3	.1	7.1	1.7	3.4	.2	.0	16.9	26.6
	17.0	26.0	20.0	32.0	34.0	26.0	17.0	32.0	17.0	22.0	20.0	19.0		
5	.1	1.1	3.2	3.0	.6	.4	.1	4.5	3.7	8.0	3.2	.8	28.5	45.0
	16.0	25.0	34.0	43.0	32.0	29.0	17.0	25.0	20.0	53.0	41.0	32.0		
6	1.1	1.3	4.9	2.6	1.4	.1	.0	.3	12.7	8.7	2.7	.2	36.0	56.7
	23.0	26.0	47.0	40.0	47.0	20.0	13.0	14.0	40.0	43.0	37.0	25.0		
7	2.4	4.3	4.9	.8	.2	.0	.0	.0	.4	.0	.0	.0	13.1	20.6
	29.0	46.0	47.0	26.0	25.0	14.0	14.0	7.0	14.0	11.0	17.0	16.0		
8	3.0	4.6	5.2	2.7	.6	.0	.0	.7	5.8	1.1	.0	.0	23.8	37.5
	32.0	52.0	53.0	41.0	32.0	13.0	13.0	16.0	23.0	17.0	14.0	20.0		
9	2.8	4.3	5.3	3.5	.1	.1	.1	4.5	10.5	4.8	.0	.1	36.1	56.8
	31.0	47.0	56.0	50.0	22.0	20.0	17.0	25.0	31.0	25.0	16.0	22.0		
10	2.2	4.3	5.3	3.0	.1	.3	.1	6.8	9.5	8.3	.7	.1	40.8	64.4
	28.0	46.0	55.0	44.0	23.0	26.0	19.0	31.0	29.0	37.0	25.0	22.0		
11	.5	3.8	5.3	3.0	.4	.4	.1	7.7	.0	8.3	.2	.0	29.7	46.8
	20.0	41.0	55.0	43.0	29.0	28.0	19.0	34.0	11.0	37.0	20.0	16.0		
12	.5	3.0	5.1	2.7	.9	.2	.1	6.8	7.2	7.3	.0	.1	33.9	53.5
	20.0	35.0	50.0	41.0	37.0	22.0	19.0	31.0	25.0	32.0	10.0	22.0		
13	1.6	.3	1.3	.3	.1	.2	1.4	1.1	9.0	.0	.0	.0	15.3	24.1
	25.0	20.0	25.0	22.0	23.0	22.0	29.0	17.0	28.0	5.0	8.0	20.0		
14	3.5	4.6	5.3	3.0	.0	.1	.0	.3	7.8	.7	.3	.2	25.8	40.6
	35.0	55.0	55.0	43.0	10.0	20.0	13.0	14.0	26.0	16.0	22.0	25.0		
15	3.3	4.6	5.0	3.8	.0	.9	.1	5.0	11.6	3.4	.5	1.0	39.1	61.7
	34.0	59.0	70.0	56.0	17.0	43.0	19.0	26.0	34.0	22.0	23.0	34.0		
16	3.0	4.6	5.0	3.8	.4	.7	.2	6.2	12.8	5.2	.7	1.3	43.9	69.2
	32.0	58.0	71.0	58.0	29.0	37.0	20.0	29.0	44.0	26.0	25.0	37.0		
17	1.8	4.4	5.3	3.3	.9	.6	1.4	7.7	12.3	7.3	.3	1.0	46.5	73.2
	26.0	49.0	58.0	47.0	38.0	34.0	29.0	34.0	37.0	32.0	22.0	34.0		
18	1.6	4.3	5.3	3.7	1.5	.6	2.4	8.7	7.2	6.4	.0	.8	42.4	66.8
	25.0	47.0	55.0	53.0	50.0	34.0	35.0	40.0	25.0	29.0	17.0	32.0		
19	.1	3.8	5.3	3.5	1.4	.4	2.2	8.7	3.7	.3	.1	.4	29.8	46.9
	16.0	41.0	56.0	50.0	47.0	28.0	34.0	40.0	20.0	14.0	19.0	28.0		
20	.0	3.0	4.9	3.7	1.1	.2	.9	5.8	10.5	.0	.3	.1	30.5	48.0
	11.0	35.0	47.0	53.0	40.0	23.0	26.0	28.0	31.0	10.0	22.0	23.0		
21	4.3	4.6	5.1	3.3	.0	.0	2.7	.7	10.5	5.2	.3	.1	36.9	58.1
	43.0	56.0	68.0	47.0	14.0	8.0	37.0	16.0	31.0	26.0	22.0	23.0		
22	4.1	4.6	5.0	3.6	.8	.0	3.7	1.1	12.3	7.8	1.3	.2	44.5	70.2
	40.0	61.0	70.0	52.0	35.0	13.0	46.0	17.0	37.0	34.0	29.0	26.0		
23	4.1	4.6	5.0	3.7	1.7	.0	3.8	6.2	12.8	7.3	.9	.4	50.4	79.4
	40.0	62.0	70.0	55.0	56.0	13.0	47.0	29.0	44.0	32.0	26.0	28.0		
24	2.4	4.6	5.0	3.7	1.6	.0	3.2	8.3	12.7	8.0	1.7	.2	51.3	80.9
	29.0	62.0	71.0	53.0	53.0	16.0	41.0	37.0	46.0	35.0	31.0	26.0		
25	1.6	4.6	5.1	3.7	1.8	.2	1.8	8.9	11.9	7.1	1.7	.0	48.1	75.8
	25.0	53.0	68.0	53.0	62.0	23.0	31.0	44.0	35.0	31.0	31.0	20.0		
26	.9	4.3	5.3	3.9	1.6	.5	2.2	8.7	9.0	4.8	1.7	.0	42.8	67.4
	22.0	46.0	62.0	61.0	53.0	31.0	34.0	40.0	28.0	25.0	31.0	16.0		
27	.1	4.5	5.2	3.9	1.1	.3	1.4	8.9	11.9	3.4	1.7	.0	42.3	66.7
	17.0	50.0	53.0	59.0	41.0	26.0	29.0	43.0	35.0	22.0	31.0	14.0		
28	4.1	4.3	5.3	3.3	1.3	.0	.4	8.6	12.3	7.8	1.7	.4	49.4	77.8
	40.0	46.0	62.0	47.0	44.0	10.0	22.0	53.0	37.0	34.0	31.0	28.0		
OP	4.4	4.6	5.3	3.9	1.8	1.2	4.2	8.9	12.8	8.7	4.5	3.1	63.5	
	49.1	56.9	57.8	65.1	68.8	68.5	60.4	45.4	42.7	42.8	62.5	70.3		

FIG 9.04 UTILISATION FOR FEB

FOR BEGINERS

AVERAGE EFFICIENCY =53.2

	WIND DIRECTION													
LOC	0	30	60	90	120	150	180	210	240	270	300	330	ALL	EFF
1	.0	2.5	2.8	.1	.0	.0	.0	.0	.0	.0	.1	.0	5.6	8.7
	22.0	44.0	40.0	22.0	7.0	20.0	11.0	16.0	8.0	13.0	17.0	17.0		
2	.2	1.5	1.8	.4	.0	.0	.0	.6	.5	.4	.0	.1	5.4	8.4
	28.0	38.0	35.0	25.0	14.0	17.0	23.0	22.0	17.0	16.0	13.0	23.0		
3	.1	.6	.3	.5	.1	.0	.0	.7	7.8	.1	.0	.0	10.1	15.7
	25.0	31.0	25.0	26.0	25.0	23.0	16.0	23.0	32.0	14.0	11.0	20.0		
4	.0	.1	.0	1.2	.5	.1	.0	2.2	.5	3.2	.3	.0	8.1	12.7
	17.0	26.0	20.0	32.0	34.0	26.0	17.0	32.0	17.0	22.0	20.0	19.0		
5	.0	.1	1.6	2.8	.4	.1	.0	1.0	1.4	14.0	4.5	1.1	27.0	42.1
	16.0	25.0	34.0	43.0	32.0	29.0	17.0	25.0	20.0	53.0	41.0	32.0		
6	.0	.1	4.1	2.4	.9	.0	.0	.0	10.9	13.7	3.8	.3	36.3	56.6
	23.0	26.0	47.0	40.0	47.0	20.0	13.0	14.0	40.0	43.0	37.0	25.0		
7	.2	2.8	4.1	.5	.1	.0	.0	.0	.1	.0	.1	.0	7.9	12.3
	29.0	46.0	47.0	26.0	25.0	14.0	14.0	7.0	14.0	11.0	17.0	16.0		
8	.4	3.7	5.1	2.5	.4	.0	.0	.0	2.9	.7	.0	.0	15.7	24.5
	32.0	52.0	53.0	41.0	32.0	13.0	13.0	16.0	23.0	17.0	14.0	20.0		
9	.3	3.0	5.5	3.5	.0	.0	.0	1.0	7.3	5.3	.0	.1	26.1	40.7
	31.0	47.0	56.0	50.0	22.0	20.0	17.0	25.0	31.0	25.0	16.0	22.0		
10	.2	2.8	5.4	2.9	.1	.1	.0	2.1	6.2	12.0	1.1	.1	32.9	51.4
	28.0	46.0	55.0	44.0	23.0	26.0	19.0	31.0	29.0	37.0	25.0	22.0		
11	.0	2.0	5.4	2.8	.3	.1	.0	2.5	.0	12.0	.3	.0	25.4	39.7
	20.0	41.0	55.0	43.0	29.0	28.0	19.0	34.0	11.0	37.0	20.0	16.0		
12	.0	1.1	4.7	2.5	.6	.0	.0	2.1	4.0	9.7	.0	.1	24.7	38.6
	20.0	35.0	50.0	41.0	37.0	22.0	19.0	31.0	25.0	32.0	10.0	22.0		
13	.1	.0	.3	.1	.1	.0	.1	.1	5.6	.0	.0	.0	6.4	10.0
	25.0	20.0	25.0	22.0	23.0	22.0	29.0	17.0	28.0	5.0	8.0	20.0		
14	.6	4.2	5.4	2.8	.0	.0	.0	.0	4.5	.4	.5	.3	18.6	29.1
	35.0	55.0	55.0	43.0	10.0	20.0	13.0	14.0	26.0	16.0	22.0	25.0		
15	.5	4.6	6.7	3.9	.0	.4	.0	1.2	8.7	3.2	.7	1.4	31.4	49.0
	34.0	59.0	70.0	56.0	17.0	43.0	19.0	26.0	34.0	22.0	23.0	34.0		
16	.4	4.5	6.8	4.0	.3	.3	.0	1.7	11.8	6.0	1.1	1.8	38.7	60.4
	32.0	58.0	71.0	58.0	29.0	37.0	20.0	29.0	44.0	26.0	25.0	37.0		
17	.1	3.3	5.8	3.2	.6	.2	.1	2.5	9.9	9.7	.5	1.4	37.4	58.4
	26.0	49.0	58.0	47.0	38.0	34.0	29.0	34.0	37.0	32.0	22.0	34.0		
18	.1	3.0	5.4	3.8	1.0	.2	.2	3.3	4.0	8.0	.1	1.1	30.0	46.8
	25.0	47.0	55.0	53.0	50.0	34.0	35.0	40.0	25.0	29.0	17.0	32.0		
19	.0	2.0	5.5	3.5	.9	.1	.2	3.3	1.4	.1	.2	.6	17.8	27.8
	16.0	41.0	56.0	50.0	47.0	28.0	34.0	40.0	20.0	14.0	19.0	28.0		
20	.0	1.1	4.1	3.8	.7	.0	.0	1.5	7.3	.0	.5	.1	19.2	30.0
	11.0	35.0	47.0	53.0	40.0	23.0	26.0	28.0	31.0	10.0	22.0	23.0		
21	1.2	4.3	6.6	3.2	.0	.0	.3	.0	7.3	6.0	.5	.1	29.5	46.0
	43.0	56.0	68.0	47.0	14.0	8.0	37.0	16.0	31.0	26.0	22.0	23.0		
22	.9	4.8	6.7	3.7	.5	.0	.5	.1	9.9	10.8	2.0	.4	40.3	62.9
	40.0	61.0	70.0	52.0	35.0	13.0	46.0	17.0	37.0	34.0	29.0	26.0		
23	.9	4.9	6.7	3.9	1.1	.0	.5	1.7	11.8	9.7	1.3	.6	43.3	67.6
	40.0	62.0	70.0	55.0	56.0	13.0	47.0	29.0	44.0	32.0	26.0	28.0		
24	.2	4.9	6.8	3.8	1.1	.0	.4	2.9	12.1	11.2	2.5	.4	46.3	72.2
	29.0	62.0	71.0	53.0	53.0	16.0	41.0	37.0	46.0	35.0	31.0	26.0		
25	.1	3.9	6.6	3.8	1.2	.0	.1	3.6	9.1	9.2	2.5	.0	40.1	62.6
	25.0	53.0	68.0	53.0	62.0	23.0	31.0	44.0	35.0	31.0	31.0	20.0		
26	.0	2.8	6.2	4.2	1.1	.1	.2	3.3	5.6	5.3	2.5	.0	31.3	48.9
	22.0	46.0	62.0	61.0	53.0	31.0	34.0	40.0	28.0	25.0	31.0	16.0		
27	.0	3.5	5.1	4.1	.7	.1	.1	3.6	9.1	3.2	2.5	.0	31.9	49.9
	17.0	50.0	53.0	59.0	41.0	26.0	29.0	43.0	35.0	22.0	31.0	14.0		
28	.9	2.8	6.2	3.2	.8	.0	.0	4.0	9.9	10.8	2.5	.6	41.7	65.1
	40.0	46.0	62.0	47.0	44.0	10.0	22.0	53.0	37.0	34.0	31.0	28.0		
OP	2.7	5.9	6.9	4.3	1.2	.6	.9	4.0	12.6	14.2	5.8	5.0	64.0	
	83.5	84.8	79.9	69.5	68.6	72.3	80.8	54.3	52.7	49.1	58.6	75.6		

FIG 9.05 UTILISATION FOR JUNE

FOR BEGINERS

AVERAGE EFFICIENCY =40.7

The last two rows on the Figure entitled "OP" instead of a location number, are optimum values from the theory in Section 9.2. Again the top row are values of Cumulative Probability Percentage for sailing, and the second are the values of velocity ratio (R) which would give the optimum value of

LOC	0	30	60	90	120	150	180	210	240	270	300	330	ALL	EFF
						WIND DIRECTION								
1	.9	4.2	4.2	.3	.0	.1	.0	.8	.0	.1	.0	.0	10.8	12.7
	22.0	44.0	40.0	22.0	7.0	20.0	11.0	16.0	8.0	13.0	17.0	17.0		
2	2.2	3.5	3.4	.7	.0	.0	.5	3.2	1.7	.7	.0	.1	16.0	18.9
	28.0	38.0	35.0	25.0	14.0	17.0	23.0	22.0	17.0	16.0	13.0	23.0		
3	1.6	2.3	1.3	.8	.2	.2	.0	3.7	11.1	.3	.0	.0	21.4	25.2
	25.0	31.0	25.0	26.0	25.0	23.0	16.0	23.0	32.0	14.0	11.0	20.0		
4	.1	1.3	.4	1.6	.7	.3	.1	7.3	1.7	3.4	.2	.0	17.1	20.2
	17.0	26.0	20.0	32.0	34.0	26.0	17.0	32.0	17.0	22.0	20.0	19.0		
5	.1	1.1	3.2	3.0	.6	.4	.1	4.6	3.7	11.0	3.2	.8	31.7	37.3
	16.0	25.0	34.0	43.0	32.0	29.0	17.0	25.0	20.0	53.0	41.0	32.0		
6	1.1	1.3	5.2	2.7	1.4	.1	.0	.3	13.9	9.9	2.7	.2	38.8	45.7
	23.0	26.0	47.0	40.0	47.0	20.0	13.0	14.0	40.0	43.0	37.0	25.0		
7	2.4	4.5	5.2	.8	.2	.0	.0	.0	.4	.0	.0	.0	13.6	16.0
	29.0	46.0	47.0	26.0	25.0	14.0	14.0	7.0	14.0	11.0	17.0	16.0		
8	3.0	5.0	5.8	2.8	.6	.0	.0	.8	5.8	1.1	.0	.0	24.9	29.4
	32.0	52.0	53.0	41.0	32.0	13.0	13.0	16.0	23.0	17.0	14.0	20.0		
9	2.8	4.6	6.1	3.7	.1	.1	.1	4.6	10.6	4.8	.0	.1	37.5	44.2
	31.0	47.0	56.0	50.0	22.0	20.0	17.0	25.0	31.0	25.0	16.0	22.0		
10	2.2	4.5	6.0	3.1	.1	.3	.1	6.9	9.6	8.8	.7	.1	42.5	50.1
	28.0	46.0	55.0	44.0	23.0	26.0	19.0	31.0	29.0	37.0	25.0	22.0		
11	.5	3.9	6.0	3.0	.4	.4	.1	7.9	.0	8.8	.2	.0	31.2	36.8
	20.0	41.0	55.0	43.0	29.0	28.0	19.0	34.0	11.0	37.0	20.0	16.0		
12	.5	3.0	5.5	2.8	.9	.2	.1	6.9	7.2	7.5	.0	.1	34.7	40.9
	20.0	35.0	50.0	41.0	37.0	22.0	19.0	31.0	25.0	32.0	10.0	22.0		
13	1.6	.4	1.3	.3	.1	.2	1.4	1.1	9.1	.0	.0	.0	15.4	18.2
	25.0	20.0	25.0	22.0	23.0	22.0	29.0	17.0	28.0	5.0	8.0	20.0		
14	3.5	5.2	6.0	3.0	.0	.1	.0	.3	7.9	.7	.3	.2	27.3	32.2
	35.0	55.0	55.0	43.0	10.0	20.0	13.0	14.0	26.0	16.0	22.0	25.0		
15	3.3	5.5	6.9	4.2	.0	.9	.1	5.0	12.0	3.4	.5	1.0	42.8	50.4
	34.0	59.0	70.0	56.0	17.0	43.0	19.0	26.0	34.0	22.0	23.0	34.0		
16	3.0	5.4	6.9	4.3	.4	.7	.2	6.2	14.9	5.2	.7	1.3	49.4	58.2
	32.0	58.0	71.0	58.0	29.0	37.0	20.0	29.0	44.0	26.0	25.0	37.0		
17	1.8	4.8	6.2	3.4	.9	.6	1.4	7.9	13.0	7.5	.3	1.0	48.9	57.7
	26.0	49.0	58.0	47.0	38.0	34.0	29.0	34.0	37.0	32.0	22.0	34.0		
18	1.6	4.6	6.0	3.9	1.6	.6	2.4	9.4	7.2	6.4	.0	.8	44.5	52.5
	25.0	47.0	55.0	53.0	50.0	34.0	35.0	40.0	25.0	29.0	17.0	32.0		
19	.1	3.9	6.1	3.7	1.4	.4	2.2	9.4	3.7	.3	.1	.4	31.7	37.3
	16.0	41.0	56.0	50.0	47.0	28.0	34.0	40.0	20.0	14.0	19.0	28.0		
20	.0	3.0	5.2	3.9	1.1	.2	1.0	5.8	10.6	.0	.3	.1	31.3	36.8
	11.0	35.0	47.0	53.0	40.0	23.0	26.0	28.0	31.0	10.0	22.0	23.0		
21	4.5	5.3	6.8	3.4	.0	.0	2.7	.8	10.6	5.2	.3	.1	39.8	46.9
	43.0	56.0	68.0	47.0	14.0	8.0	37.0	16.0	31.0	26.0	22.0	23.0		
22	4.2	5.6	6.9	3.9	.8	.0	3.8	1.1	13.0	8.0	1.4	.3	48.8	57.6
	40.0	61.0	70.0	52.0	35.0	13.0	46.0	17.0	37.0	34.0	29.0	26.0		
23	4.2	5.7	6.9	4.1	1.8	.0	3.9	6.2	14.9	7.5	.9	.4	56.3	66.4
	40.0	62.0	70.0	55.0	56.0	13.0	47.0	29.0	44.0	32.0	26.0	28.0		
24	2.4	5.7	6.9	3.9	1.7	.0	3.2	8.7	15.3	8.3	1.7	.3	58.1	68.5
	29.0	62.0	71.0	53.0	53.0	16.0	41.0	37.0	46.0	35.0	31.0	26.0		
25	1.6	5.1	6.8	3.9	2.0	.2	1.8	10.2	12.3	7.1	1.7	.0	52.7	62.1
	25.0	53.0	68.0	53.0	62.0	23.0	31.0	44.0	35.0	31.0	31.0	20.0		
26	.9	4.5	6.5	4.5	1.7	.5	2.2	9.4	9.1	4.8	1.7	.0	45.7	53.9
	22.0	46.0	62.0	61.0	53.0	31.0	34.0	40.0	28.0	25.0	31.0	16.0		
27	.1	4.8	5.8	4.4	1.1	.3	1.4	10.0	12.3	3.4	1.7	.0	45.4	53.6
	17.0	50.0	53.0	59.0	41.0	26.0	29.0	43.0	35.0	22.0	31.0	14.0		
28	4.2	4.5	6.5	3.4	1.3	.0	.4	11.4	13.0	8.0	1.7	.4	54.7	64.5
	40.0	46.0	62.0	47.0	44.0	10.0	22.0	53.0	37.0	34.0	31.0	28.0		
OP	5.7	6.2	7.2	5.4	2.5	1.7	5.7	12.1	16.9	11.4	6.0	4.1	84.8	
	75.1	85.6	86.8	97.0	103.0	100.6	90.9	68.3	64.6	64.9	94.1	106.6		

FIG 9.06 UTILISATION FOR FEB

FOR EXPERT SAILORS

AVERAGE EFFICIENCY =42.7

Probability. The Probability values are summed for all wind directions under the "ALL" column. A new term, the "efficiency", is now introduced. This is the ratio of the Cumulative Probability that sailing is possible, divided by the optimum value of Probability. Values of Efficiency for every location are

WIND DIRECTION

LOC	0	30	60	90	120	150	180	210	240	270	300	330	ALL	EFF
1	.0	2.5	2.8	.1	.0	.0	.0	.0	.0	.0	.1	.0	5.6	6.6
	22.0	44.0	40.0	22.0	7.0	20.0	11.0	16.0	8.0	13.0	17.0	17.0		
2	.2	1.5	1.8	.4	.0	.0	.0	.6	.5	.4	.0	.2	5.4	6.3
	28.0	38.0	35.0	25.0	14.0	17.0	23.0	22.0	17.0	16.0	13.0	23.0		
3	.1	.6	.3	.5	.1	.0	.0	.7	7.8	.1	.0	.0	10.1	11.9
	25.0	31.0	25.0	26.0	25.0	23.0	16.0	23.0	32.0	14.0	11.0	20.0		
4	.0	.1	.0	1.2	.5	.1	.0	2.2	.5	3.2	.3	.0	8.2	9.6
	17.0	26.0	20.0	32.0	34.0	26.0	17.0	32.0	17.0	22.0	20.0	19.0		
5	.0	.1	1.6	2.8	.4	.1	.0	1.0	1.4	16.8	4.5	1.1	29.8	34.9
	16.0	25.0	34.0	43.0	32.0	29.0	17.0	25.0	20.0	53.0	41.0	32.0		
6	.0	.1	4.2	2.4	.9	.0	.0	.0	11.2	14.4	3.8	.3	37.4	43.8
	23.0	26.0	47.0	40.0	47.0	20.0	13.0	14.0	40.0	43.0	37.0	25.0		
7	.2	2.8	4.2	.5	.1	.0	.0	.0	.1	.0	.1	.0	7.9	9.3
	29.0	46.0	47.0	26.0	25.0	14.0	14.0	7.0	14.0	11.0	17.0	16.0		
8	.4	3.8	5.2	2.5	.4	.0	.0	.0	2.9	.7	.0	.0	15.8	18.6
	32.0	52.0	53.0	41.0	32.0	13.0	13.0	16.0	23.0	17.0	14.0	20.0		
9	.3	3.0	5.7	3.6	.0	.0	.0	1.0	7.3	5.3	.0	.1	26.3	30.9
	31.0	47.0	56.0	50.0	22.0	20.0	17.0	25.0	31.0	25.0	16.0	22.0		
10	.2	2.8	5.5	2.9	.1	.1	.0	2.1	6.2	12.2	1.1	.1	33.3	39.0
	28.0	46.0	55.0	44.0	23.0	26.0	19.0	31.0	29.0	37.0	25.0	22.0		
11	.0	2.0	5.5	2.8	.3	.1	.0	2.5	.0	12.2	.3	.0	25.7	30.2
	20.0	41.0	55.0	43.0	29.0	28.0	19.0	34.0	11.0	37.0	20.0	16.0		
12	.0	1.1	4.7	2.5	.6	.0	.0	2.1	4.0	9.8	.0	.1	24.8	29.1
	20.0	35.0	50.0	41.0	37.0	22.0	19.0	31.0	25.0	32.0	10.0	22.0		
13	.1	.0	.3	.1	.1	.0	.1	.1	5.7	.0	.0	.0	6.4	7.6
	25.0	20.0	25.0	22.0	23.0	22.0	29.0	17.0	28.0	5.0	8.0	20.0		
14	.6	4.2	5.5	2.8	.0	.0	.0	.0	4.5	.4	.5	.3	18.8	22.0
	35.0	55.0	55.0	43.0	10.0	20.0	13.0	14.0	26.0	16.0	22.0	25.0		
15	.5	4.7	7.3	4.1	.0	.4	.0	1.2	8.8	3.2	.7	1.4	32.3	37.9
	34.0	59.0	70.0	56.0	17.0	43.0	19.0	26.0	34.0	22.0	23.0	34.0		
16	.4	4.6	7.4	4.3	.3	.3	.0	1.7	12.5	6.0	1.1	1.9	40.3	47.2
	32.0	58.0	71.0	58.0	29.0	37.0	20.0	29.0	44.0	26.0	25.0	37.0		
17	.1	3.3	5.9	3.3	.6	.2	.1	2.5	10.1	9.8	.5	1.4	37.8	44.3
	26.0	49.0	58.0	47.0	38.0	34.0	29.0	34.0	37.0	32.0	22.0	34.0		
18	.1	3.0	5.5	3.9	1.0	.2	.2	3.3	4.0	8.0	.1	1.1	30.3	35.6
	25.0	47.0	55.0	53.0	50.0	34.0	35.0	40.0	25.0	29.0	17.0	32.0		
19	.0	2.0	5.7	3.6	.9	.1	.2	3.3	1.4	.1	.2	.6	18.1	21.2
	16.0	41.0	56.0	50.0	47.0	28.0	34.0	40.0	20.0	14.0	19.0	28.0		
20	.0	1.1	4.2	3.9	.7	.0	.0	1.6	7.3	.0	.5	.2	19.4	22.7
	11.0	35.0	47.0	53.0	40.0	23.0	26.0	28.0	31.0	10.0	22.0	23.0		
21	1.2	4.3	7.1	3.3	.0	.0	.3	.0	7.3	6.0	.5	.2	30.1	35.3
	43.0	56.0	68.0	47.0	14.0	8.0	37.0	16.0	31.0	26.0	22.0	23.0		
22	.9	4.9	7.3	3.8	.5	.0	.5	.1	10.1	10.8	2.0	.4	41.3	48.4
	40.0	61.0	70.0	52.0	35.0	13.0	46.0	17.0	37.0	34.0	29.0	26.0		
23	.9	5.0	7.3	4.0	1.2	.0	.5	1.7	12.5	9.8	1.3	.6	44.9	52.6
	40.0	62.0	70.0	55.0	56.0	13.0	47.0	29.0	44.0	32.0	26.0	28.0		
24	.2	5.0	7.4	3.9	1.1	.0	.4	3.0	13.0	11.3	2.5	.4	48.2	56.4
	29.0	62.0	71.0	53.0	53.0	16.0	41.0	37.0	46.0	35.0	31.0	26.0		
25	.1	3.9	7.1	3.9	1.3	.0	.1	3.8	9.2	9.2	2.5	.0	41.1	48.2
	25.0	53.0	68.0	53.0	62.0	23.0	31.0	44.0	35.0	31.0	31.0	20.0		
26	.0	2.8	6.5	4.5	1.1	.1	.2	3.3	5.7	5.3	2.5	.0	32.1	37.5
	22.0	46.0	62.0	61.0	53.0	31.0	34.0	40.0	28.0	25.0	31.0	16.0		
27	.0	3.5	5.2	4.3	.7	.1	.1	3.7	9.2	3.2	2.5	.0	32.5	38.1
	17.0	50.0	53.0	59.0	41.0	26.0	29.0	43.0	35.0	22.0	31.0	14.0		
28	.9	2.8	6.5	3.3	.8	.0	.0	4.4	10.1	10.8	2.5	.6	42.7	50.1
	40.0	46.0	62.0	47.0	44.0	10.0	22.0	53.0	37.0	34.0	31.0	28.0		
OP	3.7	7.9	9.4	5.8	1.6	.8	1.3	5.2	16.8	18.5	7.6	6.7	85.4	
	125.6	127.8	119.9	104.7	103.2	108.3	121.4	82.4	79.5	74.6	88.8	113.4		

FIG 9.07 UTILISATION FOR JUNE

FOR EXPERT SAILORS

AVERAGE EFFICIENCY =31.3

presented in the last column under the heading “EFF”. In the rubric a value for the Average Efficiency is presented, on the assumption that each location represents an equal area. A weighted average could be produced if the areas were different.

The purpose of repeating the velocity data on the same Figure as the Probability data becomes clear: these same data are presented for the optimum conditions in the last row. A comparison between the optimum value of R and that measured for the location shows whether more time is lost (or there is a decrease in Probability of sailing) because the local wind is too low or too high. For example consider location 1 for wind direction 0 (North) on Figure 9.04. The optimum time was 4.4%, but only 0.9% was achieved. The actual velocity percentage was 22, but it would require a velocity percentage of 49.1 for optimum sailing time. The loss in sailing at this location in this wind direction is due to the wind speed being too low. To improve the utilisation, the building around the water should increase wind speeds here. This is a turn round, the wind engineer is usually being asked to reduce wind speeds in inhabited areas!

Comparison of Figures 9.05 and 9.07, both for June, but the first for beginners and the second for expert sailors show a very interesting result. The average time when sailing is possible for all wind directions for beginners is 26.1% and for expert sailors is 31.2% , an increase for expert sailors as would be expected. But, because most of the restriction is when the wind is not strong enough and this applies to both kinds of sailors, the difference is small On the other hand the efficiencies for beginners and expert sailors are

FIG 9.08 PLOT OF EFFICIENCIES
FOR BEGINERS IN FEB

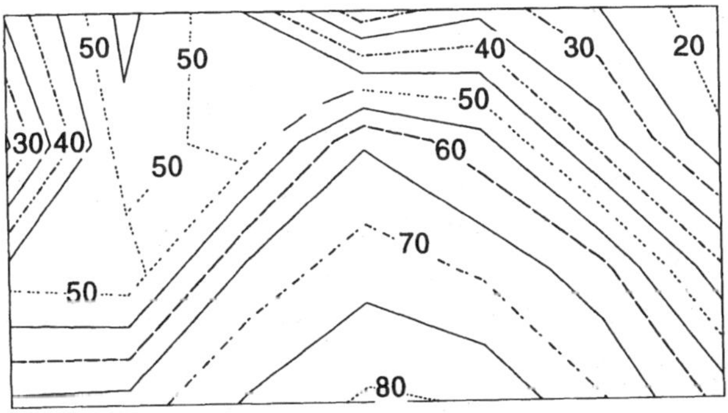

40.7% and 31.3%; it is more efficient for beginners because the optimum time for experts (85.4%) is much higher than that for beginners (64.0%) because of the extended useful time during higher wind speeds.

Figures 9.04 and 9.05 apply to Beginners, and Figures 9.06 and 9.07 refer to experienced sailors. Figures 9.04 and 9.06 are for February, a winter month, and Figures 9.05 and 9.07 are for June, a summer month. The presentation of these four Figures is to show the difference in utilisation possible for Winter and Summer, and for the different types of user.

Some clients prefer pictorial presentations rather than tables, which are more condensed. A contour plot can be produced, Figure 9.08 for example,

FIG 9.09. VELOCITY PERCENTAGES FOR WIND DIRECTION 270º

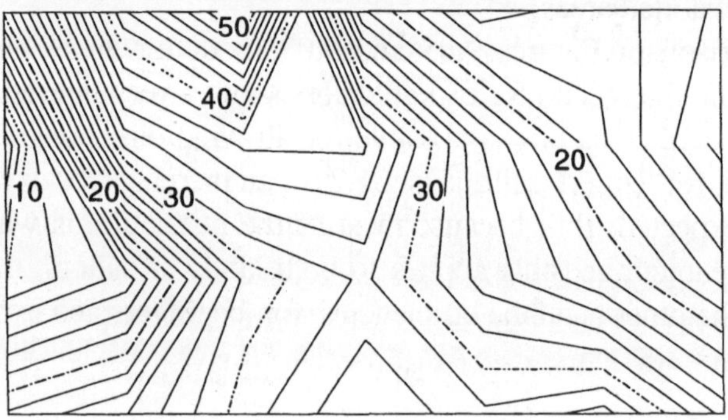

which can be superimposed on a photograph of the water. This form of presentation has the advantage that it emphasises the importance of some stretches of water over others. The location of the Boat Club Houses is important, because if they are in becalmed waters, then it is difficult to get from the club house into sailing water, and the utilisation of the sailing water falls. This applies especially to beginners.

This graphical presentation also assists the assessment of any areas where shear could be a problem. It is possible to produce a contour plot of the velocity percentages for each wind direction, and the close spacing of contours would show shear. This has been done in Figure 9.09 for wind direction 270°, and in Figure 9.10 for wind direction 180°, both for the same project as Figure 9.08. Comparison between Figures 9.09 and 9.10 suggest that areas of shear vary with wind direction, which is so. The picture is further complicated by the fact that the value of the reference wind speed to which the percentages of velocity relate have different probabilities for the different wind directions, so the value of the shear is not directly comparable from figure to figure. The problem is that, if the restriction is based on too high a wind speed, then the important data are for the prevailing wind directions which provides much of the high wind speeds. If, however, the

FIG 9.10. VELOCITY PERCENTAGES FOR WIND DIRECTION 180°

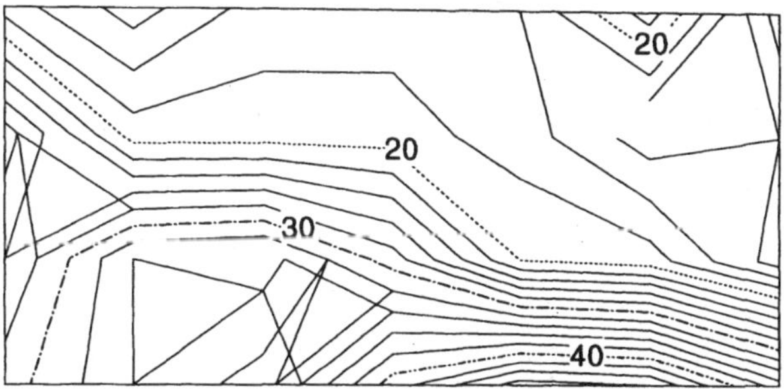

restriction is because of low speeds, then the directions with low reference wind speeds are more critical. As the value of Efficiency takes all these into weighted account, close contours of efficiency in Figure 9.08 would appear to be the better data on which to consider which areas are affected by shear, and the sizes of the areas which are thus affected.

10. Experimental Methods

Experimentation in aerodynamics started with Wind Tunnels, and still the majority of the experimental work is carried out in them. The new contender is Computer Fluid Dynamics (CFD): this science is developing and has its own advocates: the author is not one of these. Consequently any reader wishing to learn about CFD and its application to Building Aerodynamics will have to consult a book on that subject, he will find no help in these pages.

Building Aerodynamics is a very experimental subject, and has grown out of Aircraft Aerodynamics. The description of the wind is very complex, compared to the still air through which aircraft fly for most of their life. The wind has shear and turbulence which can only be described in statistical terms, and can approach from any direction. The shapes used are bluff shapes which cause the air to separate as it flows around them, rather than smooth sleek shapes, like wings and fuselages, to which the flow is attached.

Even with agreeable conditions, the aircraft aerodynamist had to resort to experimental measurements to quantify the parameters which theory showed were important

The aircraft engineers developed wind tunnel techniques which solved their problems satisfactorily, and, by the middle of the twentieth century, the body of techniques and experience was impressive.

By the middle of the twentieth century buildings, other than cathedral and similar buildings, were beginning to increase in size and reduce in weight so that wind loads began to form an important part of the total loading. At the same time new materials were becoming available, new light materials whose weight and thickness was no longer a sufficient stabilising factor. Wind loads were required with an accuracy greater than previously available.

At the end of World War 2 a considerable number a wind tunnels, which had been involved in the aircraft industries around the world, became lightly used or redundant, and work for them was sought in many fields, and the building field appeared a God sent opportunity to use the excess capacity.

However, the early results were not encouraging, in spite of being produced by the famous names in the aircraft industry. Aircraft techniques were not satisfactory, and new techniques were required. But before the new techniques were developed, the reason why the aircraft techniques failed had to be established.

The differences have been listed at the start of this Chapter: bluff shapes, shear and turbulence in the wind. Aircraft used some bluff shapes, and quite a lot was known about them. The problem was to understand the relevance of the shear and turbulence in the wind. Because of these fundamental differences Building Aerodynamics is now considered to be a field entirely separate from Aircraft Aerodynamics.

10.1. Wind Tunnels.

10.1.1 The Effect of Shear and Turbulence.

10.1.1.1. Shear

The importance of shear was first explained by Jenson in Denmark and Baines in Canada, and subsequently many workers have refined their early concepts.

When a body is placed in a moving air stream, the wind speed on the surface is zero to satisfy the non-slip requirements of the molecules on the surface. Over a small distance from the surface, the velocity rapidly increases to a value, which will be discussed below. In this region of rapid change of velocity, the viscosity of the air, and, to a greater extent, because the sizes involved in Building Aerodynamics ensure turbulent flow, the Reynolds Stresses, produce shear forces which are of the same order of magnitude as other forces on the elements of moving air, and thus play an important part in their movement. This layer of air close to the surface of the body in which viscous and Reynolds stresses are important is called the "boundary layer". Outside the boundary layer the shear stresses are small with respect to the other forces on the elements of air and can be ignored; this region is described as experiencing "potential flow". The value of wind speed at the edge of the boundary layer is calculated from potential flow studies around the body. On the surface of most bodies this boundary layer is very thin, the order of centimetres on aircraft, and of the order of 1 meter on buildings. It is ignored in the potential flow studies around the building.

The earth's surface with wind blowing over it is just another surface and has its own boundary layer which is called the "atmospheric boundary layer". By comparison with the boundary layers on the aircraft or building, the atmospheric boundary layer is thick, of the order of 1 km. A building, with its own boundary layers, is within the atmospheric boundary layer, with its vertical dimension normal to the velocity profile of the atmosphere.

The interaction of the building and the atmospheric boundary layer creates three-dimensional flow; that is to say that vertical components of velocity, along the span of the building, are produced, which in turn alter the other components of velocity, and therefor the pressure at all heights of the building.

Before the importance of shear was appreciated, aircraft type wind tunnels, which do not contain shear, were used, and the data acquired from them were wrong, and the use of wind tunnels for the study of buildings fell into disrepute.

The first "Industrial" tunnels were designed with the whole atmospheric boundary layer present; this meant a tall working section with a small building therein. The tall boundary layer required a long fetch for it to be grown, so the new industrial wind tunnels were taller and longer than their aircraft counterparts.

Soon devices were introduced in the fetch to the working section to make the boundary grow at an increased rate, thus shortening the wind tunnel.

Work by Cook (N.J.Cook "Wind Tunnel Simulation of the Atmospheric Boundary Layer; Methods in Current Use at Bristol" Symposium of External Flows 4th to 6th July 1972. University of Bristol 1972.) showed that it was unnecessary to produce the whole height of the boundary layer, satisfactory results could be obtained with the simulation of only the lower part of the boundary layer, and this allowed lower working sections to be used.

So the new breed of wind tunnels was born.

But then the question of what shear should be introduced, and how important was the exact shape of the velocity profile? The measurement of actual profiles during storms, when the highest winds usually occur, showed a variety of shapes, these have been discussed in Chapter 1. The shapes of the profile in Hurricanes and Thunderstorms are different.

10.1.1.2. Turbulence.

Except where "Clear Air Turbulence" occurred, the aircraft aerodynamist had not to contend with turbulence: to his Wind Engineer counterpart it is an every day ingredient.

Apart from the obvious effect of producing a time-varying value for velocities, pressures and forces, turbulence affects the actual flow patterns around bluff bodies.

On a streamlined body separation is controlled by Reynolds Number, Turbulence in the air stream, the pressure gradient along the surface, and the Roughness of the surface. In a bluff body, separation occurs at the sharp corner.

Reattachment, or the approach to reattachment, is controlled by Turbulence in the air stream and the pressure gradient along the surface. This is explained in Section 2.1.2.2. To model reattachment correctly in the wind tunnel, turbulence must be correctly represented.

To represent turbulence correctly, both its magnitude and frequency, or scale, need to be modelled. The turbulent eddies in the atmosphere are centred on those of 100m in size. Every piece of turbulence is unique, so modelling its statistical properties is the best that can be achieved, and, when the actual variations which can occur in real life (Figure 1.04) are considered, is quite good enough.

10.1.2. Generation of an Atmospheric Boundary Layer in the Wind Tunnel.

Over the brief history of Wind Engineering there have been many different devices used to generate the required boundary layer. The earliest was to have a long fetch and let the boundary grow naturally, but this took a long distance and only produced one boundary layer.

A helping hand was provided, this took the form of all sorts of devices attached to the floor of the approach to the working section of the wind tunnel. "Spires", semi-ellipses and all sorts of three-dimensional shapes were devised, and used by their creators: the one appeared as good as the next. The advent of these additions was a step forward, because different devices could be quickly added to a wind tunnel to simulated boundary layers of different scales (because all models were not to the same linear scale), and the differences of a city environment to a rural profile could be undertaken.

In Bristol we used a grid-barrier-roughness method described by Nick Cook in "Wind Tunnel Simulation of the Adiabatic Boundary Layer by Roughness, Barrier and Mixing Device Methods" in Volume 3 numbers 2/3 of the Journal of Industrial Aerodynamics July 1978. We developed the mixing devices on a series of boards with cones (ice cream tubs and coffee cups) attached. It was our philosophy to place these in a random fashion over the surface. Size of cup and their spacing controlled the scale of the turbulence to a major extent, and the number of cups per unit area affected the intensity of turbulence, although all three variables are interrelated.

Routine situations were provided by pairs of the standard boards. In the early days of CP3, the simulation, as the definition of site roughness in Table 3, was city, wherever the site was within the city, and a city simulation was used. Gradually the significance of being on the edge of the city was appreciated, and combinations of boards were used, so that, when BS 6399 came into use, the wind tunnel was ahead of the requirements.

We have always used Volume 1 of the Wind Engineering series of the ESDU Data Sheets for the benchmark data for all our simulations.

Other workers use many other schemes which are just as good as those in use at Bristol. A regular pattern of elements is used by some. More recently rows of flat plates extending normal to the floor, a each row of which could be raised to a different height, have been designed in the fetch region of at least one wind tunnel, the plates being raised to different heights in different rows to simulate different scales and conditions of boundary layer.

At least one wind tunnel has used air jets blowing vertically upwards to create the required simulation.

The ingenuity of man is endless!

However the simulation is achieved, the object is for the finished product to conform to the requirements of Annex A of BS 6399.

10.1.3. Measurement of Velocity.

10.1.3.1. Pitot-Static Tubes.

The classic method of measuring velocity was with a Pitot-Static tube. In subsonic flow, the velocity is given by

$$V = \{(p_o - p_s) / 1/2\rho\}^{1/2} ,$$

where p_o is the total pressure, p_s is the static pressure and ρ is the density of the air.

The major problem with using a pitot-static tube for the measurement of velocity is that it is not very accurate below about 1 m/s. This cuts out a range of velocities often of great importance in wind engineering. Because it is so robust it does have its uses for several applications such as measuring the value of the reference wind speed in the wind tunnel.

There can also be a restriction on the frequency response of the instrument, associated with the size of the tube and the length of flexible tubing connecting the pitot-static tube to the measuring pressure device. This will be considered in section 10.1.4.1.

A pitot-static tube is especially useful in measuring the reference wind speed in an investigation involving the measurement of pressures. If the pitot and static pressures are measured by the same electronic instruments with which the pressures on the model are measured, values of pressure coefficient can be obtained by subtracting and dividing voltage outputs; no exact calibration of gain and zero setting needs to be made provided only that the voltage output is proportional to velocity.

10.1.3.2. Hot Wire Anemometers.

These instruments have performed the vast majority of the high frequency measurements of velocity in wind tunnels. There are two basic types, constant temperature and constant current. Most of the instruments in current use are of the constant temperature type.

The principle is simple. A wire, originally of platinum but now usually of tungsten, is heated by an electric current to a predetermined temperature (usually about 200°C). When the wind blows on the wire, it cools, and its electrical resistance changes. The two types differ from this point onwards; in the constant temperature version, the current through the wire is increased until its resistance returns to its pre-set value, when the current through the wire is a measure of the wind speed (Kings Law relates the current to the velocity). In the constant current version, the resistance is related to the velocity, but the relationship is not so well developed, and it is for this reason that this version is not favoured.

The miniature wire usually used in building aerodynamics is about 3mm long and 5 microns (1 micron is 10^{-6} meters) in diameter. Because it is so small, its heat capacity is also very small and it can respond to fluctuations of the order of 10^5 Hz. Hardware is supplied with the anemometer which produces an output voltage proportional to the velocity. These instruments have been in use for a long time and are extremely reliable.

Single Hot Wire anemometers have two large drawbacks in wind engineering; both based on the fact that they cannot distinguish wind direction. The output from the wire is a measure of the modulus of the velocity (even this is not absolutely true because the stem of the instrument and the wire supports introduce a directional response). In a separated or wake flow a component of velocity may vary rapidly from a positive to a negative value, but the output of the anemometer, reading the modulus value, is always positive.

To enable components of velocity to be measured, a Cross Wire anemometer was introduced. This instrument works on the principle that the cooling effect of the wind is proportional to the cosine of the angle of yaw (the angle between the flow direction and the normal to the wire: this proportionality breaks down when the angle becomes too large due mainly to the effect of the wire supports). The cross wire anemometer consists of two identical wires inclined at an angle to each other: each wire being monitored separately. When the flow direction is along the bisector of the two wires, the output from each wire is the same, so the sum of the outputs from the wires gives a measure of the component of velocity along the bisector, and the difference in outputs gives a measure of the component of velocity at right angles to the bisector. Because the wires are already yawed to the direction of flow, the directional deviation allowed before interference from the supports, and other non-linear effects, reduces the output and this means that an X wire can only respond accurately to a limited level of turbulence. In addition their response to velocities in the third direction requires attention.

Three wires can be incorporated to produce a "Three Component Hot Wire". These exist, and have been used satisfactorily, but require great care in their operation. With modern computing capacity, the outputs from the black boxes attached to the three wires can be fed into a computer which outputs the three components of velocity directly.

The three component instrument has gone a long way to solve the difficult problems in wind engineering, but at the cost of a complicated, expensive and delicate instrument. In many applications a single Hot Wire provides suitable data, and its shortcomings are forgiven because of its simplicity.

10.1.3.3. Hot Wire Anemometer Variations.

Two such variations will be discussed here; the McGill probe and the Pulsed Wire Anemometer.

In the McGill probe, two wires are placed parallel to each other and a short distance apart. The wires are then enclosed in an annulus or cowl, the purpose of which is to accept through the cowl only the component of velocity along the axis of the cowl, and to ensure that the direction of flow over the wires is exactly along this direction. The instrument works by measuring the velocity at each wire separately, and, by assuming that the wire recording the lower velocity must be in the wake of the other wire, the upwind wire measures the correct magnitude, and the direction is from the wire with the higher reading to the other wire. Computer programs can easily detect the higher reading and put the appropriate sign to the correct value of velocity. The drawback to this instrument is that the size of the cowl limits the upper frequency limit to about 100Hz in a wind speed of 6 m/s for a cowl of practical size.

The Pulsed Wire Anemometer has three wires, the outer two are parallel and the third is midway between and at right angles to them. The outer two wires are the sensor wires and the central one is the pulse wire. The instrument works by measuring the time for the pulse of heat emitted by the pulse wire to reach one of the sensor wires. The identity of the receiving wire demonstrates the direction of the flow, and the time delay the velocity. Such instruments have a limited frequency response. Commercial instruments were produced by Bradshaw, and their use is described in I.P.Castro, G.F.S.Wiggs "Pulsed-Wire Anemometry on Rough Surfaces with Application to Desert Sand Dunes" Journal of Wind Engineering Vol 52 pp 53 - 71: 1994.

10.1.3.4. Laser Doppler Anemometers.

These instruments have the advantage that there is no intrusion into the flow by any measuring head.

The flow to be measured is seeded with particles. The one dimensional instrument consists of a pair of laser beams which intercept at the measurement point. The use of lasers ensures that the volume where the two beams intersect is very small. As the seeded particles pass through the "volume", they reflect the laser light, and this is received by a "photodetector". In the measurement volume the two laser beams interfere to form fringes, so that the particles, as they pass through, are illuminated at the interference or Doppler Frequency. The frequency of signal received by the photodetectors is directly related to the angle between the laser beams, the wave length of the light and the velocity of the particles. The instrument measures the component of velocity perpendicular to the intercepting laser beams, but the sign of the velocity is undetermined. To overcome this problem, the frequency of one of the beams is shifted by a sufficient amount by a Bragg Cell so that the velocity calculated above is always positive. This shift is allowed for in the analysis of the signals received from the instrument, giving an output with the correct sign and velocity.

Duplication of lasers and photodetectors allows two and three dimensional systems to be produced.

The use of these instruments is increasing, attractive adaptations are made for their use in wind tunnels. Their cost at present is high, but this will come down with their introduction to more laboratories.

Among many other uses, some very exciting measurements of velocities very close to building surfaces have been made with this type of instrument at the Wind Engineering Research Group at the University of Oxford, under the leadership of Colin Wood (see A.J.Minson & C.J.Wood "Extreme Velocities near Building Faces using Laser Doppler Anemometry" Journal of Wind Engineering Vol 52 pp 121 - 137 1994).

10.1.3.5. Scour Tests.

This technique has the advantage that it covers all locations on the ground of the model. The floor of the model is first covered with a thin even covering of powder which does not coagulate; various materials have been used including ground walnut shells. The model is lit from above, and a camera is also placed directly over the model. The wind is turned on and run up to a low speed representing a known fraction of the reference wind speed. After equilibrium conditions have been reached, the wind will have moved the "powder" from those areas where the local wind speed is above a calibrated value. A photograph is taken. The wind speed is raised to another prescribed value and the procedure repeated.

By using modern computer techniques the photographs can be superimposed in different colours producing a single photograph with areas of different colour denoting areas of different local velocity.

This is aesthetically pleasing and the coverage is good, but the accuracy leaves much to be desired; advocates of the method suggest a 30% accuracy, but my personal attempts were not as successful.

Sometimes this approach is suggested as a first approach to a study, to determine areas of high local velocity prior to conducting real measurements. My comment on this is that a competent wind engineer will determine all such areas by eye, and the process is unnecessary. In any case, I abhor the idea of dust or other particles being introduced on purpose into my wind tunnel, more than enough dirt enters unbidden.

Nick Cook discusses several papers on the use of scour tests presented in the Journal of Wind Engineering in his contribution in that Journal (volume 79 pp 307 - 309 1999).

10.1.3.6. The Irwin Probe.

A new sensor for measuring pedestrian-level wind speeds on wind tunnel models was devised by Peter Irwin (H.P.A.H.Irwin "A Simple Omnidirectional Sensor for Wind Tunnel Studies of Pedestrian-level Winds" Journal of Wind Engineering Vol 7 pp 219 to 239 1981). The instrument is surface mounted, has a cavity (called the Sensor Hole of diameter D and depth H) through the centre of which protrudes a flat topped Sensor tube (internal diameter d_1 and external diameter d), extending a short distance above the surface (h). The standard configuration was for

$$h / d = 1.0$$
$$H / d = 3.1$$
$$d_1 / d = 0.72$$
$$D / d = 1.56$$

Most of the development work was conducted with 16 gauge hypodermic tubing of diameter d = 1.65mm. A unique relationship between the pressure difference between that in the tube and that in the cavity with the velocity at a short distance above the surface was obtained.

The instrument had the advantage that the instrument could be placed in parts of the model where access by other instruments was extremely difficult, if not impossible.

10.1.4. Measurement of Pressure.

The measurement of fluctuating pressures is an essential part of wind loading studies and techniques have to be developed to cover all situations. As all pressures in wind engineering are of a fluctuating nature, the only suitable device is a pressure transducer. This is a device which converts an applied pressure into an electric voltage. Not only does this allow rapidly fluctuating values of pressure to be measured, it also allows statistical, or any other, evaluations to be performed directly on the data.

The first requirement is for the pressure to be measured at a great many locations on a model. This means that it was physically impossible to mount sufficient individual transducers within the model, and some means had to be found to transfer the pressure from the location on the model to a place where the transducer can be housed. Tubing is an essential, and the next few sections deal with the problem they introduce.

With the large number of locations to be studied, there must either be a bank of transducers, or a means whereby the output from many locations can be switched to a single transducer. The latter solution was used extensively in the aircraft industry, and so was the first to be used in wind engineering. The switch is called a "Scanivalve", which is the trade name of the first successful manufacturer. This device will be discussed in its own section.

However, the Scanivalve has the drawback that it measures the pressure at locations sequentially. Simultaneous measurement of pressure is required for some applications. This can be achieved by running several Scanivalves in parallel, the data collection system obtaining a reading from a series of Scanivalves in very rapid rotation (instantaneous in the times involved in wind engineering). This allows correlation of pressure from two or more locations, depending upon the number of Scanivalves available. This is enough for most applications.

If correlations from more locations are required, simultaneously multi-transducer banks are being used. This is discussed in Section 10.1.4.4.

Simultaneous averages of pressure over finite areas are required in some instances, and for this application "Pneumatic Averagers" have been developed, and these are discussed in Section 10.1.4.5. An interesting application of Pneumatic Averages is to obtain values of Shear Force and Bending Moment on buildings directly by pressure measurement rather than resorting to the use of Wind Tunnel Balances.

10.1.4.1. The Use of Tubing: Attenuation and Amplification.

The measurement of a fluctuating pressure is made by an electronic transducer: all other forms of manometer have too low a frequency response. The electronic transducer is a device which converts fluctuating pressure into an electric signal. In the transducer the pressure is applied to a surface of finite size which deflects, and the movement is sensed electrically. For the measurement of high frequencies, the size of the diaphragm must be very small.

The ideal situation would be to place a separate transducer just below the surface of the model at every measurement location: this is impractical, if not impossible. The measurement locations have to be connected to the transducer by a length of tubing, the shorter the better. This means that the transducer needs to be as close to the measurement surface as possible; either within the model or immediately below it.

The pressure signal is attenuated down a tube, the longer the tube, the greater the attenuation. However, what is not so obvious is that there will be amplification as well due to the presence of standing waves in the tube. These standing waves, sometimes called "organ pipe" resonance, will occur at definite frequencies depending on the tube and the details of its ends. Basically the model end will be open, and the transducer end will be sealed by the face of the transducer in its cavity. The fundamental wave will be generated at the open end, pass down the tube and be reflected 180° out of phase at the face of the transducer. It will then be reflected at the open end of the tube in phase with the signal. So the standing wave will have a fundamental wave length four times the length of the tube. There will be a first harmonic of that wave which is reflected at the face of the transducer, then reflected in phase once at the open end, and again reflected at the face of the transducer. There will be an infinite number of harmonics; getting weaker the greater number of transits down the tube.

The volume of the transducer cavity is also of importance because the way that the pressure is built up in the tube, and is therefore measured at the transducer, is by the pumping of air through the tube into the cavity. The transducer cavity is at the end of the tube, so the extra air which is required to fill this cavity to increase its pressure has to pass down the tube, with the frictional losses involved. A large transducer cavity will prevent the measurement of high frequencies.

All this amounts to the fact that the tubing connecting the measurement location on the model to the transducer is frequency dependent, and the mathematical correspondence of response to input is sometimes called the "transfer function". It can be determined for any complex tube/transducer arrangement. If spectra are to be measured, the frequency dependence is unimportant, because, provided that it is known, the measured spectra can be corrected frequency by frequency. But most measurements are average, quantile or statistical values, such as the "standard deviation". These values are composed of all frequencies. Many attempts have been made since the 1920's to obtain a theoretical solution to this problem, success was achieved in 1965 by Bergh & Tijdeman (H.Bergh, H.Tijdeman "Theoretical and Experimental Results for the Dynamic Response of Pressure Measuring Systems" Report NLR-TR F238 National Aerospace Laboratory (The Netherlands) 1965). In 1981 this theory was used by S.J.Gumley at the University of Oxford ("Tubing Systems for the Measurement of Fluctuating Pressures in Wind Engineering" Oxford University Engineering Labs Report Number 1370.81") to design optimum tubing systems for minimising distortion in pressure measurements. This analysis has been carried out for a tubing system composed of a brass insert in the model, a 450 mm length of flexible tubing, and a transducer. The results, over a frequency range of 0 to 400 Hz are presented in Figure 10.01.

For this tubing system the amplification is obvious. If spectra are to be measured, then it would be possible to correct this response, but, if values of mean pressure and standard deviation are to be obtained, then this tubing would be unacceptable.

The major improvement required is to correct the amplification. This is usually carried out by the use of one or more restrictors in the tubing, which will be discussed in the next section.

FIG 10.01 FREQUENCY RESPONCE OF PLAIN TUBING

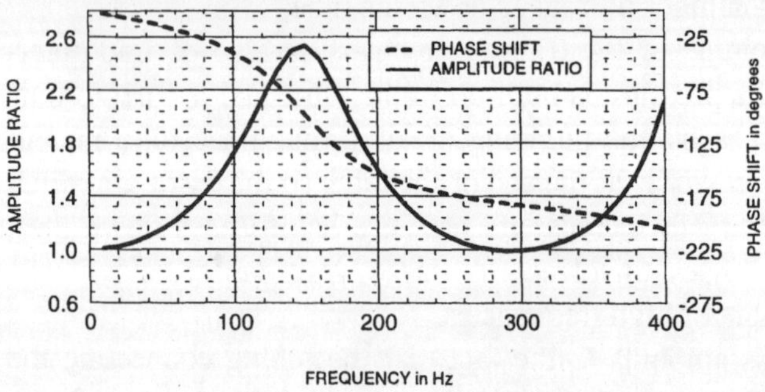

10.1.4.2. Restrictors.

The need is for a device within the tubing system which would correct the amplification of the pressure signal in the tubing. The original idea for such a device was put forward by Peter Irwin (H.P.A.H.Irwin, K.R.Cooper, R.Girard "Correction of Distortion Effects caused by Tubing Systems in Measurement of Fluctuating Pressure" Journal of Wind Engineering Vol 5 (1/2) October 1979), and consists of a restrictor placed in the tubing, breaking up the standing waves therein.

Most laboratories have their own standard lengths of tubing, depending upon the distances from the surface of the model in their tunnels to the place where it is convenient to locate the pressure transducer.

An example of Gumley's analysis applied to standard tubing at Bristol is presented as Figure 10.02. In this figure the frequency range is restricted to 50 Hz because the signal is filtered at 33.3 Hz prior to processing to remove any noise which might be induced into the data by other equipment in the laboratory. The overall data for the tube system is plotted in Figure 10.03. In Figure 10.02 the performance of each part of the tubing system is quoted separately so that, in case of alterations to the system being required to improve its performance, the part of the system which would be most efficient to make the change can be identified quickly.

The object is to produce standard tube combinations for which the pressure ratio (location on the model to transducer) is unity over the required frequency range: the tube arrangement analysed in Figure 10.02 meets that requirement. It is not sufficient to ensure that the amplitude ratio of output to

J	L	D	VW	SIG= 3.00
1	30.000	1.000	.000	
2	175.000	1.500	.000	
3	10.000	1.000	.000	
4	3.200	.300	.000	
5	10.000	1.000	.000	
6	275.000	1.500	.000	
7	40.000	1.000	.000	
8	10.000	.300	1.000	

FREQ	TOT	1	2	3	4	5	6	7	8	9	10
5.	.999	1.000	1.001	1.000	.998	1.000	1.001	1.000	1.000	.000	.000
	-4.	-0.	-0.	0.	-3.	0.	-0.	0.	0.	0.	0.
10.	.998	1.001	1.003	1.000	.992	1.000	1.002	1.000	1.000	.000	.000
	-7.	-1.	-1.	-0.	-5.	-0.	-0.	0.	-0.	0.	0.
15.	.996	1.001	1.006	1.000	.982	1.001	1.005	1.000	1.000	.000	.000
	-11.	-1.	-1.	-0.	-8.	-0.	-1.	0.	-0.	0.	0.
20.	.995	1.002	1.011	1.000	.971	1.001	1.009	1.000	1.000	.000	.000
	-14.	-1.	-1.	-0.	-10.	-0.	-1.	0.	-0.	0.	0.
25.	.995	1.004	1.016	1.000	.960	1.002	1.014	1.000	1.000	.000	.000
	-18.	-2.	-2.	-0.	-12.	-0.	-1.	0.	-0.	0.	0.
30.	.997	1.006	1.022	1.001	.947	1.003	1.020	1.000	1.000	.000	.000
	-21.	-2.	-2.	-0.	-14.	-0.	-1.	0.	-0.	0.	0.
35.	1.001	1.008	1.029	1.001	.935	1.004	1.027	1.001	1.000	.000	.000
	-25.	-2.	-3.	-0.	-16.	-0.	-1.	0.	-0.	0.	0.
40.	1.007	1.010	1.037	1.001	.922	1.005	1.035	1.001	1.000	.000	.000
	-28.	-3.	-3.	-1.	-18.	-1.	-2.	0.	-0.	0.	0.
45.	1.014	1.013	1.046	1.002	.908	1.006	1.044	1.001	1.001	.000	.000
	-31.	-3.	-4.	-1.	-20.	-1.	-2.	0.	-0.	0.	0.
50.	1.022	1.015	1.055	1.002	.895	1.008	1.054	1.001	1.001	.000	.000
	-35.	-4.	-5.	-1.	-22.	-1.	-2.	-0.	-1.	0.	0.

FIG 10.02 PRESSURE LOSSES IN TUBING SYSTEM

FIG 10.03 RESPONSE OF PRESSURE MEASURING SYSTEM

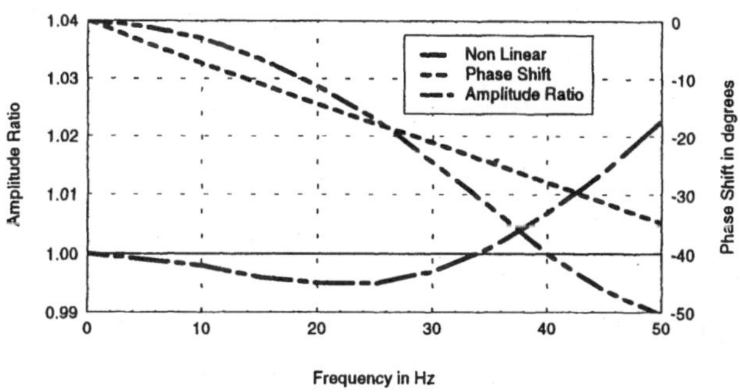

input signal is as near unity as practical for all frequencies considered, but that the phase shift is linear with frequency for the following reason.

Consider a single frequency pressure variation at the measurement location (p_i) and at the transducer (p_t) given by

$$p_i = p_{io} \cos(\omega t)$$

$$p_t = p_{to} \cos(\omega t + \delta)$$

where p_i and p_t are the pressures at inlet and transducer respectively, p_{io} and p_{to} are the peak values at inlet and the transducer respectively, and δ is the phase shift. Over the frequency range of interest it is possible to arrange that p_{io} / p_{to} is unity, or as near as matters. But now imagine two frequencies which have peak values at inlet at time zero. If it is assumed for the moment that the phase shift is proportional to the frequency, viz.

$$\delta = c \times \omega$$

the value of the pressure at the transducer can be written

$$p_t = p_{to} \cos \omega (t + c)$$

in other words all frequencies are delayed by the same time. Thus, if the two frequencies had simultaneous peaks at inlet, there would be simultaneous peaks at the transducer. The sum of all frequencies at a given instant at inlet would be the same at the transducer some fraction of a second later (in the illustration below 0.00194 seconds). The requirement is that the phase shift shall be proportional to frequency.

10.1.4.3. Scanivalves.

This is essentially a switch which connects the tubing from a number of locations on a model to a single transducer. The requirements are that the volume of the transducer cavity is minimal, that the internal paths are of minute cross sectional area, that there are no leaks, that identification of measuring location is certain and that the operation is reliable.

The commercial instrument meets all these requirements: do not try to make your own.

To facilitate the study of vast numbers of locations, the tubes from the locations are connected to rings, which house 48 inputs. Each ring is then attached to the Scanivalve in turn, obviating the attachment of the tubing in cramped conditions.

The normal operation is for the computer carrying out the computations to control the Scanivalve, performing an automatic sweep through the 48 locations and the storing of data or the reduction of results as required. It is also necessary to investigate individual locations for calibration or checking purposes, and the driving mechanism must allow for this to be simply performed.

Scanivalves are well proven over many years of operation.

10.1.4.4. Multi-banks of Transducers.

Pressure scanning switches, like the Scanivalve, make optimum use of what used to be expensive resources. A single transducer could be used to measure the pressure at up to 48 locations. If three of the locations were used to measure reference conditions in the wind tunnel, no absolute calibration of the transducers was required.

Recent years have seen the development of inexpensive solid-state pressure transducers, and a rapidly decreasing cost of digital data storage on large capacity media such as CDR.

The latest trend for multi-channel pressure measurement is to connect each of many surface tappings to its own transducer, and to digitise the signals at high scan rates. By this means each scan gives an instantaneous snapshot of the pressure distribution over the whole building model.

The principal drawback is that the absolute calibration of each transducer needs to be known, but the stability of modern transducers is so good that this no longer poses a problem.

The principal advantage is that simultaneous reading are available at a vast number of points on the building model which means that extensive correlations of pressure over all the building can be calculated with no additional measurements. A subsidiary advantage is that the data, once stored, can be used to calculate a variety of different functions, although the required sampling rate may differ for the calculation of different statistical quantities.

10.1.4.5. Pneumatic Averagers.

It was shown many years ago that, if several fluctuating pressure inputs were connected to a small volume, then the output from that volume was a pressure which was an instantaneous average of the input pressures. This is a simpler approach to determining the instantaneous pressure over a finite area than taking individual measurements and applying correlation coefficients. The devices are small, very simple, cheap and commercially available.

They have the drawback that the average is a true average, without any weighting. Consequently, when applied to an area, the locations must be associated with equal surface areas. In determining the measurement locations on a model, it is customary to position a denser pattern of measurement locations where large pressure gradients occur: this cannot be done when using averagers.

However, this drawback can be turned to advantage. To measure a Bending Moment for example, if the areas represented by the pressure tapping are graded so that the product of the area and the moment arm about the ground is the same for all, as shown in Figure 10.04, then the output from the averager is a measure of the Bending Moment about the ground. The phase relationship of all the inputs, as discussed in sections 10.1.4.1 and 10.1.4.2, must be suitably adjusted.

FIG 10.04 PNEUMATIC AVERAGER LOCATIONS FOR BENDING MOMENT

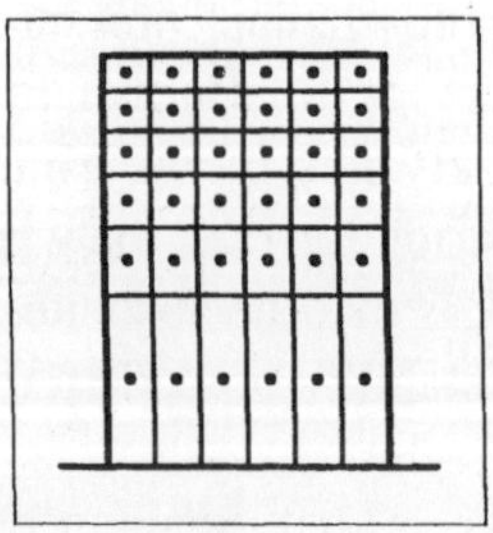

10.1.5. Measurement of Quasi-Static Loads.

Because wind speeds are fluctuating, wind loads will also always be fluctuating. However, if the building does not react in a dynamic fashion, that is to say does not store energy from one cycle to another, then it is sensible to design the building to the peak applied loads which it will be expected to bear in its lifetime. This type of loading is called Quasi-Static, and is discussed in the introduction to Chapter 3.

There are two ways in which this load can be measured in a wind tunnel context, and these will be discussed in the following two sections.

10.1.5.1. Balances.

The advantage of using a balance is that an overall value for the loads and moments can be obtained quickly on a simple model. If changes are made to the model, then the cost of both the new model and the investigation is small.

Most balances work on the principle that a rigid model is mounted on a platform which is free to move, and is restrained from moving by springs or flexures, the deflection of the spring or flexure being a measure of the load. The simplest example of this type is a spring balance.

This is satisfactory if the load in only one direction is required. But loads in three directions may be required, and, in addition, moments in three directions may also be required. This makes six components in all.

There are two varieties of this type of balance, the first is to let the model deflect and measure its deflection, the second is to apply an equal and opposite force to return the suspension to its original position: this is rather difficult with a fluctuating force.

If the platform is mounted at several points, it is possible, by combining the forces in each mounting to derive the force in one direction and components of up to two moments. If the ends of the flexures are attached to a second frame which is suspended from flexures allowing movement in a second plane, then the forces in the second direction can be measured by the deflection of these flexures, and another frame again will allow the forces in the third dimension to be measured.

So, if the model is mounted on a platform which is mounted by flexures to a frame, which in turn is mounted by flexures to another frame, which is fastened to earth (a firm foundation) by more flexures, a six component balance is achieved.

But the device is flexible and probably heavy. Because the wind is fluctuating, the forces on the model will be fluctuating, and it has been placed on a flexible support. If any natural frequencies of the balance with the mass of the model added are excited, and an oscillation is produced, then the forces and moments measured by the deflections of the flexures will be a measure of the deflection of, and not the force on the flexures, and therefor on the model. Because the oscillations are due to the balance, they bear no semblance to oscillating forces on the model

The two parameters of significance are stiffness and mass. The frequencies of the balance are functions of (stiffness / mass). The stiffness of the flexures should be as great as possible, but, the stiffer the flexure, the less sensitive the measurement of deflection. This measurement can either be made with strain gauges mounted on the flexure, or by restraining the movement of the flexure by a load cell which is mounted so as to apply a force only in the required direction (the stiffness in this case is the stiffness of the combined flexure and load cell). The mass includes that of the live frames and all the load cells attached to the live frames. A balance has been built at the University of Western Ontario with a fundamental frequency of about 350 Hz without model.

An all-purpose six component balance is out of the question, and the simplest possible balance for the particular experiment is the correct solution.

The lowest frequency of the balance with the model mounted should be higher than any frequency required in the data, and it is preferable for the higher frequencies to be damped out in the balance rather than being removed digitally from the data. This necessitates more mass on the live frames.

A special type of balance uses Piezo-electric crystals for the measurement of load. Because the movements involved are extremely small, their high frequency response is excellent, and the restrictions on model mass are not serious. But they are expensive, and have the drawback that they cannot measure static loads. This can be overcome by measurement techniques and procedures. Readers interested in this type of balance should read "A Sensitive 6 component High Frequency Range Balance for Building Aerodynamics" J Physics: Scientific Instruments Vol 6 pp 390 - 393 1983.

10.1.5.2. Integration of Pressures.

The straightforward integration of pressure over the surfaces of the model is a simple matter when the values of pressure coefficients are already in the computer. Values of pressure (not coefficient) have to be averaged over the correct period depending upon the size of the surface. The TVL formula should be used for this purpose.

$$T \times V = 4.5 \times L,$$

where L is the diagonal of the area over which correlation is required, and V is the hourly-average value of the wind speed at the top of the building. To be pedantic, a different value for L should be used for each face of the building separated by a shear layer (see section 3.1.4), and that several summations are made as described in section 3.1.9, using the 0.85 factor where necessary. But my experience would suggest that if the value for L is the diagonal of the

LOC	AX	X	AY	Y	AZ	Z
1	.00	.00	.00	.00	.00	.00
2	.00	.00	.00	.00	.00	.00
3	.00	.00	.00	.00	.00	.00
4	.00	.00	.00	.00	.00	.00
5	.00	.00	.00	.00	.00	.00
6	.00	.00	.00	.00	.00	.00
7	.00	.00	.00	.00	.00	.00
8	.00	.00	.00	.00	.00	.00
9	.00	.00	.00	.00	.00	.00
10	.00	.00	.00	.00	.00	.00
11	.00	.00	.00	.00	.00	.00
12	.00	.00	.00	.00	.00	.00
13	.00	.00	.00	.00	.00	.00
14	.00	.00	.00	.00	.00	.00
15	-240.50	49.00	-240.50	4.50	.00	25.00
16	-450.75	40.00	-450.75	13.50	.00	25.00
17	-450.75	31.00	-450.75	22.50	.00	25.00
18	-450.75	22.50	-450.75	31.00	.00	25.00
19	-450.75	13.50	-450.75	40.00	.00	25.00
20	-240.50	4.50	-240.50	49.00	.00	25.00
21	.00	.00	.00	.00	.00	.00
22	.00	.00	.00	.00	.00	.00
23	.00	.00	.00	.00	.00	.00
24	.00	5.00	276.25	.00	.00	25.00
25	.00	16.00	573.75	.00	.00	25.00
26	.00	27.00	573.75	.00	.00	25.00
27	.00	38.00	573.75	.00	.00	25.00
28	.00	49.00	275.75	.00	.00	25.00
29	-138.00	50.00	-138.00	3.50	.00	60.00
30	-265.25	42.50	-265.25	11.50	.00	60.00

FIG 10.05 AREAS and MOMENT ARMS

FIG 10.06 AXES FOR AREA MEASUREMENT

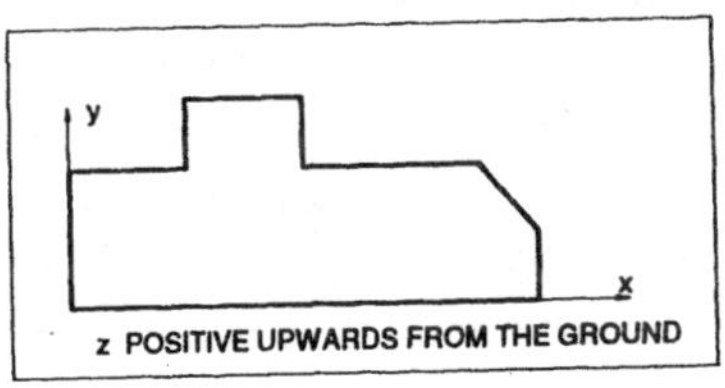

building, then an integration over the whole building in one step is satisfactory.

To obtain the complete set of loads and moments shown in Figure 3.08, it is necessary to produce a table of components of areas and moment arms appropriate to each measurement location. An example of part of such a table is shown in Figure 10.05; this must be accompanied by a diagram showing the axes, Figure 10.06. The sign of the component of the X area should be positive if a positive pressure on that face would give a force in the direction of the positive x axis.

Confusion can occur when names such as "Pitching Moment", Yawing Moment" are given to moments, in Bristol we define all moments as, for example, "X force multiplied by Y moment arm". The total "Pitching Moment" can be obtained by subtracting the "Z force × y arm" from the "Y force × z arm": taking care of the signs of each.

Pneumatic Averagers can be used to obtain average values of pressure over large areas containing many measurement locations. To obtain a correct average, the areas represented by each location must be equal. This prevents the distribution of measurement locations more closely in areas where the pressure is changing more rapidly; this is a drawback. The advantage is that the simultaneous values of pressure are integrated, so that a measure of the fluctuating pressure over the whole area is available if required. Calibrations between the integration of measurements at individual locations, using the TVL formula, and those from pneumatic averagers show good agreement.

10.1.6. Measurement of Dynamic Loads.

Direct measurement of mildly-dynamic loads in a wind tunnel is extremely difficult and expensive. The reason is that it is extremely costly to produce a model which has the correct flexibility characteristics.

The measurement of dynamic loads is impossible, because it this case, the final state deflection cycle is a measure of the energy which the building can store from cycle to cycle, and the work done by the wind on the building is equal to the energy dissipated by damping. Most buildings are sufficiently large for the wind load to be little changed by the movement of the building, so that the use of quasi-static wind data is of at least the same accuracy as the rest of the calculation.

10.1.7. Concentrations in Emissions.

The subject of Emissions from Buildings is covered extensively in Chapter 8. In that chapter most of the studies were of the recording of smoke emissions from the chimneys, or other outlets from buildings. This procedure has the advantage that the photographs can be appreciated by anyone and show which areas are subject to pollution. Much is made in that chapter that only "Near Field" studies in wind tunnels have real significance.

Concentrations of about 0.5% of the concentration at emission can be detected by smoke observations. For some toxic or obnoxious emissions this level of concentration is insufficient. Recourse must be made to the addition of a different tracer into the emission, and the measurement of concentration at chosen locations.

Several schemes have been used in the past, but the one which appears to have achieved the widest and longest use is the "Flame Ionisation Detector".

In my experience, the laboratory most advanced in this technique is the Wind Engineering Research Group in the Department of Engineering at the University of Oxford, and the following remarks are based upon their experience.

A "Stack Gas" comprising 1% by volume of Propane (monitored very accurately) is emitted from the chimney under study. A continuous flow of air from the location under study is burnt in a polarised hydrogen flame. During the combustion process, compounds containing carbon-hydrogen bonds form ions, and a voltage applied between the flame and the collector electrode causes migration of the ions to the electrode. The resulting current is used to provide an output voltage proportional to the concentration of hydrocarbon in the sample.

Measurement of the background concentration in the wind tunnel at all times is essential.

The process is continuous, so, with knowledge of the collection and sampling rate, an averaging time (in wind tunnel time) can be attributed to the measurement of concentration. These data can thereafter be integrated over longer periods to obtain concentration data to compare with acceptable levels such as those presented in "Occupational Exposure Limits 1988: Guidance Note EH 40/88 from the Health and Safety Executive" for the UK.

10.2. Computer Fluid Dynamics.

No book on Building Aerodynamics would be complete without mention of the new CFD, or other initials, which have been developed over the last few decades. This is an altogether different approach which requires its own introduction and derivation: and a description of its merits should be put forward by someone who believes strongly in the approach. I am not in that position, and I would recommend that the reader turns to CFD literature for an introduction to its charms and procedures.

11. Necessary Statistics

This chapter gives a brief introduction to the statistics necessary for an understanding of the analyses performed on the data. The variation of a parameter with time will be called a signal.

A signal which varies with time has two dimensions, its magnitude or size, and its frequency or variation with time. Statistical terms must be defined to describe both these attributes.

The first section defines the terms, the second describes how magnitude is defined, the third how time or frequency is considered, the fourth deals with the interrelation of two fluctuating signals, and the last with extreme value analysis.

11.1. Definitions.

Assume that the time varying function $X(t)$ can be written as

$$X(t) = \bar{x} + x(t),$$

where $\bar{x}$ is the constant part, and $x(t)$ is the fluctuating part which has zero mean value.

11.1.1. Magnitude or Size.

The **Mean** ($\bar{x}$) value of a signal is the average value over the length of the sample

$$\bar{x} = \int_0^T X(t)\, dt$$

The **Root Mean Square** ($\overline{X^2}$) value of the signal is the average value of the integral of the square of the signal over the sample:

$$\overline{X^2} = (1/T) \int_0^T X(t)^2 \, dt$$

The **Standard Deviation** (σ_x) is the square root of the average value of the square of the difference between the value of the signal at that time and the mean value of the signal:

$$\sigma_x^2 = (1/T) \int_0^T \{X(t) - \bar{x}\}^2 \, dt = (1/T) \int_0^T [x(t)]^2 \, dt$$

$$\sigma_x^2 = \overline{X^2} - (\bar{x})^2$$

it is also equal to the square root of the difference between the Root Mean Square and the square of the Mean.

The **Variance** (σ_x^2) is the square of the Standard Deviation.

The **Stationary Length** is the minimum length of sample which will yield unique values for its mean and standard deviation.

The **Probability Density Function (p(x))**. $p(x_o)dx$ is the probability that the value will be between $(x_o - dx/2)$ and $(x_o - dx/2)$. It follows that

$$1 = \int_{-\infty}^{\infty} p(x)\,dx$$

The **Cumulative Distribution Function ($P(x_0)$)** is the probability that a value is less than or equal to a threshold value x_o and is equal to the integral of the Probability Density Function from $-\infty$ to the value x_0:

$$P(x_0) = \int_{-\infty}^{x_0} p(x)\,dx.$$

$$0 < P(x_o) < 1$$

The **Probability of the Exceedence of a threshold** **($Q(x_0)$)** is given by $Q(x_o) = 1 - P(x_o)$ and is written as

$$Q(x_0) = \int_{x_0}^{\infty} p(x)\,dx$$

Sometimes $Q(x_o)$ is incorrectly called "Cumulative Probability".

11.1.2. Frequency or Time.

The **Spectral Density Function ($S_{xx}(n)$)** defines how the magnitude of the signal, expressed in terms of its variance, is distributed across the frequency band. Thus:

$$\sigma_x^2 = \int_0^{\infty} S_{xx}(n)\,dn$$

$S_{xx}(n)$ is called the Spectral Density Function of the variable x.

The **Autocorrelation Function ($R_{xx}(\tau)$)** is defined as

$$R_{xx}(\tau) = \overline{[\ \overline{x} + x(t)] \times [\ \overline{x} + x(t+\tau)]}$$

The **Autocovariance Function** ($C_{xx}(\tau)$) is defined as

$$C_{xx}\ (\tau) = \overline{x\ (t) \times x\ (t+\tau)}$$

The **Autocorrelation Coefficient** ($r_{xx}(\tau)$) is defined as

$$r_{xx}\ (\tau) = R_{xx}\ (\tau)\ /\ \sigma_x^{\ 2}.$$

The **Autocovariance Coefficient** ($c_{xx}(\tau)$) is defined as

$$c_{xx} = C_{xx}\ (\tau)\ /\ \sigma_x^{\ 2}$$

The **Integral Time Scale** (T_x) is defined as

$$T_x = \int_0^{\infty} c_{xx}(\tau)\ d\tau$$

The **Covariance** ($\sigma_{xy}^{\ 2}$) is comparable to the variance, but refers to either two variables or two points in space

$$\sigma_{xy}^{\ 2} = \overline{x(t) \times y(t)}\ .$$

The **Cross Covariance Function** ($C_{xy}\ (\tau)$) mirrors the autocovariance function, this function is defined as

$$C_{xy}(\tau) = \overline{x(t) \times y(t+\tau)}\ ,$$

The **Cross Covariance Coefficient** ($c_{xy}(\tau)$) is defined as

$$c_{xy}(\tau) = C_{xy}\ /\ \sigma_x\,\sigma_y.$$

There is now the complication that these functions are not symmetric with respect to τ and have to be studied from $-\infty$ to $+\infty$.

The **Spatial Covariance** ($\sigma_{x1\,x2}$) is defined as

$$\sigma_{x1x2} = \overline{x(t,r_1)\times x(t,r_2)},$$

where $r_1\ (x_1, y_1, z_1)$ and $r_2\,(x_2, y_2, z_2)$ represent two points in space.

The **Cross Spectral Density Function** (S_{xy} **(n)**) is the equivalent of the Spectral Density Function, but this is asymmetric and given by

$$S_{xy}(n) = 2\int_0^{\infty} C_{xy}(\tau)\exp(-i2\pi n\tau)\,d\tau$$

$$= P_{xy}(n) - iQ_{xy}(n)$$

where $P_{xy}(n)$ is called the "cospectrum" and $Q_{xy}(n)$ is called the "quadspectrum". The polar form of the Cross Spectral Density Function is sometimes used.

$$S_{xy}(n) = [\,|S_{xy}(n)|\,]\exp[i\theta_{xy}(n)]$$

where $|S_{xy}(n)|$ is called the "modulus of the cross spectral density function, and $\theta_{xy}(n)$ is called the phase angle.

$$[\,|S_{xy}(n)|\,] = P_{xy}^{\ 2}(n) + Q_{xy}^{\ 2}(n),\ \text{and}$$

$$\theta_{xy}(n) = tan^{-1}[Q_{xy}(n)/P_{xy}(n)]$$

The **Cospectrum** (**P_{xy}(n)**) defined above.

The **Quadspectrum** (**Q_{xy}(n)**) is defined above.

The **Coherence Function** (**γ_{xy}(n)**) is used to measure the correspondence of the pressure at two points on the face of a building. It is given by:

$$\gamma_{xy}^{\ 2}(n) = [\,|S_{xy}(n)|\,]^2/[S_{xx}(n)\times S_{yy}(n)]$$

The **Integral Scale Lengths** (**^xL_u etc.**) are used as a measure of the scale of turbulence. There are nine of them relating the *x,y* and *z* dimensions with the *u, v* and *w* velocities. The Integral Length Scale for the u component of turbulence in the x direction should be called $L_u(x)$, but ESDU have used the symbol ^xL_u and this symbol will be used here.

$$^xL_u = \int_0^\infty \{\sigma_{x1x2}^{\;2} / \sigma_x^{\;2}\}\, dx$$

where σ_{x1x2} is defined as

$$\sigma_{x1x2}^{\;2} = \overline{x(t, x) \times x(t, x+dx)}$$

The other lengths are defined in similar manner.

11.2. Measurement of Magnitude.

The signal is composed of a time-constant part, and a fluctuating part.

$$X(t) = \bar{x} + x(t)$$

The time-constant or mean part is obvious and is expressed as the mean value. The fluctuating part is composed of a range of values about the mean value. An overall measure of the fluctuating part is the Standard Deviation. However, the distribution within the range can be important, and differs from one situation to another. More information can be given by defining the shape of the range of values, this is called the **Probability Density Function.** It is presented as the variation of the probability density function $(p(x))$ against the values of the variable. A typical curve for a Normal or Gaussian Distribution is shown in Figure 11.01.

11.2.1. Moments of the Probability Density Function.

The probability that the value of a function lies between $X\text{-}dX/2$ and $X+dX/2$ is defined as $p(X)\, dX$. Thus, it follows by definition that

FIG 11.01 GAUSSIAN PROBABILITY DENSITY FUNCTION

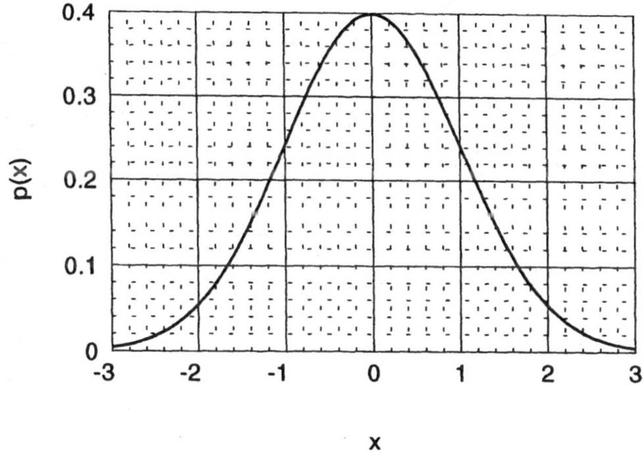

$$\int_{0}^{\infty} p(X)\, dX = 1$$

The first four moments of *p(X)* have a use and are defined as follows

$$\int_{-\infty}^{\infty} X(t)\, p(X)\, dX = \overline{x}$$

$$\int_{-\infty}^{\infty} X(t)^2\, p(X)\, dX = \overline{X}^2$$

$$\int_{-\infty}^{\infty} x(t)^2\, p(x)\, dx = \sigma_x{}^2$$

$$(1/\sigma_x{}^3) \int_{-\infty}^{\infty} x(t)^3\, p(x)\, dx = skewness$$

$$(1/\sigma_x^4) \int_{-\infty}^{\infty} x(t)^4 \, p(x) \, dx = kurtosis$$

The use of the mean value, Root Mean Square and Variance are obvious, skewness is a measure of asymmetry, and a high value of kurtosis shows that there are either several high values in the tail of the distribution, or that there is one very high value. This latter is a useful way to determine whether there is a rogue value in the data.

11.2.2. Transformation of Variables.

When two variables are related, then their distributions are also related. Let the variables be x and y, related by the expression

$$y = f(x),$$

then, provided that the relationship is monotonic,

$$p(x)\, dx = p(y)\, dy \text{ or}$$

$$p(y) = p(x)\, |dx / dy|.$$

11.2.3. Special Distributions.

11.2.3.1. Gaussian or Normal Distribution.

When a variable is composed of a very large number of different components, each of which can be described by its own distribution function, then the central limit theory shows that the composite variable will follow a Gaussian distribution, whose probability density function is given by

$$p(X) = [1/(\sqrt{2\pi} \times \sigma_x)] exp[-(X - \bar{x})^2 / 2\sigma_x^2],$$

where σ_x is the standard deviation, and x is the mean value. A simpler version can be presented in a new variable z, where

$$z = (X - \bar{x}) / \sigma_x$$

the expression is

$$p(z) = (1/2\pi)^{1/2} \exp(-z^2/2).$$

In this form it is possible to present a single table for values of z. Even in this simpler form this equation cannot be integrated to obtain a function for the Cumulative Distribution Function; values can be obtained from tables widely available.

The Normal distribution is applied in most situations where the variable is affected by many mechanisms. The Probability Density Function is shown in Figure 11.01.

11.2.3.2. Weibull Distribution.

This family of distributions was defined by an engineer, Weibull, who was studying fatigue. Wind data are found to follow this distribution closely, and it is always used for this purpose. It is defined by its Cumulative Distribution Function

$$P(x) = 1 - \exp[-\{(x/c)^k\}],$$

k is called the Weibull slope, and c was originally called the characteristic life, but is now called the mode. This expression can be differentiated to obtain an expression for the Probability Density Function.

$$p(x) = (k/c)(x/c)^{k-1} \exp[-\{(x/c)^k\}].$$

The mean value and standard deviation of the distribution are given by

$$\bar{x}/c = \Gamma[(1/k)+1], \quad \text{and}$$

$$\sigma_x^2/c^2 = \Gamma[(2/k)+1] - \{\Gamma[(1/k)+1]\}^2$$

where $\Gamma\ [a]$ is the Gamma Function which is equal to *a!* and can be calculated to great accuracy by a polynomial expression for 0 < x > 1, and factored for higher values of x.

These functions are plotted in Figure 11.02.

FIG 11.02. WEIBULL PROBABILITY DENSITY FUNCTIONS

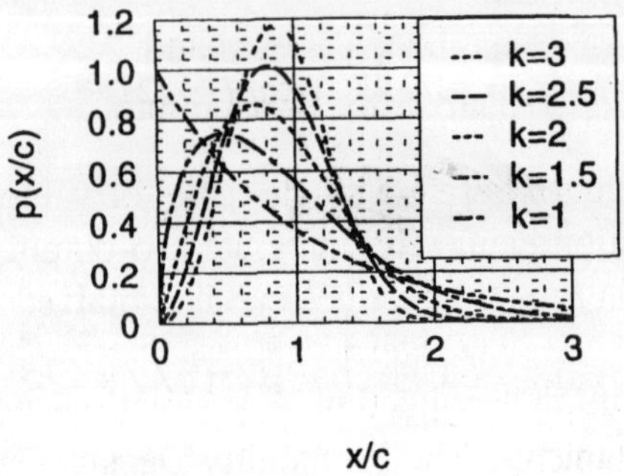

11.2.3.3. Exponential Distribution.

This is simply the expression

$$p(x/c) = exp(-x/c) \text{ for } 0 > x/c > \infty$$

$$p(x/c) = 0.5\ exp(x/c) \quad \text{for } -\infty > x/c > \infty$$

FIG 11.03. EXPONENTIAL PROBABILITY DENSITY FUNCTION

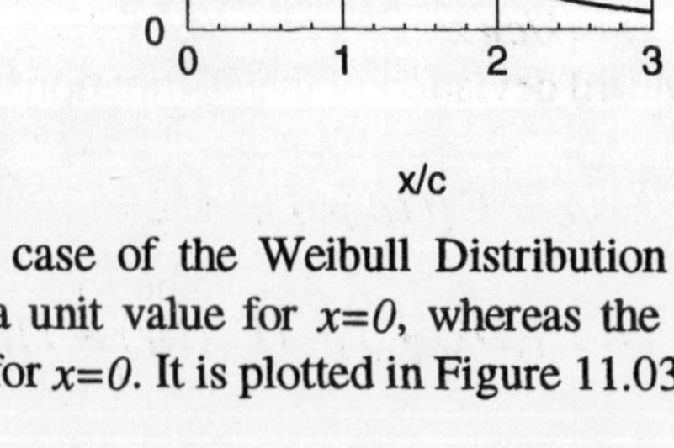

and is a special case of the Weibull Distribution for *k=1*. Note that this distribution has a unit value for *x=0*, whereas the Weibull Distribution has zero probability for *x=0*. It is plotted in Figure 11.03.

11.2.3.4. Mixed Distribution for Negative Pressures.

The negative tails of the distribution of negative pressure at the corners of buildings follow an exponential distribution. To obtain a complete distribution for this area of a building it is necessary to compound two distributions, the Normal Distribution for values of pressure in the core and an Exponential Distribution for larger values.

The distributions merge where their values and slopes are equal. It is also required that the area under the density distribution for $0 < x > \propto$ to be 0.5, so that the distribution is symmetric.

These requirements are satisfied by an inner (Gaussian) probability density function

$$p_1(x) = 0.3420\, exp\, (-x^2\, /\, 2),$$

and an outer (exponential) probability density function of

$$p_2(x) = 0.5639\, exp\, (-x).$$

These are both shown on Figure 11.04.

FIG 11.04 MIXED PROBABILITY DENSITY FUNCTION

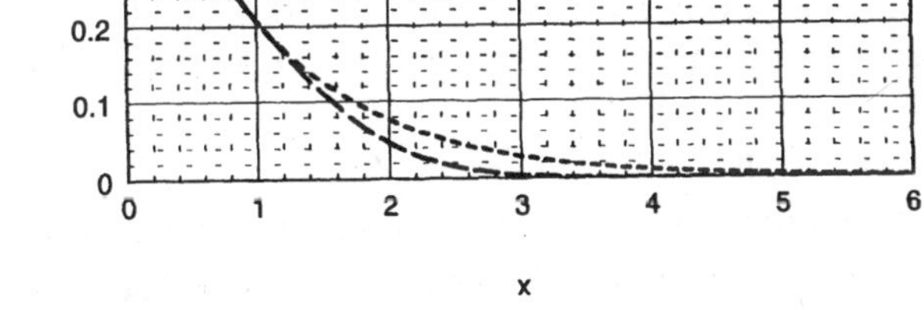

11.2.3.5. Rayleigh Distribution.

This can be considered a special case of the Weibull Distribution with a value of 2 for k. The value of the mode value is given by

$$c = 2\sigma_x / (4 - \pi)^{1/2} .$$

This distribution is shown on Figure 11.05.

This distribution is used for wind speeds very close to the ground where only two degrees of freedom exist.

FIG 11.05 RAYLEIGH PROBABILITY DENSITY FUNCTION FOR x/c

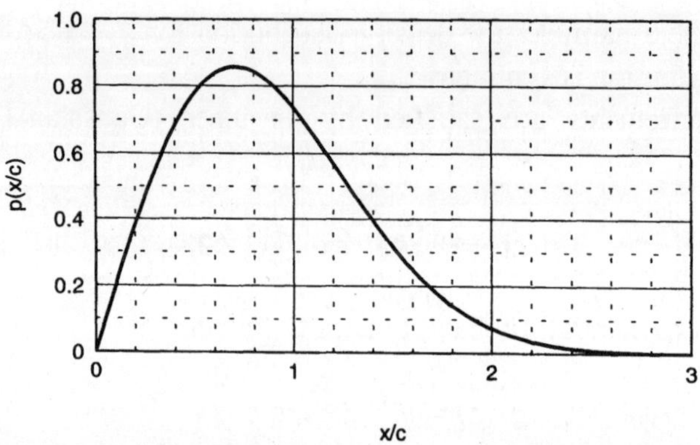

11.2.3.6. Binomial Distribution.

This distribution is basic to probability theory. Unlike the former distributions which referred to a continuous variable, the binomial distribution refers to discrete events.

Consider the following example: Suppose that a die is thrown 10 times. At each throw, which constitutes a trial, the probability of throwing a 6, provided the die is unbiased, is 1/6 in any one throw. The probability of not throwing a 6 in one throw is 5/6. Then the probability of not throwing a 6 in 10 throws would be $(5/6)^{10}$.

The probability of throwing a 6 in the first throw is 1/6. To throw one 6 in 10 throws would require you not to throw a 6 in the next 9 throws, i.e. $(5/6)^9$. But it would not matter in which throw you threw the 6 so the overall probability of throwing the 6 would be ${}_{10}C_1 (1/6)(5/6)^9$ or $10(1/6)(5/6)^9$, where

$${}_N C_r = \{N(N-1)...(N-r+1)\} / \{1(2)...(r)\}$$

Repeating the argument for two 6's would give the probability of

$$_{10}C_2\,(1/6)^2\,(5/6)^8 \text{ or } 45(1/6)^2\,(5/6)^8 .$$

Think then of the series expressed by

$$[1/6 + 5/6]^{10} .$$

The probability of throwing n 6's is the (N-n+1)th term of the series.

If $Q_1(x_0)$ is the probability that the variable will have a value greater than x_0 in 1 trial, and $P_1(x_0)$ is the probability that the value will be less than x_0, then

$$[P_1\,(x_0) + Q_1\,(x_0)] = 1$$

thus the probability that the value will be greater than x_0 r times in N trials will be

$$_N C_r \times P_1(x_0)^{N-r} \times Q_1\,(x_0)^r$$

or more specifically, the probability that a value will be less that x_0 in N trials will be $P_1\,(x_o)^N$, Thus

$$P_N\,(x_o) = P_1\,(x_o)^N .$$

This relationship is of importance in "Once in 50 Years" arguments.

11.2.3.7. Other Distributions.

Many other distributions are used in different applications, for instance

The Log Normal Distribution
The Chi-Square Distribution
The Student-t Distribution
The Maxwell Distribution

Details of these distributions are available in many textbooks on Statistics, or in volume 2 of my own book called "Wind Effects on Buildings".

11.2.3.8. Joint Probability.

If two variables are completely unrelated, the joint probability of an event is the product of the two separate probabilities, thus

$$P(x_o\ ,\ y_o) = P(x_o) \times P(y_o).$$

If the variables are perfectly correlated then

$$P(x_o\ ,\ y_o) = P(x_o) = P(y_o).$$

If the variables are partially correlated between these two limits, the relationship is very complex and the joint probability is a function of the separate probabilities and the covariance coefficient $c_{xy}(0)$.

11.2.3.9. Mixed Populations.

11.2.3.9.1. Mutually Exclusive Events.

Sometimes the data comes from two different mechanisms which can occur at different times and are thus uncorrelated. For example, wind speeds in Hong Kong come from either Extratropical Storms or from Hurricanes. It would be wrong to lump all the data together and obtain a single distribution, because, by and large, the higher wind speeds come from Hurricanes.

The procedure is to split the data into Extratropical Storms and Hurricanes, and derive the probability for each type of storm. Having divided the data into two types, a probability density function can be derived for each type separately. Thus, providing a Weibull Distribution applied to both extratropical storms and hurricanes, the cumulative probability function for the combined effects would appear as

$$P(V_o) = p_1 \times P_1(V_o) + p_2 \times P_2(V_o)$$

where p_1 is the probability of extratropical storms occurring and $P_1(V_o)$ is the probability that the wind speed will be less than V_o in extratropical storms: p_2 is the probability of hurricanes occurring and $P_2(V_o)$ is the probability that V_o will be exceeded in the hurricanes. It follows that

$$p_1 + p_2 = 1$$

11.2.3.9.2. Mutually Inclusive Events.

When two events are perfectly correlated, then

$$P(V_o) = P_1(V_o) \times P_2(V_o)$$

11.3. Measurement of Time or Frequency.

Frequency is the reciprocal of time, and engineers, because the response of structures is usually calculated in terms of frequency, mostly use frequency. However there are occasions when terms which are really dependent on time are expressed in units of length: these are discussed in section 3.1.3.

The usual way to express the frequency content of a signal is in the form of the Spectral Density Function.

11.3.1. Spectral Density Function.

The Spectral Density Function $(S_{xx}(n))$ describes how the signal is distributed across the frequency range, and is related to the magnitude scale by the expression

$$\sigma_x^2 = \int_0^\infty S_{xx}(n)\ dn$$

For presentation purposes, the Spectral Density Function is often presented as

$$\int_0^\infty n \times S_{xx}(n)\ d(\ln n) = \sigma_x^2 ,$$

where the area under the curve is the variance in both cases.

The Spectral Density Function is often presented in its "Normalised" form by dividing by the variance, thus:

$$\int_0^\infty n \times (S_{xx}(n) / \sigma_x^2)\, d(\ln n) = 1$$

or the area under the curve is unity. A typical Spectral Density curve is presented in Figure 11.06.

11.3.2. Two-sided Spectral Density Function.

The Spectral Density Function described above is one-sided because the integral is from 0 to ∞. There is a two-sided Spectral Density Function, usually denoted by *G(n)*, which goes from $-\infty$ to $+\infty$.

The idea of $-\infty$ is difficult to conceive until it is converted into circular measure

$$2\pi n = \omega = \theta$$

FIG 11.06 WIND SPECTRAL DENSITY FUNCTION

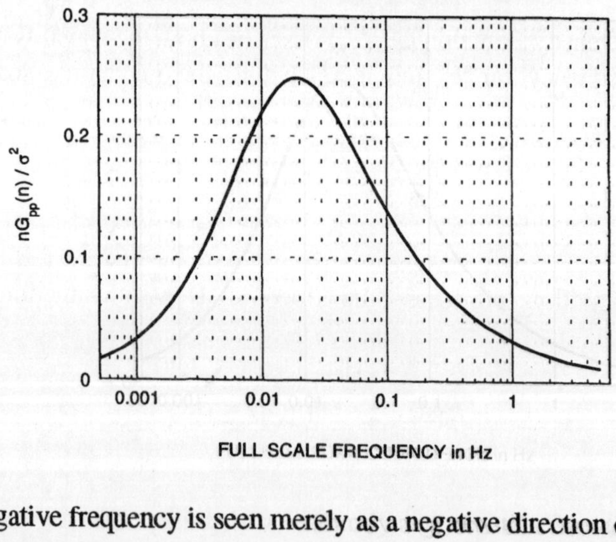

when negative frequency is seen merely as a negative direction of rotation.

11.3.3. Aliasing.

Care must always be taken when sampling fluctuating signals. Suppose that a high frequency signal is being measured, but that the frequency of measurement is less that the frequency of the signal. This situation is shown in Figure 11.07. The frequency of 1/6 Hz has been sampled 1500 times in 60 seconds (every 0.04 seconds) and the full curve results. Then the same frequency was sampled 19 times in 60 seconds (every 3.15 seconds) and the dotted curve resulted. Any conclusions from the dotted curve could be grossly misleading.

FIG 11.07 SIGNALS SHOWING ALIASING

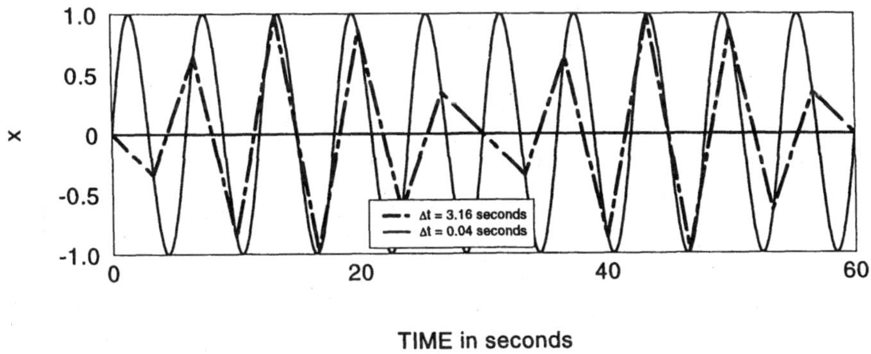

Frequencies in the signal of less than n/2, where n is the digitisation frequency, are correctly represented in their contribution to $S(n)$. The signal frequencies from n/2 to n contribute to values of $S(n)$ from n/2 to 0 (A signal of frequency n digitised at frequency n will appear as a constant value, i.e. zero frequency). The contribution to $S(n)$ from frequencies n to 3n/2 will be added to the values of $S(n)$ from 0 to n/2 and so on.

The signal must be <u>analogue</u> filtered at n/2 before digitisation for aliasing not to occur.

11.3.4. Effect of Instrumentation Averaging Time and Sample Length.

Consider a signal represented by

$$x(t,n) = I_1\ (n)\ \cos 2\pi nt\ +\ I_2\ (n)\ \sin 2\pi nt.$$

The average at time t_1 over a time s is given by

$$x(t_1, n, s) = (1/s) \int_{t_1 - s/2}^{t_1 + s/2} [I_1(n)\cos 2\pi nt + I_2(n)\sin 2\pi nt]\, dt$$

$$= [\sin(\pi n s)/\pi n s]\, x(t_1, n).$$

By similar arguments the effect of a sample length of τ on the evaluation of variance is

$$[\sigma^2_x, \tau_0] = \int_0^\infty S_{xx}(n)\, \{1 - [\sin(\pi n \tau) / \pi n \tau]^2\}\, dn$$

The joint effect of instrument sampling time and sample size is shown in Figure 11.08 for a sampling time of 10 seconds and an instrument averaging time of 0.01 seconds. It can be seen that a satisfactory response occurs between frequencies of 0.1 and 10 Hz. To improve the response up to 50 Hz, the averaging time of the instrument must be reduced from 0.01 seconds.

FIG 11.08 PERFORMANCE OF MEASURING INSTRUMENTS AVERAGING TIME 0.01s SAMPLE TIME 10s

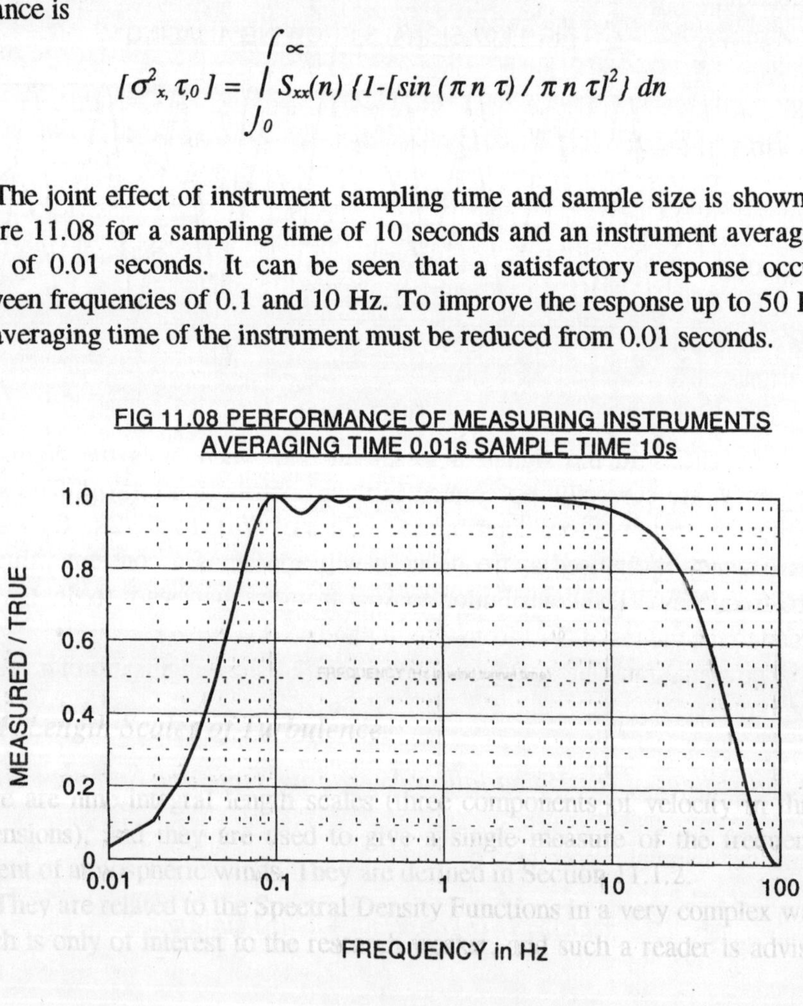

11.3.5. Accuracy of the Fast Fourrier Transform.

When the FFT relationship for the function is substituted into the expression for the Spectral Density Function it becomes

$$S_{xx}(n) = (1/T)\int_0^T \{[I_1^2(n) + I_2^2(n)]/2\}\,dt$$

The differences from the mean values of $I_1^2(n)$ and $I_2^2(n)$ have Gaussian distributions, so the estimates of $S_{xx}(n)$ will have a Chi-Square distribution with two degrees of freedom. Consequently

$$\sigma_{[S_{xx}(n)]} / S_{xx}(n) = (2n)^{1/2} / n = (2/n)^{1/2} ,$$

and for n = 2, the standard deviation of the estimate is equal in magnitude to the best estimate; an unacceptable situation.

The solution is both to take "ensemble averages" (where many complete samples are taken and the average values for each value of $S_{xx}(n)$ are taken) and "frequency smoothing" (whereby the value for every value of frequency is smoothed using the values for frequencies on either side, using a Hanning or other filter).

11.4. Two Point Correlation.

These can either be one point in space at two times, or at two points in space at one time, or can concern two different variables.

The main term most used is the Cross Spectral Density Function defined above. It appears in several forms, but the polar one is of interest because the Coherence Function, which is used to define the correspondence of pressure at two points, is derived from it.

The lengths scales of turbulence are based on two-point measurements of a component of velocity, and are a measure of an average size of eddy or structure of the turbulence.

11.5. Extreme Values.

The ordinary Probability Density Distribution is often called a "parent" distribution because it is composed of data which has been measured. Data might only have been measured over a short period (several years in the case of Meteorological data), but estimated values are required for longer periods of time.

If one sample of N values from the population, is measured, then the distribution will be a standard parent distribution, say a Weibull Distribution, and there will be one extreme value, the largest of the sample N. If another sample is measured, the parent distribution will be the same, but there will be a second extreme value. In the process a new probability distribution for the extreme values is formed. As the number of samples is increased, then the probability of larger values increases. Probability Density Functions for the parent and for multiple parents are shown in Figure 11.09.

FOG 11.09 PARENT AND EXTREME PROBABILITY DENSITY FUNCTION

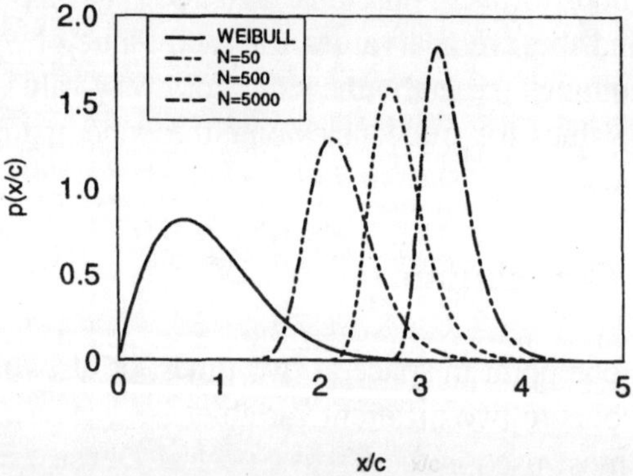

If data exists for a long time, it is possible to take measured maximum values in each of a succession of events and plot it in such a way that the data can be extrapolated to a greater number of events, this will be considered in section 11.5.2.

If the data has been reduced to the definition of the parent distribution, values of maximum values in the events having been lost, then there is a need to derive extreme data from the parent distribution. This is considered in section 11.5.3.

A discussion of the theories used will take place in section 11.5.1.

11.5.1. Basic Theories.

A textbook on Extreme Value Analysis should be studied for an account of the theories, only snippets will be included here.

Because it is possible that the second largest value in one sample could be larger than the largest value in another sample, then it would be preferable to consider several highest values in each sample, and to allow for this number in the value of the reduced variate. This is considered in section 11.5.2.2.

Fisher and Tippett produced the first complete analysis of extreme values, and they studied three cases, which they called "Types". Type 1 was where the values were unrestricted, in Type 2 the solution was bounded by $X > X_1$, and in the Type 3 analysis, the solution was bounded by $X < X_1$.

Gumbel also contributed a vast amount of work in this field, and his nomenclature was First, Second and Third Asymptotes, because the solutions were asymptotes to the parent distributions obtained as $N \rightarrow \infty$.

11.5.1.1. Fisher Tippett Type 1 Solution (Asymptote as N tends to ∞).

Most situations in Wind Engineering are based on the Type 1 solution, so only this will be presented.

The solution is usually written

$$P(X) = exp[\, -exp(\, -y)], \qquad \text{where}$$

$$y = \alpha\,(X - U), \quad \text{and}$$

y is called the "Reduced Variate", α is called the "Dispersion" and U is called the "Mode". The value of the reduced variate can be rewritten as

$$y = \; - \ln[\, - \ln\{\, P(X)\}].$$

11.5.1.2. Rates of Convergence.

The convergence from a multiple parent distribution to the extreme value distribution depends upon the shape of the parent distribution: an exponential distribution gives the fastest convergence.

For this reason, in the case of wind speed which has a Weibull Distribution, with the power k close to 2, a more rapid convergence is achieved if the square of the wind speed is used as the variable, and not the wind speed itself. Most recent analyses use this procedure. The fastest convergence would occur if the variable v^k were used.

11.5.1.3. The Return Period or the Mean Recurrence Interval.

Statistics should relate to independent data, otherwise if there is correlation in the data, the statistics become biased. The procedures which create wind have been discussed in Chapter 1, and may be described as events. Although data for the parent distribution can be collected over many events, if extreme values are to be extracted from it, the length of time L between each event becomes important.

The "Once in T Years" value of wind speed is defined as the value of wind speed which has a probability of $1/T$ of being exceeded in any one year; T in this context is called the "Return Period" or the "Mean Recurrence Interval".

11.5.2. Extremes Knowing Maxima of a Number of Samples.

11.5.2.1. Theory.

Let the maximum value in sample "m" be X_m. The procedure is to rank the maximum values (X) in order of magnitude. If the number of samples is N, then X_1 is the lowest and X_N is the highest. The value of the Reduced Variate (y) for the mth value is y_m, given by

$$y_m = - ln \{ -ln [P(X)] \},$$

Gumbel proposed the expression for the probability to be

$$P(X_m) = m/(N+1),$$

so that the expression for the reduced variate becomes

$$y_m = -\ln\{-\ln[m/(N+1)]\}$$

and X_m is plotted against y_m for the N values. Such a graph is shown in Figure 11.10.

FIG 11.10 GUMBEL PLOT OF REFERENCE WIND SPEED

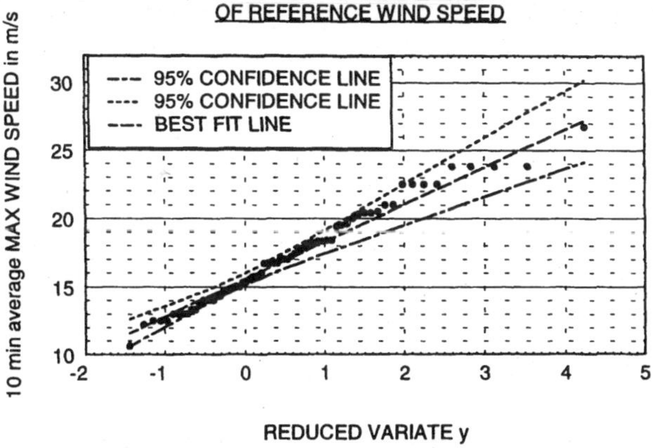

Gumbel shows that if the mean of the extreme data is $\overline{X}$ and the standard deviation is S_X, then the best line through the data is

$$X = \overline{X} + (y - 0.5772) \times 0.7797 \times S_X, \quad \text{where}$$

$$\overline{X} = (1/N) \sum_{I=1}^{N} X_i \qquad \text{and}$$

$$S_X^{\,2} = [1/(N+1)] \sum_{I=1}^{N} (X - \overline{X})^2$$

The value of the mode is equal to the value of X for y=0, and the value of the dispersion is the slope of the line. This follows from the expression derived above, that is to say:

$$y = \alpha (X - U)$$

11.5.2.2. Extremes from "Peak over Threshold Values".

As mentioned above, the use of only the extreme value from each sample can lose data when the second highest value in one sample is higher than the highest value in another. To avoid this occurrence the "peak over threshold" approach is used.

Given that all values of X above a threshold X_o are selected (i.e. $X > X_o$), and r is the sample (annual) rate, and that all values of X are independent, then

$$P(X\uparrow) = P^r(X) = \{m / (N+1)\}^r .$$

The varying value of annual rate, r, leads to a non-standard plotting procedure which makes compilation difficult.

11.5.2.3. Confidence Lines.

The scatter of the actual data from the line drawn through the data follows a Gaussian Distribution around the mode, but Type 1 at the extremes, so it is possible to draw "Confidence Lines" on either side of the best estimate line, implying the statement that there is n% confidence that the data will fall between these lines. These are also shown in Figure 11.08.

The value of the Variance of the actual values from the line is given by

$$\sigma_X^2 = (0.2643 + 0.1166y + 0.6687y^2) \times S_X^2 / N$$

and, because this has a Gaussian Distribution, the Confidence Lines are drawn on either side of the best estimate line where dX is equal to $n \times \sigma_X$, where n is the number of standard deviations which has the required value of the Cumulative Distribution. Thus,

$$P(z) = \int_{-\infty}^{z_0} (1/2\pi)^{1/2} \exp (-z^2 / 2) \, dz$$

For example, a 95% confidence line would require a value of $P(z)$ of 0.975 (2.5% in each tail), and, from tables of a Gaussian Distribution, the corresponding value of z would be 1.96. The 95% Confidence Line would then be

$$X = \bar{X} + (y - 0.5772) \times 0.7797 \times S_X \pm 1.96\, \sigma_X \,.$$

The points for the confidence line would only span the range of values of y for which values of X were available. Outside that range of values of y, the confidence lines would run parallel to the best estimate line with dX equal to that for X_1 and X_N. This is shown in Figure 11.08.

11.5.2.4. Probability Expression by Gringorton.

The probability estimator used by Gumbel is biased, and a less biased estimator was proposed by Gringorton (I.I.Gringorton "A Plotting Rule for Extreme Probability Paper" J Geophys Res Vol 68 (1963) pp 813 - 814). He suggests that the following expression be used in place of that suggested by Gumbel. Note that this only applies to Fisher-Tippett Type 1 solutions.

$$P(X_m) = (m - 0.44) / (N + 0.12)$$

11.5.2.5. Best Linear Unbiased Estimator (BLUE) Method.

For reasons given by Mann ("Point and Interval Estimation Procedures for the two parameter Weibull and Extreme Value Distributions" Technometrics Vol 10 1968 pp 231-56), the least squares method gives a biased (in the statistical sense) estimate for the mode and dispersion of a Fisher Tippett Type 1 Distribution.

This method is due to Leiblein ("Efficient Methods of Extreme Value Methodology" NBSIR 74-602. US Dept. of Commerce. October 1974) who states that unbiased values for mode and dispersion are given by

$$U = \sum_{m=1}^{N} A_m X_m$$

and

$$1/\alpha = \sum_{m=1}^{N} B_m X_m$$

where X_m is the mth ordered value for the variable, and values for the coefficients A_m and B_m are given below.

If there are 10 or more extreme values, the values for 10 points are given in Figure 11.11. For M points, where M > 10, the values for 10 points are corrected by the expressions

$$A_m = \sum_{t=1}^{10} A_t(t/m)p\{m,10,M.t\}$$

$$B_m = \sum_{t=1}^{10} B_t(t/m)p\{m,10,M,t\}$$

where A_t and B_t within the summation are values for M=10 from Figure 11.11, and $p\{m,10,M,t\}$ is the hyper-geometric probability distribution function given by

$$p\{m,10,M,t\} = [m!/(m-t)!]\times[10!/(10-t)!]\times[(M-m)!/M!]\times[(M-10)!/(M-m-10+t)!].$$

FIG 11.11 VALUES OF LIEBLEIN COEFFICIENTS FOR TEN POINTS (M=10)

(M=10)m (M>10) t	A_m A_t	B_m B_t	y
1	0.2229	-0.3478	-0.875
2	0.1623	-0.0912	0.533
3	0.1338	-0.0192	-0.262
4	0.1129	0.0222	-0.012
5	0.0956	0.0487	0.238
6	0.0806	0.0661	0.501
7	0.0670	0.0770	0.794
8	0.0542	0.0828	1.144
9	0.0417	0.0836	1.606
10	0.0289	0.0779	2.351

FIG 11.12 VALUES OF LIEBLEIN COEFFICIENTS FOR LESS THAN TEN POINTS

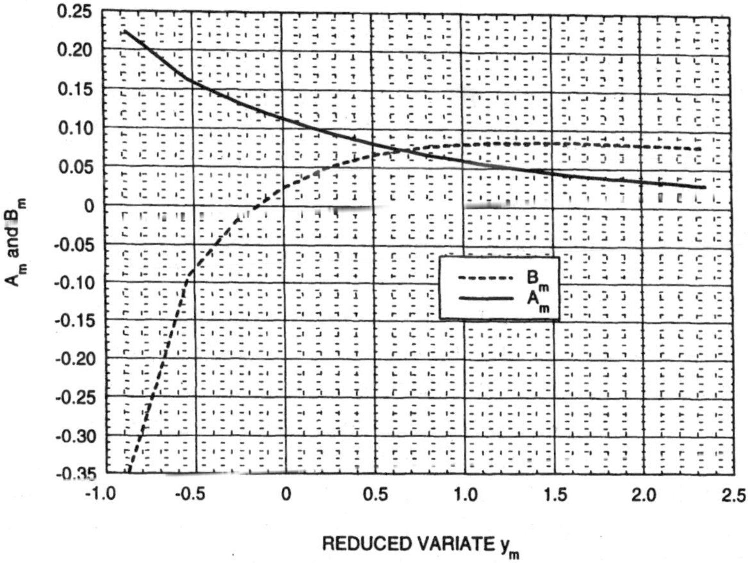

For values of M=10, the values in the table are for A_m and B_m , but, when corrections for higher values of M are required, the values in the Figure are for A_t and B_t .

Once the values have been calculated, a check should be made that

$$\sum_{m=1}^{M} A_m = 1, \quad \text{and}$$

$$\sum_{m=1}^{M} B_m = 0$$

and if these equalities do not occur, the values should be corrected to make them true.

If the number of points is less than 10, then the value of the Reduced Variate (y) for each point should be calculated and the values of A_m and B_m derived from Figure 11.12 for each point. Alternatively the values can be evaluated from the equations

$$A_m = -0.00782\, y^3 + 0.0388\, y^2 - 0.0834\, y + 0.111$$

$$B_m = 0.0228\,y^5 - 0.108\,y^4 + 0.166\,y^3 - 0.127\,y^2 + 0.103\,y + 0.0269.$$

The summation of the coefficients should then be made, and the coefficients altered so that the equalities for the summations of each is achieved.

A fuller description of this process is given in ESDU Data Item 87034 "World-wide Extreme Wind Speeds Part 1: Origins and Methods of Analysis".

11.5.3. Extreme Values from the Weibull Distribution for Wind Speed.

Annual extremes may be extracted from the parent wind data over the annual rate of events. The annual rate of events must be determined from the wind data. Rice started the analytic study with measurements of the number of "up-crossings", the subject was advanced by the work of Alan Davenport, and many papers have appeared in the scientific literature in recent years.

From all the literature I have read, I have decided to use a value of 300 events a year as an acceptable value. As there are 8766 hours in the year (we are interested in hourly-average values), and if there are 300 events a year, each "sample" will be of 29 hours duration.

The largest value of hourly-average wind speed (V_o) will have a probability of exceedence in one sample of 1/30. Thus the probability that the wind speed will be less than V_o in the sample will be

$$P_1\,(V_o) = 1 - exp\{-(V_o\,/c)^k\} = 29/30\,.$$

Therefor the probability that the wind speed will be less than V_o in one year will be

$$P_Y\,(V_o) = \{P_1\,(V_o)\}^{300}\ ,$$

and the probability that the wind speed will be less than V_o in T years will be

$$P_T\,(V_o) = [P_Y\,(V_o)]^T = [P_1\,(V_o)\,]^{300T}\ .$$

and this, by definition of the Return Period is

$$P_T\,(V_o) = 1 - 1/T\,,$$

where V_o is the "Once in T Years" Wind Speed.

Thus, if c and k are known for the parent distribution,, a value of V_o can be calculated for any value of T.

It has been mentioned in Section 11.5.1.2 that an exponential distribution converges most rapidly to the Type 1 Extreme Value Analysis where the extreme value of wind speed is a linear function of the Reduced Variate. Thus, if $V_o{}^k$ is used as the variable then its value can be expressed as

$$V_o{}^k = Mode\,(V^k) + Dispersion\,(V_o{}^k) \times y\,,$$

where y is the Reduced Variate, and equal to

$$y = -\,ln\{-\,ln[1 - 1/T]\}.$$

Because the value for k varies from location to location, and becausc its value is close to 2, it is common for the square of the extreme value to be calculated; thus

$$V_o{}^2 = Mode\,(V^2) + Dispersion\,(V^2) \times y\,.$$

References

1. Abernathy F.H., Kronauer R.E. "The Formation of Vortex Sheets" J.Fluid Mech Vol 13 pp 1 - 20 1962 (page 41)
2. Bergh H., Tijdeman H. "Theoretical and Experimental Results for the Dynamic Response of Pressure Measuring Systems" Report NLR-TR F238 National Aerospace Laboratory (The Netherlands) 1965 (page 235)
3. BRE "Building Research Establishment Environmental Assessment Method", published as a BRE Report (page 124)
4. BSI "Code of Practice for Assessing exposure of Walls to Wind-driven Rain" BS 8104: 1992. (pages 143 & 146)
5. BSI "Guide to the Evaluation of Human Exposure to Vibration and Shock in Buildings" Draft for Development number DD32:1974, which was subsequently republished as BS 6841:1987. (page 136)
6. BSI "Loading for Buildings Part 2 Code of Practice for Wind Loads" BS 6399 Part 2 1997.
7. Calvert J.R. "Experiments on the Flow Past an Inclined Disc" J. Fluid Mech Vol 29 pp 691 - 703 1967 (page 41)
8. Castro I.P., Wiggs G.F.S. "Pulsed-Wire Anemometry on Rough Surfaces with Application to Desert Sand Dunes" Journal of Wind Engineering Vol 52 pp 53 - 71: 1994 (page 230)
9. Committee of Wind Loading, Society of Steel Constructors of Japan in 1975 under the heading "Wind Resistant Design Regulations: A World List".(page 57)

10. Cook N.J. "The Designer's Guide to Wind Loading of Building Structures. Part 1 Background, damage survey, wind data and structural classification" Butterworths 1985 (page 24)
11. Cook N.J. "Wind Tunnel Simulation of the Adiabatic Boundary Layer by Roughness, Barrier and Mixing Device Methods" Volume 3 numbers 2/3 of the Journal of Industrial Aerodynamics July 1978 (page 227)
12. Cook N.J. "Wind Tunnel Simulation of the Atmospheric Boundary Layer; Methods in Current Use at Bristol" Symposium of External Flows 4th to 6th July 1972. University of Bristol 1972 (page 225)
13. Cook N.J. discusses several papers on the use of scour tests presented in the Journal of Wind Engineering in his contribution in that Journal (volume 79 pp 307 - 309 1999 (page 232)
14. Den Hartog J.P. "Mechanical Vibrations" 4th Edition McGraw Hill, New York 1956 (page 89)
15. ESDU "Characteristics of Atmospheric Turbulence Near the Ground: Part ii Single Point data for Strong Winds (neutral atmosphere)". ESDU Data Item 85020 (page 19)
16. ESDU "World-wide Extreme Wind Speeds Part 1: Origins and Methods of Analysis" ESDU Data Item 87034. (page 274)
17. ESDU Data Item "A Guide to Fan Selection and Performance" Item number 79037 Amendment A 1980 (page 174)
18. ESDU "Mean Forces, Pressures and Flow Field Velocities for Circular Cylindrical Structures: single cylinder with two-dimensional flow" ESDU Data Item 80025 Amend C 1986.
19. Gerrard J.R. "The Mechanics of the Formation Region of Vortices behind Bluff Bodies" J. Fluid Mech Vol 25 pp 401 - 413. 1966 (page 41)
20. Gringorton I.I. "A Plotting Rule for Extreme Probability Paper" J Geophys Res Vol 68 (1963) pp 813 - 814 (page 271)
21. Gumley S.J. "Tubing Systems for the Measurement of Fluctuating Pressures in Wind Engineering" Oxford University Engineering Labs Report Number 1370.81 (page 235)
22. Health and Safety Executive "Occupation Exposure Limits 1988: Guidance Note from the Health and Safety Executive (page 199)
23. Health and Safety Executive "Occupational Exposure Limits 1988: Guidance Note EH 40/88" from the Health and Safety Executive (page 245)

24.HMSO "Tables of Surface Wind Speed and Direction over the United Kingdom" Met o 792 HMSO 1968.

25.Holland D.J. "Rain Intensity Frequency Relationships in Britain" Meteorological Office Hydrology Memo No 33 1964 with Appendix 1968 (page 146)

26.Irwin H.P.A.H. "A Simple Omnidirectional Sensor for Wind Tunnel Studies of Pedestrian-level Winds" Journal of Wind Engineering Vol 7 pp 219 to 239 1981 (page 232)

27.Irwin H.P.A.H., Cooper K.R., Girard R. "Correction of Distortion Effects caused by Tubing Systems in Measurement of Fluctuating Pressure" Journal of Wind Engineering Vol 5 (1/2) October 1979), (page 236)

28.Lacy R.E. "Driving-rain Index" Building Research Establishment Report 1976 (page 143)

29.Lawson T.V. "Wind Effects on Buildings Vol 1 Design Applications, Vol 2 Statistics and Meteorology" Applied Science Publishers 1980.

30.Lawson T.V. "The Determination of the Wind Environment of a Building Complex before Construction" Department of Aerospace Engineering, University of Bristol Report Number TVL 9025 May 1990 (page 124)

31.Leiblein J. ("Efficient Methods of Extreme Value Methodology" NBSIR 74-602. US Dept. of Commerce. October 1974 (page 271)

32.Mann N.R. "Point and Interval Estimation Procedures for the two parameter Weibull and Extreme Value Distributions" Technometrics Vol 10 1968 pp 231-56 (page 271)

33.Mayne J.R., Walker G.R. "The Response of Glazing to Wind Pressure" BRE Current Paper 44/76 HMSO June 1976 (page 65)

34.Minson A.J. & Wood C.J. "Extreme Velocities near Building Faces using Laser Doppler Anemometry" Journal of Wind Engineering Vol 52 pp 121 - 137 1994 (page 231)

35.Newberry C.W., Eaton K., Mayne J.R. "Wind Loading on Tall Buildings: further results from Royex House" BRE Current Paper 29/73 HMSO November 1973 (page 65)

36.Novak M., Tanaka H. "The Effect of Turbulence on Galloping Instability" Boundary Layer Wind Tunnel Laboratory Report 2-73 Faculty of Engineering Science, University of Western Ontario, Canada. May 1973 (page 91)

37.Pasquill Frank "Atmospheric Diffusion". Van Nostrand 1962. (page 21)

38. "Sensitive 6 component High Frequency Range Balance for Building Aerodynamics" J Physics: Scientific Instruments Vol 6 pp 390 - 393 1983 (page 242)
39. Sherlock R.H. and.Stout M.B. in 1931 and 1933 and were reported in the Journal of Aeronautical Science Vol 5 No 2 pp 53 to 61 December 1937 (page 13)
40. Simpson A. "On the Flutter of a Smooth Circular Cylinder". Aero Quart. Vol 22(1) February 1971 (page 89)
41. Simpson A. "Wake Induced Flutter of Circular Cylinders - Mechanical Aspects" Aero Quart Vol 22(2) Mat 1971 (page 89)
42. Steffens R.J. "Structural Vibration and Damage" a BRE Report dated 1974 (page 126)
43. Van der Hoven I. "Power Spectrum of Horizontal Wind Speed in the Frequency Range 0.0007 to 900Hz" J. Meteorology Vol 14 NO 160 1957.

Subject Index

The numbers in brackets refer to Sections, and the other numbers refer to pages.